COURSES FOR HORSES

For Nicolette, Rebecca and Laura

COURSES FOR HORSES

A Journey Round the Racecourses of Great Britain and Ireland

NICHOLAS CLEE

WEIDENFELD & NICOLSON

First published in Great Britain in 2023
by Weidenfeld & Nicolson

1 3 5 7 9 10 8 6 4 2

A CIP catalogue record for this book
is available from the British Library.

ISBN (HB) 9781474618427
ISBN (eBook) 97814746618441

Typeset by Input Data Services, Bridgwater, Somerset

Printed in Great Britain by Clays Ltd, Elcograf S.p.A.

Weidenfeld & Nicolson

The Orion Publishing Group Ltd
Carmelite House
50 Victoria Embankment
London
EC4Y 0DZ
An Hachette UK Company

www.orionbooks.co.uk

CONTENTS

INTRODUCTION

The pioneers of horseracing were as likely to stage their contests over flat, oval circuits as they were to set up flat, oval circuits for hunting foxes. Horsemanship was a country pursuit, and horsemen raced their horses over the countryside. The land, even parkland, tended to rise and fall. The contours dictated irregularly shaped layouts. The result, once there were a few poles in the ground to mark the routes, was the glorious individuality, in some cases you could call it eccentricity, of British and Irish racecourses.

They come in many forms, and in distances range from one mile round to over two miles round. They may be left-handed (the horses run anti-clockwise) or right-handed. Some are not round, but U-shaped or L-shaped; in certain races at two downland courses, the horses race away from the spectators up the straights, descend into loops, turn a circle, re-enter the straights, and race back up them. Two courses describe figures of eight; one of them is on an island. There is a course with no grandstands. The venues for the most important race in the British jumps calendar (the Gold Cup) and the most important race in the flat racing calendar (the Derby) have pronounced upwards and downwards slopes; at the Derby venue, there's also a sideways slope. The views from the stands may take in miles of South Downs, the English Channel, the Wicklow Mountains, Roman walls, housing estates, railway lines, or the A1. There are posh courses and modest courses; there's a course – Fakenham – that is both.

There are fifty-nine of them in Britain, and twenty-six in Ireland. I would have been happy to visit them all, and I have a few regrets: Cartmel sounds fun, I gather Limerick is beautiful, and Haydock and Kempton stage important races. But this is not a completist's memoir or a guidebook.

It's about, as well as the venues, racing people, who are similarly various. There's the well-fed owner and the lightweight jockey. There's

1

royalty, and all classes down. There are insiders – no longer 'horsemen', in the era of outstanding figures such as jockeys Rachael Blackmore and Hollie Doyle, and trainers Venetia Williams and Jessica Harrington – and there are enthusiasts like me. A racecourse is a complex world, with numerous interacting cogs: grooms, trainers, jockeys, vets, farriers, doctors, racecourse executives, ground staff, administrators, caterers, bar staff, camera operators and other technicians, stewards, commentators, broadcasters, journalists, bookmakers, punters. A number of these people have kindly given me insights into their roles as I've travelled – with a fourteen-month interruption while the Covid pandemic shut down all sports and then compelled them to take place behind closed doors – to courses both prestigious and unassuming, picturesque and nondescript, smart and functional.

It's been a lovely job. Entering the racecourse gates, you arrive in another world, with its own procedures obscuring, for an afternoon or evening, your everyday concerns. You're on holiday. Some like to spend their holiday in the bar, a one-stop shop for betting and watching the racing (on monitors) as well as drinking. I like to stroll between parade ring, pre-parade ring, grandstand and rails, close to the horses as they thunder past. Each race, whether you bet or not, is an intriguing puzzle, with clues that give you some chance of solving it; getting it right is exhilarating, and your love goes out to the magnificent animal who was on your side. The respect that horses engender, and the sense of privilege one has from getting close to them as they parade and race, never go stale.

WETHERBY

Jumps (also stages flat racing)

27 December 2019

Crackerfull of sprouts

I seem to be the only person travelling to Wetherby racecourse by bus from Leeds, an hour-long journey costing less than a fiver. You must ask to be dropped specially at the Spring Lane entrance. It's a half-mile walk up the narrow road to the course; every time a car wants to pass there is no choice but to jump sharply out of the way into ankle-deep mud. In preparation, I am stuffing my trouser bottoms into my socks when a driver takes pity, and offers me a lift. He is a racing journalist, and when we get to the course he finds for me, perhaps because I tell him that I'm writing a racing book, a spare member's badge and a racecard – please don't mention my name as your benefactor, he says, because the management may not approve. I happen to be looking for the Wetherby CEO, Jonjo Sanderson, I say. 'That's him, who just walked past,' the journalist replies. So that's nearly twenty quid saved, and I'm able to grab twenty minutes with a man who, later, would probably be too busy to see me. Things are going well so far.

I sort of knew that my luck would last only as long as it took to complete the first race – leg one of the Tote Placepot, a bet that I fail to resist, despite experience, every time I visit a course. According to the Tote, lots of other mugs – sorry, racegoers – fall for it – sorry, play it – too: it is 'Racing's most popular bet', a claim that, subjected to proper scrutiny, would probably collapse.

The Jackpot invites you to pick the winners of six races. You've got to get them all: there are no consolation prizes. For the Placepot, you pick horses to be placed, which usually means finishing in the first three. From the runners at Wetherby, I mark on the Placepot card two horses in each of the six legs (races). That's two to the power of six: sixty-four lines, or potential combinations. Plenty, one should think. And the horses do not even have to win! Just let them make the frame – is that too much to ask?

In my case, mostly yes. The last time my Placepot came up was at Newbury in summer 2018. My outlay was £6.40 (yes, I hazard only 10p a line, I'm not suicidal); after I had seen selections get placed in six races, the cashier gave me back £9.20. A £2.80 profit! 'Buy yourself a cup of tea,' she suggested. My last win before that was . . . I cannot remember. Derby Day 2000, that was one: I made about £30, I think. Oh yes: there was that occasion at Wetherby about twelve years ago, when I bought a trilby to celebrate.

The racing journalist David Ashforth once defined a Placepot as – I'm quoting roughly – an accumulator in which five of your six selections come up before the sixth misses out by a short head. I should be so lucky. Race one at Wetherby today is the 888Sport Novices' Hurdle (Class 4), over two miles. I go for College Oak, forecast to be favourite and some way clear of his rivals according to the *Racing Post*'s ratings; and for Neville's Cross, who is, in the view of both the *Racing Post* and the racecard, 'open to improvement'. Vying for favouritism is Black Pirate, who has not raced for twenty months but is expected to run well. Black Pirate wins. College Oak is fourth of the seven runners and Neville's Cross is fifth ('challenged when [made] mistake two [hurdles] out and lost momentum, weakened [slowed almost to a standstill] last', the *Racing Post* reports). Oh well. That's the end of the afternoon, betting-wise. I wonder whether I can go through the entire research period for this book without winning a single Placepot? Precedent indicates that I have a shot at it.

Before the race, I ask a bookmaker – whose pitch is some way down from the prime position – what business was like yesterday, the first of the two days of the meeting. Not brilliant, she confides. As we chat, a woman approaches nervously, says she's never done this before, and asks for £2 on Black Pirate. Then a man has £2.50 each way on Clondaw Pretender, who is to finish sixth. These bets would be too puny for many bookmakers at the grander courses to accept, and you wonder how someone could prosper on such takings. Nevertheless, the bookmaker tells me later that business has picked up. These racegoers, though outnumbered by the Boxing Day crowd, are more enthusiastic punters.

There are about 5000 people here today, and yesterday there were about 8500: committed racegoers, families escaping from overheated sitting rooms with permanently active TVs, men escaping from over-heated families. The numbers are not what they once were; but then the market town of Wetherby and the racecourse itself used to boast railway stations, until the savage mid-twentieth-century cuts to the network put paid to them. Now, it's the Leeds bus from one direction, and, from the other, a free shuttle bus from Wetherby town centre.

The course has occupied the site since 1891, having moved from a place known as Wetherby Ings on the banks of the River Wharfe, home more recently to Wetherby Golf Club. Steeplechase racing first took place at the Ings in the 1840s, while there are claims that the history of racing here dates back to Viking and even to Roman times, with the prolific (Yorkshire-born) writer John Fairfax-Blakeborough asserting that the Wharfe banks hosted the first organised horse races to have taken place in the British Isles. Why steeplechase? Because the sport has developed from matches held over hunting land, fences and ditches included, between prominent points in the landscape, usually church steeples. At Wetherby, before racing started at the Ings, the landmarks were Kirk Deighton Church and Walton Church, the latter still visible from the course. The origins of the sport in hunting also explain the term National Hunt.

Lord Montagu of nearby Ingmanthorpe Hall owned the land of the new site. Ingmanthorpe Hall is now apartments, and the racecourse is owned by a private, independent company, the Wetherby Steeplechase Company. Jonjo Sanderson's family business, International Racecourse Management, runs Wetherby as well as fellow Yorkshire courses Catter-ick, Thirsk and Redcar.

Sanderson and his immediate predecessors have done a great deal to improve Wetherby's facilities, which, when I began visiting the course in the nineties, were somewhat dingy. The standard paddock enclosure consisted of a series of shed-like structures, none of them inviting – though the canteen served an excellent steak and kidney pie, the best hot food I've ever enjoyed on a racecourse. I am afraid that I cannot give you a review of Wetherby's current hot food offerings, as I find that after

Christmas Day and Boxing Day I have no appetite for another round of meat and two veg. But I can say that the bar of the Bramham Hall (opened in 2007) is a much pleasanter place – indeed, more congenial than the packed and noisy Marston Moor bar of the Millennium Stand (1999), entrance to which requires a more expensive, day member's badge. A third recent structure – if you count 1999 as 'recent' – is the Millennium West Stand, opened in 2017. Recognising these improvements, the Racecourse Owners' Association has given Wetherby its Gold Standard award.

Then there are the additional attractions. Today, Wetherby is offering, as well as the trad jazz band that seems to be an obligatory feature of race meetings, various entertainments. There is a 'Christmas Cracker' draw, one of the lucky winners of which gets to take home a bag of sprouts; by way of compensation, he is appointed to assess the horses in the paddock for the 'best turned-out' prize before one of the races. In the marquee, there are circus performers, and a circus workshop. I catch a few minutes of Dr Phantasma's Sideshow ('You won't believe your eyes!'), where Ramona the gypsy queen suspends my disbelief with her ascent of a ladder of razor-sharp swords. Next door, children are rushing around on tricycles and unicycles, and ignoring a burly man in a striped red coat who is trying to interest them in a tightrope lesson. His jolly persona is slipping. 'That's right, ladies and gentlemen, don't bother closing the door!' he booms, as the icy wind blows in from outside. He, and possibly some parents and unlucky punters, might benefit from a quiet talk with one of the chaplains who are, the racecard advertises, patrolling the stands, ready to offer 'a listening ear' to those 'of all faiths and none'.

Six or seven races and the wherewithal to get drunk do not seem to be enough by way of incentives to come racing these days. Racecourses, in common with other venues, must provide 'experiences'. On Wetherby's January fixture list is 'Christmas jumper Saturday', with prizes for the best/worst examples of these gifts. 'William Hill Medieval Day, featuring the Towton Novices' Chase' promises to evoke for racegoers the bloodiest battle to have been fought on British soil. There is 'Wear a Hat Race Day', and a spring favourite is 'Family Raceday, featuring the Mascot Gold Cup' – yes, a race for mascots. In the summer, 'Ladies' Evening' is a riot of, according to the unwoke blurb, 'Fillies, fashion and fizz'. And so on.

All this requires a good deal of work. Wetherby, which stages racing on nineteen days a year, has a staff of twelve. Today, a further 150 or so are employed: commentators, caterers, bar staff, stewards and other officials, a medical team (for horses and people), a farrier, a judge (to confirm results), the aforementioned chaplains, and others. Then of course there are all the busy outsiders: jockeys, trainers, stable staff, journalists, camera crews, bookmakers and betting shop staff, perhaps even the odd person who tries to make a living from backing horses. Horseracing is a significant employer nationally: the British Horseracing Authority, which runs the sport, reckons that there are more than 17,000 racing people in full-time employment, with the number going up to 85,500 if you count workers in associated businesses such as bookmaking catering and and journalism.

Wetherby employs six full-time ground staff. Looking after the ground at a racecourse involves a great deal more than throwing down some seed and replacing divots, as Jonjo Sanderson is particularly well placed to attest. In 2006, two years before he took up his job here, the adjoining A1 was widened, and encroached on the far turn of the course. The ground staff relaid a third of the turf, calling on, the Pitchcare website informs me, a Blec Aerovator and Agrovator, verti-draining, the Gwazae compressed air system, topdressing with 1000 tonnes of Mansfield Sand/ organic matter 50/50 mix, calcium carbonate to encourage flocculation, and other treatments including pig and poultry manure to increase organic matter. To summarise in layperson's terms: it was a job for people who knew what they were doing. Nevertheless, some nine years were to elapse before certain trainers, who had been alarmed by the new racing surface, were prepared to enter their horses at Wetherby again.

Even without such challenges, the ground at racecourses is a constant worry. It's either raining too much, or not enough. This autumn, it's been too much, and where there haven't been abandonments, horses round the country have been compelled to race through hock-deep mud. 'We had a lovely summer,' Sanderson tells me, 'and then it started raining in mid-September, and it hasn't really relented since. I think we've had about fourteen to fifteen inches since then.

'The track does take the water very well, because it drains off to the dykes, and the dykes drain into the river. But the problem areas are the car parks, which don't have that kind of drainage.

'When I first checked, this was going to be a bright, sunny week. Thank you, I thought. Then towards the beginning of the week, it started to rain again, and half an inch of rain was forecast for Boxing Day and last night. Please no. But we got less than a millimetre. So thank you. Thank you.' One gets the picture: it's a nervy business. Sanderson and his chief groundsman were here on Christmas Day, walking the course. Today, he is mostly engaged in tackling problems, while making sure that owners, trainers and the public are happy. 'We've had a lady stuck in a loo already,' he reports. While we're talking, a colleague interrupts to tell him that the Wi-Fi hotspot at the turnstiles has gone down. And jockeys who have walked the course have advised that they would like to see some of the running rails moved.

Back in October, the dykes burst their banks, and only a week before the Charlie Hall meeting, Wetherby's most important event of the year, the back straight was under water. The course generates 60 per cent of its turnover between October and the end of December, but does not insure against lost fixtures. 'The premium is pretty much the same as our profit,' Sanderson explains. 'So in effect we self-insure: we build in an abandonment provision for every fixture, and every time a fixture takes place we write that expense back into the books.' The two-day Charlie Hall meeting did go ahead, with the flood having left its traces only at one back-straight fence, which the runners bypassed.

In the summer, the clay soil gets too firm, certainly for steeplechase horses. It meant until recently that Wetherby could not expand its fixture list. Then came the A1 road widening, a nuisance in many respects but bringing the unexpected gift of enabling the course to stage flat races. On the previous course, the horses galloped towards the road before turning sharply round what was for them a hairpin bend – a manoeuvre that was manageable for jumpers but that would have compelled flat racers, who tend to run faster and over shorter distances, to shift down into first gear. The new course has a gentler oval.

Horseracing is a traditionalists' sport, and there was grumbling in 2015 when Wetherby, to that point the only course in Yorkshire de-voted entirely to jumps racing, staged its first flat meetings. But trainers and the public have supported the initiative, Sanderson reports. The figures tell the story of this popularity: the course attracts about sixty entries a day for its jumps fixtures, and eighty-eight runners a day for its flat fixtures. 'About two seasons ago, we had a three-way photo finish between a Hamdan Al Maktoum horse, a Khalid Abdullah horse and a Godolphin horse,' he says. [He's referring to two leading owners and to Sheikh Mohammed's training operation.] 'I'd thought that we'd be staging fairly modest races for the northern flat fraternity, not that we'd see photo finishes involving horses from Lambourn and Newmarket.'

They come from all over, too, for Wetherby's most important race, the Charlie Hall Chase, which in recent years has featured equine superstars Cue Card (Dorset), Silviniaco Conti (Somerset) and Bristol de Mai (Gloucestershire). Today's highlight is the Castleford Chase, described by course commentator Darren Owen, a tad economically with the truth, as 'a race with a rich history'. In fact, the race I saw the great Viking Flagship win twice in the nineties has transferred to Kempton, where it is called the Desert Orchid Chase. The Castleford Chase now run at Wetherby on 27 December is a handicap for horses rated up to 145. Viking Flagship was once rated by the British Horseracing Authority in the high 170s, meaning that a runner with the highest possible rating in today's field would have no chance against him, unless Viking Flagship were given at least two and a half extra stone to hump round the course.

Still, the Castleford winner today, Marracudja, looks impressive enough in this context. Trained by Dan Skelton at Alcester in Warwickshire and ridden by his sister-in-law Bridget Andrews, Marracudja goes into the race with recent form figures of 055, and the racecard suggests that he might benefit from being allowed to take the lead. That is exactly what Andrews does, in an expertly judged ride that is further evidence of what experts have known for some years – the best female jockeys are as good as the best men. Her victory comes as, at Leopardstown in Ireland, Rachael Blackmore cements her place among the elite of either sex by riding her second Grade 1 winner in two days, bringing her tally of victories at the highest level this year to six.

There is a lot of high-quality racing on today, and I spend the afternoon shuttling between the grandstand, the paddock and the Bramhall Hall, where I watch the action from Leopardstown, two races from Kempton, and the Welsh Grand National from Chepstow – seventeen horses and riders ploughing through mud for three miles and six furlongs. Again the racecard is prescient: 'likely to be staying when others have cried enough' it says of Potters Corner, first of twelve finishers, the last of whom crawls over the line some 43 lengths behind. (The others were pulled up – there were no fallers.)

Wetherby is a decent track for the spectator. The grandstand stanchions can get in the way, and when the runners are on the far side of the course by the A1 they are more than half a mile distant; but you can resort to the big screen, which, unlike those at some other courses, has a sharp image. The racecourse commentary is somewhat blurry, though, and during the final furlong, when the racegoers are yelling at the horses carrying their money, inaudible.* This is the point during a race when I get the impression that everyone on the course apart from me has backed the winner. It is somewhat lowering to watch people jumping up and down with their arms in the air, when neither of the two horses you've put in your Placepot ever got into contention.

This is one of my most useless ever days of Placepot betting. My selections come up in only two of the six races – one of which has only three runners, and two of them are my selections (the third being an outsider), while in the second, my placed horse was the odds-on favourite. The dividend that I failed to enjoy was £56.10 to a £1 stake, so if I'd managed to get one horse placed in each race I'd have taken home £5.61 – a loss of 79p. This book is not a story of high-rolling.

To cheer me up a little, quite a few people come unstuck in the last, a conditional [apprentice] jockeys' handicap hurdle. The racecard comment on Bolton Boy is, 'best to look elsewhere', with a prediction that the horse will start as the 33/1 outsider (a £1 bet would return £33, plus the £1 stake). Whoops: the market appears to have information that the racecard tipster lacked, because Bolton Boy goes off as 11/4 favourite (a £4 bet would return £11, plus the £4 stake). But the market was not so smart, after all. Bolton Boy never travels particularly well and falls at the seventh. Groans all around me. The winner is Pray for a Rainbow (12/1), who has some supporters. As I leave the course, I pass various

---

* I learn from my travels that there are spots on most racecourses where the announcements are unclear. If you're under the roof of a modern grandstand, you may find that the tannoys are on the edge of the roof and facing away from you. Older grandstands have more helpful acoustics.

people slapping each other on the back. Sickening. No, I don't mean that really. Well done them.

I head back along the muddy Spring Lane roadside as the uninterrupted line of traffic motors past, and take my solitary place by Walton Road in the descending darkness. Buses have sailed past me here before. I recommend that as soon as you see the return bus approaching, you activate the flashlight on your phone and wave your arms about like a shipwreck victim who has spotted a trawler.

FAKENHAM

Jumps

23 January 2020

Welsh wonders in Norfolk

Fakenham, like Wetherby, is a town that has lost its rail links. Indeed, Fakenham once had *two* railway stations: Fakenham West, closed in 1959, and Fakenham East, closed in 1964. There is talk of including the village in a Norfolk Orbital Railway, a project to bring back trains to the railway-starved north of the county; but this route may not be of much use to Londoners who get an ambitious – you might say ambitious – notion to pay a visit to Fakenham racecourse by public transport. So here I am, boarding the 07:42 train from King's Cross to King's Lynn – a service that, I am told, the Queen favours when she travels to Sandringham. Arriving at 09:34, I walk to the bus station (five minutes) and catch the 10:00 bus to Fakenham – a fifty-minute journey across countryside that is not, as Noël Coward's Amanda summarises in *Private Lives*, very flat, but gently rolling. At Fakenham, where the alighting passengers thank the driver *by name*, I head down an alley, cross a road and a vehicle repair shop forecourt, walk along a muddy path by the River Wensum, and arrive at a road that leads directly to the course. I am willing to bet – it would be the only bet I'd have any confidence about winning – that no other person at Fakenham races today has come by this route.

If you're a soft Londoner, you think you're entitled to call yourself intrepid after such a journey. But more than three hours before my alarm clock went off, the trainer Christian Williams had been wakened at his home in the Vale of Glamorgan. By 3.45 a.m., he and his seventeen-year-old apprentice jockey Jack Tudor were on the road, at the start of a five-hour, 270-mile drive. Williams had sent ahead three horses. It's as if he knew something.

The first race is the Barnham Primary School Selling Handicap Chase – 'sellers' are low-grade races after which the winners are put up for sale. Williams's Strictlyadancer, ridden by Adam Wedge, races into the lead before the last and finishes six lengths clear. Strictlyadancer jumps well and gallops exuberantly to the line, but earns for his owners only £3665, failing to attract any bids at the £4000 they had been hoping to earn from him at auction. In race two, the Sky Sports Racing Conditional Jockeys' Handicap Hurdle, Jack Tudor is hard at work on board Massini's Dream from some way out, and looks to be a clear second favourite, as Very Intense coasts into the lead. But as they reach the finish, Tudor manages to get his horse up by half a length. There's a similar story with Williams's third runner, though this time Tudor's mount Cap du Nord rounds the home turn in third place and looks to be third favourite to win: Cap du Nord lands awkwardly after the last, dips his head like a drunk whose legs have failed to keep pace with the upper part of his body, rallies, takes the lead, gets headed again, and rallies once more, to win by a head. It looks as though Tudor is one of those rare jockeys who can make winners out of horses who would be losers in other hands.

Stupidly, I ask Williams, a former jockey who started training in 2017, if this has been his best day at the races. He reminds me that on 27 December his horse Potters Corner won the Welsh Grand National. (During the coronavirus lockdown, Potters Corner is to win the Virtual Grand National.) But it is the first time he has saddled a treble. Fakenham, he says, fearless about offering a hostage to fortune, has been his lucky track: to date, he has sent thirty-three runners to the course, and thirteen have been winners. Yes, but wouldn't sending those horses to win at Chepstow, just fifteen miles from home, have been less arduous? 'I could go to Chepstow and be racing in eighteen-runner fields for half the prize money,' he replies. The total reward for the three Fakenham victories is £13,652, and the number of runners in the races is eight, eight and nine. (Later, I check some Chepstow results. What Williams argues seems to apply to hurdle races rather than to chases, and to say that Chepstow's prize money is half Fakenham's is a bit of an exaggeration. Still, there's the priceless 'lucky track' factor.)

It's a good story, one that makes for excellent PR for chief executive David Hunter and his team. 'Welsh wonders Williams and Tudor make long Fakenham trek pay again', is the headline in the *Racing Post*, which illustrates the piece with an internet map showing the route and the estimated driving time (four hours fifty-two minutes). 'I'm delighted to do it at Fakenham,' Williams tells the paper. 'They put on good prize money and we like to support it and give our owners value for money.' Just the message that a small country course wants to get across.

Hunter and Williams have different priorities when it comes to field sizes, however. Williams is happy to have less competition; Hunter, who is clerk of the course as well as CEO, wants to get as many horses racing at Fakenham as possible. 'There are fewer runners coming here than there were when I arrived in this job [towards the end of the nineties],' he says. 'We put up decent prize money, we often offer the best racing ground available, and I like to think that we look after owners and trainers properly – we've got our ROA (Racehorse Owners' Association) gold standard award for the umpteenth year, which we're really proud of. But it's partly a reflection of the general racehorse population, and partly because of our location. I think some of the newer owners tend not to think, "Owning this horse gives me an opportunity to visit different parts of the country", as they did in previous generations.' Even with a car, the journey may not be an attractive prospect. Beyond Cambridge and Peterborough, you're mostly on single-lane roads. A friend tells me: 'Fakenham is a bit like Aberystwyth. The longer you drive towards it, the further away it seems to get.'

As Hunter and I talk, a colleague arrives to say that Olly Murphy – who trains horses at Stratford-upon-Avon, more than 140 miles away, and who nevertheless is another regular here – has arrived with several owners, all wanting badges (of admission). 'Err on the side of generosity,' Hunter tells her. 'He's a good supporter of ours.' On top of this kind of generosity, Fakenham does not charge entry fees to its races – Hunter believes that Newton Abbot is the only other British course to employ such a policy.

Hunter is generous to me too, issuing an invitation to return to his compact office at any time during his absence to inspect the Fakenham minute books and any other objects that may be of interest. I find, in the earliest minute book, an 1886 letter from an equerry to the Prince of Wales, later Edward VII, saying that 'it will give [the prince] much pleasure' to accept presidency of the West Norfolk Hunt Club – though HRH hopes the club will be 'particular' about whom it admits to

membership, and goes on to apologise for being 'bothered with neur-
algia' and unable to write the letter himself. The club began staging
steeplechases in East Winch near King's Lynn, and moved to Fakenham
in 1905, with committee members attracted by the better drainage on
the site, and undeterred by the argument that it would be 'very difficult
to keep the public out'. I'm afraid that I didn't find the record of the
meeting at which Fakenham members decided that they would condes-
cend to let the public in. They continue to enjoy royal patronage: the
current patron is Prince Charles, who took over the role from his mother
in 2002. Sandringham is not far away. In between there and the course
lies the village of Anmer, a name that may be familiar: King George
V's Anmer was the horse that the suffragette Emily Davison tried to
intercept during the 1913 Derby, with fatal consequences.

The committee members who thought better drainage was desirable
have been proved right. 'Since the first of January, we've had 75 millimetres of rain, and last week, the course was flooded,' Hunter says. 'I've
never seen anything like it in my time here. There was water across the
chase and hurdle course at the two-furlong marker, and it was pouring
off the side of the course in a waterfall. But it has all receded, and now
we have good to soft ground – so it does drain well.' Frost is a greater
threat. Fakenham has not invested in frost covers for the entire course,
in part because of the expense and in part because it cannot call on the
manpower that laying and then lifting the covers would involve. 'All our
ground repairs are done by local people,' Hunter says. 'It's not always
that easy to get local staff to do it at this time of year – many of them are
retirees who also work for quite a few days a week with the local shoots.'
In any event, Hunter reckons, if the overnight temperature sank to
minus four or five, the frost would probably get into the ground whether
there were coverings or not.

Like other small, independently run tracks, Fakenham takes a relatively big hit when it loses even one of its modest number of fixtures
– there are twelve or thirteen a year in Fakenham's case. The course is
owned by the West Norfolk Sporting Trust. Hunter has no financial
interest in the trust, and in theory works part-time. (Like many of us
with part-time jobs, he finds that the work is often full-time.) He has
lived with horses all his life, and is an ex-army captain who later in the
afternoon of my visit will present the prize for the RMA Sandhurst

Louts' 30th Anniversary Dinner Maiden Hurdle – being a Lout himself. There are ten racecourse directors, some of them with names that
have been associated with Fakenham for generations, and who all work
voluntarily.

The course, at about one mile round, is the smallest National Hunt
racecourse in the country, and vies with Chester for the accolade of being
the smallest racecourse overall. The shortest sections are the home and
back straights, and the horses are turning either gently or sharply left
for a good portion of the circuit. 'Horses here need to be well balanced,
and to race on their left leads,' Hunter says, assuming I'll know what
he means. I do, as far as someone who has never sat on horseback can.
If you watch these horses' front legs at the gallop round a Fakenham
turn, you should see their right legs hitting the ground first, with the left
following and extending beyond. Some horses prefer leading with their
near (left) legs, meaning they're happy turning left-handed, and some
prefer leading with their off (right) legs. The celebrated grey Desert
Orchid, for example, was uncomfortable racing left-handed, famously
overcoming that handicap as well as his dislike of galloping on mud
when he won the 1989 Cheltenham Gold Cup.

The Fakenham grounds host, as well as the racecourse, a caravan
site, which offers another source of income. There's also a sports centre,
which lays on tennis, squash, archery, shooting and golf. Several holes of
the nine-hole golf course are inside Fakenham's running rails – but the
golfers, to the relief of horses and riders, do not send balls flying about
on racedays. The centre pays rent to use this land. 'The arrangement
was set up, certainly to the sports centre's advantage, fifty years ago,'
Hunter explains.

It is market day in Fakenham, and there is something of a market day
atmosphere, too, on the course, which boasts a remarkably high ratio
of stalls to racegoers. There is a country clothing outlet, and, opposite, David 'Mouse' Cooper, equine artist, is selling his paintings and
prints. The food on offer ranges from the expected hog roast and fish
and chips to Punjabi cuisine in the bar next to the parade ring, and to
the menu at the stall named 'Norfolk Thai' – an intriguing fusion. For
£60 a head, and probably only for those who have booked in advance,
there is the Firth Restaurant, with dishes provided by the Crown Inn at
East Rudham ('the quality of the food is second to none', according to a

happy customer on Tripadvisor). I opt for a £3.50 steak and kidney pie from the Jean's Home Bakery stall, where proprietor Jean Seppings has already taken orders from her regular spot at the village market before setting up at the course. The pie is superb, with tender, gristle-free meat, and I return for cake, washed down with Americano from the next-door Cuppa Jo Jo – also excellent and cheap. You don't often get this quality, or these prices, at the grander courses.

The atmosphere is unique. It's the Norfolk set, I suppose. I should guess that there are more than a thousand people here, and they make far less noise than do comparable crowds elsewhere. When the horses enter the final furlong at most tracks, the racecourse commentary is drowned out by the desperate urgings of punters – but not today. A good many racegoers have brought their dogs, who appear to be used to having horses near them and are perfectly behaved. I've never seen dogs on a racecourse before (but shall see them again, at Perth). Public announcements are sparse, and the bookmakers, perhaps resigned to slow business, do not shout the odds with their usual urgency. I don't see many racegoers who look like serious punters, and a bookmaker confirms my impression. 'You can sum up today in one word: desperate,' he says. 'It can be like that here. There was a huge crowd on New Year's Day, and they all left their money at home.' But it's not only a Fakenham phenomenon, he adds. Since the new year, there have been complaints about slow trading from racecourse bookmakers all round the country.

Fakenham's grandstand is a simple brick and corrugated iron affair, with steppings leading up to a press box resembling a stationmaster's office on an unmodernised railway platform. There are plans to re-develop this area of the course, bringing it into line with the Prince of Wales stand, a two-storey wood and glass edifice in the members' enclosure – available for hire for weddings. In between the two stands is a green commentary tower, with, poking his head out of the top window, Tommo, or 'TV's Tommo' as Derek Thompson was known during his stint at Channel 4 Racing. Tommo will be seventy this year, had a brush with cancer eight years ago, and cuts a more subdued figure than he did when presenting the racing in the style of an ebullient gameshow host. He has a companionable style as a race caller, and betrays a rather touching concern for the horses' welfare, overriding his brief to tell you exactly what is going on. 'Let's see how they jump this . . . yep, they're all over safely,' he announces with relief, quite often. (There are no fallers this afternoon; one horse unseats his rider.)

Olly Murphy saddles Oscar Academy, the winner of the last race at 3.45, so he gets rewarded for his long journey. As for Christian Williams, he may not arrive home until midnight. 'Tomorrow, I'm going to spend the time with my family,' he says.

There are two things the user of public transport should note before travelling home from Fakenham: if you miss the 15:45 bus, your choice is either to board the 16:00, which after a leisurely tour of the North Norfolk coast will not arrive in King's Lynn for another two hours and twenty-six minutes, or to wait until 18:00 for the next, last bus; and if you buy a return ticket on the 49, you won't be able to use it if the return service is the 49A. Bearing this in mind, I choose to miss what will be Oscar Academy's moment of glory. I am back to North London just after 19:00.

PLUMPTON

Jumps

27 January 2020

Good form

Plumpton: it sounds cosy, welcoming and villagey – a bit like Trumpton, setting of the 1960s children's TV classic. The train service from London Victoria is hourly, and drops you right next to the East Sussex village of Plumpton Green on one side, and the racecourse on the other. (Plumpton village is two miles to the south.) It costs £18 to get into the grandstand: no distinctions here between the grandstand and a members' or premier enclosure. Everyone, from the stewards to the Tote staff to the bar staff, smiles at you.

Plumpton was once less welcoming to jockeys, many of whom dreaded the railway side of the course. Here, they and their charges were required to jump fences while galloping down a precipitous incline. In 1954, the Cuckfield Novices Chase, the last race on the card, was declared void after all seven runners had failed to finish: a horse called Struell Well, the last one standing, fell at the fifth last, allowed his jockey to get back on board (this was legal until 2009) but refused at the third last, jumped it after being persuaded to try again, and refused definitively – who can blame him? – at the next. By this time, Roy Gill reports in his book *Racecourses of Great Britain*, 'many of the crowd had gone home'. In 1971, all six runners in the Keymer Chase fell, but on this occasion there was a winner, because after hitting the deck at the last, Major Share was remounted and allowed to trot past the post alone.

No doubt with these precedents in mind, trainers declined to send their best horses to race at Plumpton. But the racecourse management has been steadily making improvements to track safety and to the quality of the facilities. In the 2005–06 season, Voy Por Ustedes claimed

Plumpton's £60,000 Cheltenham Bonus by winning a designated chase at the course and going on to win the Arkle Chase at the Cheltenham Festival; he proved himself to be an outstanding horse by winning the festival's two-mile showcase, the Queen Mother Champion Chase, the following season. No horse has managed to win a race in the bonus series and go on to win at the festival since, but Kalashnikov was made joint favourite for the 2019 Arkle Chase after a Plumpton victory, and a month later Master Dino also won a qualifying race and became favourite for Cheltenham's JLT Chase.

Plumpton's CEO Dan Thompson might admit to feeling relief that these recent efforts were unsuccessful. (Kalashnikov unseated his rider in the Arkle; Master Dino did not even make it to Cheltenham, owing to injury.) Yes, a victory would have gained publicity, and probably attracted further good horses to the course; but £60,000 is quite a lot of spare cash for a small, independent business to shell out. Like his counterparts at many other courses, Thompson does not insure: the premiums are too steep.

On the first day I hope to visit Plumpton, Hurricane Brendan puts paid to the fixture. You must expect abandonments during a British winter at a course on clay soil, which does not facilitate efficient draining; and, this time, the blow is mitigated when the British Horseracing Authority (BHA) gives Plumpton permission to hold a replacement meeting five days later. The course, which stages about sixteen days' racing a year, has been relatively lucky during recent winters. In 2015 and 2017 there were no lost fixtures; in 2018, the year of the 'Beast from the East', there were two. Thompson prays that more sophisticated techniques for battling the weather available now mean that seasons of six abandonments (1974/75, and again in 1977/78) are gone. 'But there's only so much you can do by investing in better drainage and frost covers,' he says.

The advantage of independence – Plumpton is owned by Peter Savill, once a combative chairman of the British Horseracing Board (as the BHA was then), and Adrian Pratt – is that Thompson can pursue policies such as boosting prize money without being hindered by the imperatives of a larger group. Plumpton, like Fakenham and Chelmsford City, has received praise from owners and trainers for offering decent purses, a phenomenon to be filed under the heading 'Things they never said' along with, from the same sources, 'The handicapper has been very fair.' The Sussex Champion Hurdle, run in April, has a prize fund of £50,0000, as does the Sussex Champion Chase, run the following day. Better prizes mean that the course can attract better horses, although it must be careful about this: the better must not scare away the less able. Racegoers do not get excited about seeing an odds-on shot taking on a couple of rivals; and, crucially, they're not tempted to bet on the outcome. The 2019 Sussex Champion Chase attracted just three runners – though small fields for feature races are a problem for every racecourse, with the possible exception of Cheltenham and Aintree at festivals time.

Like David Hunter at Fakenham, Thompson needs to encourage trainers to think that what may be a lengthy journey to the course will be worthwhile. 'My previous course was Exeter,' he says, 'and you've got National Hunt trainers coming out of your ears round there. Whereas Sussex isn't a hotbed of training establishments. So we invest in the track and the prize money and the facilities wherever we can.'

Plumpton has three medium-sized stands, unremarkable brick and glass affairs from the outside but containing smartly appointed bars, with polished wood floors and shining chrome surfaces. A fourth bar overlooks the paddock, and is a welcome vantage point when, later in the afternoon today, the rain comes down in torrents. At the back of the stands, facing large whiteboards outlining Plumpton's history and some of the more notable horses who have competed here, are three food trucks: Hog Roast, Thai Noodles, and Griddle & Fry, where I buy an excellent burger (6oz, £5). Inside the Southdown Grandstand, I complete my meal with a delicious walnut and carrot cake (only £1.50), and a slightly less delicious Americano (£2.50).

Right, it's time to – ha! – study the form. What do the records of the horses' previous performances tell us about how they might fare today? As you may have inferred by now, I know a bit about horseracing but am, when it comes to picking winners, and to put it in racing terms, Class 6. My usual practice is to look at what the tipsters say, check the ratings, and pretend to myself that I've come to some sort of studied conclusion. I get out the *Racing Post* and the racecard.

The racecard contains the 'cards' – the lists of runners in each race. It also has information about the course, about betting, and sometimes a tipster's column. I pay £2 for my Plumpton card; at the grander courses you'll be asked for a fiver, and sometimes more. You don't need a racecard if you have a *Racing Post*, and indeed will get less information from it; but I don't like to break the routine of buying one, just as I always want, also to my cost, to do the Placepot.

A racecard listing will tell you the horse's number (for its saddle cloth), name, age, the weight it will carry, form figures, and colour (BG, for example, is a bay gelding). It will tell you the horse's sire (father) and dam (mother) and damsire. Another way of putting this last information would be, to take an example from the Plumpton card: 'Bard of Brittany is by Sayif (IRE), out of Lily Le Braz by Montjeu (IRE)' – Montjeu is his maternal grandfather, and the bracketed abbreviations indicate that Sayif and Montjeu were foaled in Ireland. The assumption appears to be that the dam requires the authority of her paternal lineage. You also get information about headgear (BF means the horse is wearing blinkers for the first time), previous wins at the course and distance (CD, or just C, or D), jockey, owner, trainer, sponsor and breeder; and there's a torso-shaped illustration of the colours the jockey will wear. There's also a guide to how to read the racecard.

All this information comes from the family firm of Weatherbys (Perth chapter). At the majority of courses, however, a firm called Timeform supplies the racecard form comments, tips, star ratings and betting forecasts. (At some meetings, confusingly, you can also buy a 'Timeform Racecard', containing more detailed information.) Timeform was founded in 1948 by Phil Bull, who is remembered in racing much as Sir Thomas Beecham is in classical music: opinionated, egocentric and quotable. Racing was 'the great triviality',* Bull said; 'At the racecourse, keep your eyes open and your ears closed'; to a potential employee's comment on the meagre salary Timeform offered: 'If you can't make twice that sum a year from betting, you shouldn't be coming to work here in the first place.'

Timeform produces, as the name implies, time ratings and form ratings. Bull, a maths graduate, was a pioneer of the former, and made a small fortune from backing the horses that his figures highlighted. (No:

---

* I've learned that, like so many quotations, this is not quite what was said. But let's not spoil it.

he didn't start with a large fortune.) It's not simply a matter of record-ing what the stopwatch says. Racecourses have different layouts and gradients. A time achieved over five furlongs at Epsom, where a good part of the track is downhill, is not comparable to a time achieved at Ascot's five-furlong track, commonly described as 'stiff'. The ratings nerd first compiles, for every course, a set of times against which the times recorded on a particular day may be judged. Then, even trickier, he or she must decide what allowances to make for factors specific to that day: the state of the ground, the wind speed, sometimes the positions of the running rails, and the weight the horse is carrying.

I wish I could trust in speed ratings, as time ratings are usually known. Like most racegoers, I lack the dedication, resources and expertise to be a form student; but I don't want simply to follow what tipsters rec-ommend. Speed ratings have the dual appeal of being abstruse and yet apparently pure guides to horses' abilities. They are fallible, however. First, we have seen how difficult they are to compile: figures arrived at after these kinds of calculations cannot be entirely objective – and indeed, the experts often disagree. Second, races run at optimum paces, enabling the horses to attain ratings reflective of their abilities, are the minority. It is true of races involving humans too, and is why, when athletes set out to break world records, they employ pacemakers whose job is to ensure that each lap is run to schedule – as Chris Brasher and Christopher Chataway did when Roger Bannister ran the first four-minute mile. What about sprints, you ask? The answer is that there aren't any sprints in horseracing. Five furlongs is the shortest distance of a horse race, and is described as a sprint, but is in fact further than a thoroughbred can gallop at full speed. Horses that go off too fast will finish quite slowly. Again, the horses at the head of the pack dictate the pace, and finishing times will usually reflect what they do rather than the optimum times the runners might achieve.

There is a third problem, apparent as I cast a perplexed eye over today's Plumpton card in the *Racing Post*: most races at this moderate level are not run at paces capable of generating meaningful ratings.

The *Racing Post* no longer publishes the win percentage of its Top-speed selections. When it did, the figure was low. Racing Post Ratings (RPRs), the paper's form ratings, have a hit rate of about 25 per cent, without being profitable; and I can tell you, from experience, that you won't win the Placepot very often if you simply pick the top two RPRs in each race. Favourites win about a third of all races, but again are not profitable to back – not blindly, anyway. Form experts use ratings selectively; and speed ratings aficionados also call upon sectional timing – how fast the horses ran at various points in their races. It's all a bit technical for you and me.

Why am I banging on about this stuff? Because you, like me, may be tantalised by the suspicion that there is a statistics-based method of backing horses that does not require encyclopaedic knowledge and hours of study, but that nevertheless offers the satisfaction that comes from independently determined, winning choices. If you have discovered one, do let me know. I bet less and less these days, and when I do I tend to be somewhat whimsical: I'll put a few quid, for example, on a 33/1 outsider, hopelessly out of form but who, in better days, was capable of top-class performances. You can write off such a bet before the race is even run, thus anaesthetising yourself against the coming disappointment.

Perhaps we would be advised to consult an expert, after all. Philip Spink is a racecard editor at Timeform, and has written the tipping column in Plumpton's racecard for this meeting. Every day, he and his colleagues at Timeform HQ in Halifax assess the form for dozens of races. They may start with Timeform's form and speed ratings, but they also have to weigh up factors such as, er, weight, as well as recent form, jockey form, trainer form, the horses' course and ground predilections, and the comments of colleagues who have given *in situ* reports of the horses' performances. They make use, too, of sectional timing data. From all this, they compile not only form guides and tips but also betting forecasts: not their own assessment of what the odds should be, but what they think the market will decide the odds should be. Sometimes, this is an impossible task. A horse may have shown no ability on the racecourse to date; then, on the morning of the race, the owners and the stable staff, knowing or thinking they know something hitherto concealed from bookmakers and the public, pile in with their bets. But this money is not always smart, as I reported in the Wetherby chapter.

Spink is so busy studying the form that he barely has time to go racing: he gets to the track, he tells me, about four times a year, usually on days when Timeform is the sponsor of a meeting. He has been with the company for twelve years, having joined from Leeds City Council. 'You definitely have to have a love of the sport, to look at the form day in and day out,' he says. 'And you have to be thick-skinned, to take a few losses. But it's great to be paid for doing something you really love.'

How does he do today? Cap du Mathan, a strapping gelding trained by Paul Nicholls, obliges in the first. In the second, Wenceslaus makes it two out of two for Spink's column. You're not rich yet, though. Cap du Mathan went off at 8/11, meaning that a £5 bet would have earned you £3.63. Wenceslaus, to whom the handicapper has assigned 12st 2lb (2st more than the favourite, Clondaw Robin, carries), is a more generous 3/1, so you make £15. Spink's next four selections all lose – indeed, none of them is even placed; if you had backed all six at £5 to win, you'd have ended the day with a loss of £1.37. You could have done a lot worse. Spink, though, would have been slightly alarmed to hear that you had wagered your entire day's betting bank on his selections. He certainly wouldn't have done that himself.

What other system might we try? How about following the money? But the money, as we have seen, may be no more enlightened than the rest of us. In race one at Plumpton, Cap du Mathan is forecast to be second favourite, and the market gets it right when it makes him favourite at the off. In race two, Wenceslaus is forecast to be second favourite, but is overtaken in the betting by Clondaw Robin, forecast to be 5/1 but ending up with a starting price of 11/4. According to the form book report on the race, Clondaw Robin is 'ridden and [made] no impression before 3 out . . . struggling 2 out . . . some headway and went modest fourth run-in, never on terms'. That's how smart the money is.

Hang on a minute: we're still in the Placepot! As the light fades and the rain descends as if propelled by a sky-width water cannon, the runners set off for the last, kicking up so much mud that the jockeys will return looking as if they've emerged from burial in the stuff. One of my selections, Sadma, is racing prominently. Hang on again: where's my second selection, Chinwag? I search the field in vain for his black and emerald colours; I listen for a mention in the commentary: Chinwag is not there. I must have missed the announcement that he was a non-runner as I sheltered in the bar. The selection of a non-runner shifts to the favourite – Sadma. The good news is that if Sadma is placed, I get a double return; the bad news is that he's my only hope, and as the field rounds the home bend he is relegated to third place, with jockey Edward Austin desperately stoking his charge's fatigued engine. But the horses behind are weary too, and Sadma staggers past the post, 22 lengths behind the second horse but, crucially, four and a half lengths in front of the fourth. So that's two lines up, and I had two selections placed in the first race, and another two in the second. Eight lines (2 x 2 x 2)!

What stops me getting too excited is the thought that if I have won the Placepot, it cannot have been that hard, and lots of other racegoers will be sharing the payout. So it proves. A prize fund of £64,647 is divided between 3,883.19 winning units, and pays out £16.60 to a £1 stake. I, having spent 10p a line, get back £1.66 x 8 = £13.28. That's a profit from my £6.40 wager of £6.88. Still, you can spend that on an excellent burger and a moist walnut cake at Plumpton, and still have change.

If you've ever placed a winning bet on a racecourse, you'll know it's one of the most exhilarating experiences, even when the return is £6.88: victoriousness enhanced by smugness. The feeling sustains me on the cold and damp Plumpton railway platform while I wait for the Southern Rail Victoria service, which, as reliable as the 33/1 outsiders I like to back, is running forty minutes late.

CHELMSFORD CITY

All-weather flat

13 February 2020

Viewing from the inside

There is something about the bus timetable that does not inspire confidence, so I take a cab from Chelmsford station to Chelmsford City racecourse. Chelmsford City was once called, with greater geographical precision, Great Leighs; but that venture fell into administration, and the new management understandably ditched the name when they reopened in 2015. The course is some distance north of Chelmsford. Racecourse manager Fraser Garrity's generosity in comping me a ticket will only defray in part the cab fare of £27 (including tip) each way – a sum that I should not try to earn back in bets.

The driver turns out to be a regular visitor to the course. 'When it first opened [in Great Leighs days], there was a bit of a funny atmosphere,' he says. 'Now you can go there for an evening with your wife or a few mates and have a really good time.' He likes to book a table in the Fairwood Restaurant. It's one floor down from the Club Restaurant, which offers what the course website describes as a 'sophisticated culinary experience' and has a dress code; he is perfectly happy with the Fairwood's carvery. 'I like the beef or the lamb,' he says. 'It's as good as you'll find anywhere.' Let's get my single criticism of Chelmsford City out of the way here: the burger I buy from the course's third food outlet, the Grill Kitchen, is far from as good as you'll get anywhere. Carrying the recent memory of the terrific burger from the Griddle & Fry stall at Plumpton, I am disappointed.

Chelmsford City gets everything else right. The staff are super-friendly; owners, trainers and stable staff are well looked after; the grounds and flower beds are beautifully maintained – the paddock, on this dank February evening, is surrounded by vivid daffodils; the facilities gleam. The racecourse has only one apparent shortcoming, which if you were not prepared for it would startle you very soon after you arrived.

Beyond the ticket office, you take a path that descends between grass banks and enters a tunnel. Emerging on the other side, you find yourself in the centre of the course – and that is where the grandstand and paddock are. It means that you cannot see the horses from the steppings in front of the stand until they round the home turn about two furlongs from the winning post. But the limited perspective is not really a great inconvenience. Racegoers have grown used, even at courses with vantage points offering uninterrupted views, to watching substantial parts of races on big screens, turning their attention to the track only as the runners approach the line. Chelmsford City's big screen does the job.

The Chelmsford City management inherited this layout from the previous owners, who had discovered that there was a compulsory purchase order on part of the land, next to the A131, where a conventional grandstand would have been sited. They decided that the remaining land was not spacious enough, so they put up a temporary, two-tier marquee, previously used in 2006 for the Ryder Cup golf tournament, on the other side. In May 2008, a few months before the fall of Lehman Brothers and the financial crash, Great Leighs became the first new racecourse to open in Britain for eighty-one years; it also had the distinction of being the only racecourse in Essex. Eight months later, the business collapsed.

There were various failed attempts to reactivate the comatose site until, in 2013, a consortium led by Betfred proprietor Fred Done (his name rhymes with 'own') bought it. By the time the course got approval from the British Horseracing Authority to stage a challenging 2015 programme of fifty-eight fixtures, there were only a few months before the stalls were due to clang open for Chelmsford City's first race. The management decided that the way to get the job done on time was to put their new grandstand on the existing foundations. Building a stand on the more conventional side of the track is a project for the future. There is talk of a casino, too.

Great Leighs was the fifth 'all-weather' course to open in Britain, after Lingfield (1989), Southwell (1989), Wolverhampton (1993), and

Kempton (2006). An all-weather surface is not the same as the 'dirt' prevalent in US racing. Dirt is a mix of sand, clay and silt. All-weather surfaces – such as the Polytrack in use at Chelmsford City, Lingfield and Kempton, and the Tapeta at Southwell, Wolverhampton and Newcastle (which opened its all-weather course in 2016) – are mixes of sand, plastic and rubber fibres, and wax. (Southwell has switched to Tapeta from Fibresand, which didn't include the wax.) They are by reputation – and according to the statistics – safer than dirt (the least safe surface) and turf. But the principal reason for introducing them was, as the name implies, to be able to continue to maintain a healthy volume of racing fixtures even when the weather was bad.

For quite a while, this rationale affected the image of all-weather racing, which some characterised as weak contests for slow horses in near-empty courses, the unedifying spectacle designed solely to attract desperate bets from mug punters in dismal betting shops. But gradually, the all-weather programme became more prestigious. Lingfield and Wolverhampton staged Group – top quality – races. Lingfield instituted its 'All-weather Championships' on Good Fridays, with a prize fund of £1 million. The great filly Enable ran at Kempton before winning her second Prix de l'Arc de Triomphe, the richest race in Europe. Chelmsford City stages two Listed races (one rank down from Group), along with the Chelmsford City Cup, worth £100,000. And maybe the punters aren't such mugs. Some reckon that all-weather races, run on consistent surfaces and often at a decent pace, are easier to work out than those on turf. I checked *Racing Post* statistics for winning favourites and found that Chelmsford City recorded a higher percentage than did courses such as Ascot and York.

We get both aspects of all-weather racing on the Chelmsford City card this Thursday evening. There is the Good Friday Spring Country Fair Handicap Stakes, a Class 7 race – the lowest grade there is. The lowest-rated horse in the race is William Ashford, assessed by the British Horseracing Authority handicappers at 41 – on a scale that goes up to 140; nevertheless, he manages to finish third. The race has prize money of £4400, whereas the Tote UK Fillies' Conditions Stakes, later on the card, has prize money of £20,000. The Peter Andre Ladies Day Novice Stakes attracts three horses owned by Sheikh Mohammed's Godolphin, the most powerful name in UK racing; Godolphin bought one of them, Reflectionist, for 900,000 guineas. They're all beaten by Da Vinci, a 16/1 shot sent down from North Yorkshire by trainer Mark Johnston. (I did think, 'Why would they send him all this way?' And then I thought, 'If they are sending him all this way because they think he can win, why is no one backing him?' There you have a loser's thought processes.)

The Class 7 handicap has thirteen runners, the fillies' race has five runners, and the novice stakes has six. This is the issue that confronts all managers of smaller courses: you can try to attract better horses, but you may find that they scare away the competition. It matters not only because smaller fields generate less betting revenue, but also because they affect applications to stage fixtures.

If you manage Ascot or Cheltenham, you don't have to worry too much about how many racedays you'll be able to stage, because they mostly roll on from year to year. Royal Ascot and the Cheltenham Festival, and most other meetings at those courses, go into the diary automatically, like birthdays and Christmas. When the British Horseracing Authority (BHA) announced that it would license Chelmsford City to stage horseracing, it gave the course an allocation of twelve fixtures. But Chelmsford City needed many more than that to be a going concern, and had to bid for them. It still does. The allocations are based on a points system involving factors such as prize money and field sizes (races with only a few runners are not good, because they are unattractive to most punters); floodlit courses such as Chelmsford City (with Southwell, Wolverhampton, Kempton, and Newcastle) also appeal to the BHA in being able to put on races at times when otherwise there would be none. Chelmsford City has fifty-nine fixtures in the calendar this year, and has already put on an extra one. Last year, it staged sixty-five.

There are about five hundred customers here today. They have paid £17 to get in, and Chelmsford City hopes that they'll buy racecards (£2.50) as well as spending money in the bars, restaurants and with the bookies. There are also, contributing about a third again to the total attendance, all the people who are employed to make this happen. This last category includes, in Chelmsford City's case, staff to set up and patrol traffic lights on an adjoining B road separating the course from the racecourse stables. As Garrity says: 'You don't want a boy racer wiping out a million-pound Godolphin thoroughbred.'

Two points jump out at you from considering the attendance figures. The first is that if the BHA gives Chelmsford City an extra raceday at a week's notice, getting the required staff in place must be quite a job. The second is that raceday receipts will fall short of sustaining a profitable business. Vital to racecourses, and enabling them to keep afloat during the forthcoming pandemic, are pre-race data sales, media rights sales, Levy income and sponsorship deals. In the summer, Chelmsford City can attract bigger crowds, and in common with fellow racecourses it stages conferences, weddings, family fun days, fairs, concerts and other events: Madness, Rick Astley and Jools Holland have performed here.

As we have seen, there is a limit to the number of turf fixtures a racecourse can stage without ruining the ground. All-weather courses do not have the same limitation; but that is not to say that they do not require care. Garrity and his team are required to pay for a sixty-page report on the state of the track each year. When Chelmsford City reopened, horses and jockeys behind the leaders were getting sand kicked in their faces. The ground staff poured on more wax, and blended it in. When the 2017 report indicated a reduction of the fibre content of the Polytrack, the ground staff blended in more fibres. The maintenance cost stands at about £600,000 to date; and at some point, the entire surface will need to be replaced.

Meanwhile, Chelmsford City plans to install a turf track, to run inside the all-weather circuit. Getting hold of the right sort of soil has been a challenge, but Garrity hopes to lay the turf this spring. With the precedent in mind of Wetherby, where a new section of course took some time to offer an acceptable racing surface, and of Yarmouth, which had to abandon a race meeting a year after relaying its home straight, he is wary of saying that he'll be able to offer turf racing before spring 2022. (The pandemic proved him right to be wary. At the end of 2021, Chelmsford announced plans to stage mixed turf and all-weather racing in the second half of the 2022 season. Then came the exceptionally dry 2022 summer, delaying the opening of the turf course until 2023.)

There is no rush as far as owners, trainers and jockeys are concerned: they have always given good reports of Chelmsford City's Polytrack. Their staff like the course too, with the National Association of

Racecourse Staff voting it third, after Ascot and York, in a survey of the most hospitable places to work. Garrity and his team invite winning owners for a glass of champagne in a glass-fronted room overlooking the paddock, show them replays of the races, and give them video diaries to take away. (Other courses offer similar treats.) The Newmarket trainer Stuart Williams told the *Racing Post*: 'Chelmsford has been great for Newmarket trainers as it's just down the road and they put on great prize money. They make you very welcome and the people are great.'

We ordinary racegoers enjoy pleasant facilities too. The betting shop, which on some courses is a noisy, beer-puddled, concrete box, has a polished wooden floor and deep leather sofas. The sports bar has a soft carpet and rows of high wooden tables. The loos, I am amazed to discover, offer not dispensers of generic soap but a choice of Bayliss & Harding black pepper & ginseng or sweet mandarin & grapefruit. No doubt my fellow male racegoers stare at these bottles and think to themselves: 'Hmmm, it's just *so* hard to choose.' 'The ring' – the betting area and the people who do business there – is sited this evening at the end of the bar, and consists of just four bookmakers. They are not unduly busy.

On the outside of the track, the commentator's and judges' tower sits where a conventional grandstand would be. Even from his perch at the top, commentator John Hunt – a familiar voice from Radio 5 Live – may not be able to see the back straight beyond the highest part of the grandstand. I take up a position in front of the Fairview restaurant, and get a good view of the straight, though I am not sure whether I'd be so fortunate if there were an extra thousand people here. The inadequacy of my race-reading skills immediately becomes apparent. I have become used to watching chasers and hurdlers racing in heavy ground. As they come into the home straight after running for, at least, the best part of two miles, they are weary, and still have fences to jump. You have plenty of time to work out who is who. After that, a race at Chelmsford is like a fast-forwarding video. The runners flash past the post, and you think to yourself: 'What just happened?'

What has happened is my Placepot has gone down in the first again. 'First, number 3 [Garsman],' the judge announces. 'Second, number 4 [Gold Brocade].' Only the first and second qualify as placed in this six-runner contest, and neither Garsman nor Gold Brocade is on my betting slip. My amusement for the rest of the evening is trying to commentate on the races in my head. It's a shambles. How do proper commentators do it?

EXETER

Jumps

21 February 2020

The view from the tower

Richard Hoiles and I are chatting in a glass and wood cubbyhole on top of a windswept tower in the centre of Exeter racecourse when, seamlessly, he dons his headphones and microphone, and introduces the runners for the first race. 'Very good afternoon, everyone, welcome to Exeter,' he begins, his words echoing back from the tannoys on the other side of the course. 'Runners for our first of seven races are heading out for the Be Wiser Insurance Chase Novices' Limited Handicap – thanks to Be Wiser Insurance for their sponsorship of all the races here this afternoon. Without number three, Midnight Tune, a field of eight – still three places for each way betting – will make their way across the centre of the racecourse, led by Know the Score for the Angove Family, David Noonan riding for David Pipe in the hooped colours of lilac and black with white sleeves . . .'

My word: where did all that come from? Already, there's confirmation of my belief that I could never do Hoiles' job – and the horses haven't even started racing yet.

Like you, I should guess, I'd need a script to help me impart this kind of information; at best, a few minutes of quiet revision would soothe my nerves. Or would they? Perhaps I over-prepare, is one of the thoughts I take away from this afternoon observing a master of his craft. Hoiles, both relaxed and self-deprecating, says that what he is really doing is fixing the details in his own mind, because only now, a few minutes before the race, is he learning the colours of each jockey's silks. My word, again.

Exeter racecourse is six miles south of the city, on top of the Haldon

Hills, and is the highest racecourse in Britain. It is also, at two miles round, one of the longest. The tower that hosts Hoiles and me is situated in order to command the best all-round view of the course, but still loses sight of the runners as they descend a dip, behind a row of conifers, in the back straight.

Racing may have begun here during the Restoration, and it certainly took place in the eighteenth century. There is a mid-eighteenth-century anecdote about a racegoer's fury when his view of the climax of a race was obstructed by a fool dressed in motley – a servant of the last family in England to employ such a figure. It must have been for his gift for repartee: on being asked, 'Whose fool are you?', the man in motley replied: 'I am Squire Fulford's fool – whose fool are you?'

This was common land at the time, but came into the possession of Sir Lawrence Palk (later Lord Haldon) in 1823. It was named Haldon racecourse, then Devon and Exeter, and then, in 1992, just Exeter. It is now owned by the Jockey Club.

Exeter's most significant race is run in November: the Haldon Gold Cup, which over the years has attracted some of the best horses around, among them the three-times Cheltenham Gold Cup winner Best Mate. His name stirs a sad memory here. Having won the race in 2001, Best Mate competed in the 2005 Haldon Gold Cup against a field that also included Kauto Star, later to win the Gold Cup twice and the King George VI Chase five times. Best Mate wasn't going well and was pulled up by his jockey, Paul Carberry. A few moments later, he collapsed and died. His trainer, Henrietta Knight, had come in for a good deal of criticism for her delicate handling of the horse, whom she allowed to run in only a few races each season; now, it was clear that she was right to be protective of this fragile animal.

I am happy to report that there are no casualties today. It is Friday, and the course is well attended. In addition to the usual racing types, there are groups of friends having a day out, young women defying the weather in sleeveless dresses, and loud young men – from agricultural college, is my guess – in green checks and flat caps. They are keeping the bookmakers busy. This is the most crowded betting ring I've seen in a while – far livelier than the one at Wetherby, where there were twice as many people.

I have shared a taxi (£26, including tip) from Exeter St Davids with two owners, whom I had met on the train. Their horse Ocean Cove, in training with Fergal O'Brien, is top weight in the first – the race we heard Richard Hoiles introducing above. They are pleased with O'Brien: he makes owners feel involved, and unlike some trainers they could mention is always available to talk on the phone. Ocean Cove came fourth in a race at Chepstow after Christmas, and my fellow taxi passengers, along with the betting market, expect him to improve on that run today.

I've paid for a premier badge, so I may as well take advantage of the facilities, and I make my way past the Best Mate Room to the Denman Room – Denman ('The Tank'), who won a Gold Cup and two Hennessy Gold Cups, raced here in 2006. The Denman Room's fish and chips earn 7 out of 10, with a point taken off for the unavailability of tartare sauce – mayonnaise would have been acceptable, but is not on offer either. The fish has an excellent, light batter; the chips are a mixed bunch, some being light inside and crunchy outside while in others the predominant qualities are, less appealingly, dryness and floppiness.

Off to the paddock, where Richard Hoiles is outlining his fancies for the seven races to an audience of one (me). The preview is broadcast throughout the course and beyond, though, via bookmakers. Then Hoiles and I cross the track to the tower. At the top of four flights of fire escape-type stairs, we meet a man whose job is to keep his binoculars on the runners and alert the medical staff to any fallers, and a young camerawoman who has to stand in the open air next to the commentary box all afternoon; there's another camera operative on the roof above us. Hoiles has a bit of banter with them. He has always made it his business, he tells me, to understand the jobs of everyone involved in racing broadcasts, partly because otherwise commentating would be largely a solitary pursuit, and partly because knowing where the cameras are and what the director is likely to do helps him to match his words to what viewers are seeing.

Last night, he printed the cards and the form guide from the *Racing Post* site, and marked on them notes about the runners culled from his own database – which he will update with observations from today when he gets home. When he arrived at Exeter this morning, he walked the entire length of the course, in part to shake off stiffness after a long drive, in part to refamiliarise himself with the layout, and in part to assess the state of the ground. He does this at every meeting, sometimes bumping into a jockey or two out for a run.

He has a pair of Zeiss 8 x 42 binoculars (they magnify eight times, and have 42mm lenses), which at Exeter he uses as the horses negotiate the turn to enter the back straight. Otherwise, the monitor gives him a clearer view of the action, though he watches finishes with the naked eye. Next to the monitor is a bank of switches, all of which he keeps in the open position, confident that a director or technician's jabbering in his ear will not put him off his stride.

His astonishingly rapid preparation for each race begins as the horses enter the paddock. Surveying them through binoculars, he notes on the card any characteristics that he hadn't known about previously: this horse has a white blaze, that one is wearing a noseband. As we have seen, he learns the colours as he introduces the horses to the crowd. Just before the off, he mutters their names to himself. Some commentators, he says, try to learn the colours the night before, or have the racecards propped up next to their steering wheels as they drive to the course. 'You put a lot of pressure on yourself if you do that,' is Hoiles' view; better to learn something quickly and then to forget it just as quickly.

They're off! I can just about keep track of the horses in my Placepot; I've already forgotten the others. Hoiles, of course, identifies them all; but what really impresses is that he observes how they're all performing, while never losing track of the essential narrative, which is what's happening up front. Springfield Fox is 'very guessy' at the first fence; towards the back of the field, our friend Ocean Cove 'rather skied' the third; another horse puts in an extra stride before jumping a fence. Ocean Cove, I'm afraid, never looks like winning: nevertheless, fifth entering the home straight, he plods away doggedly – if a horse can be dogged – while three rivals in front of him slow down like cars running out of petrol, and finishes second. Springfield Fox, who led throughout, has cantered past the post some time earlier. Hoiles brings out the information that Springfield Fox has made further progress after graduation from successes in point-to-points. It's not just knowing and observing all this stuff; it's being able to impart it under pressure. It's a super-power, surely.

Fergal O'Brien goes on to saddle another second, the thirteen-year-old veteran Perfect Candidate, in the big race of the day, the Devon National. I have already mentioned the Sussex National, which is run at Plumpton;

in addition to the principal Grand one at Aintree there are also the Welsh Grand National (Chepstow), the Highland National (Perth), the Borders National (Kelso), the Durham National (Sedgefield), the North Yorkshire National (Catterick), the Midlands National (Uttoxeter), the Norfolk National (Fakenham), the London National (Sandown), the Irish Grand National (Fairyhouse), the Ulster National (Downpatrick), the Cork National (Cork), and most likely several others. That's marketing. The Devon version is a decent race, and at three miles and six furlongs-plus compelling as marathons tend to be, but not one to arouse much fanfare, even in the racing press.

Hoiles didn't know that he wanted to be a commentator until he applied to be one. He was an accountant, looking to move on and wondering if he could find a career in racing, when he spotted a 'looking for commentators' ad from SIS, which supplied pictures and data to betting shops, in the *Sporting Life* (now a website, but then a print publication). 'I was so naive, I didn't realise that you needed to send a demo tape with the application,' he recalls. But his mother's partner, who worked in TV, helped him to record one. By this time, SIS had already turned him down; but on getting the demo tape the company backtracked and called him in for interview. There were two jobs going: Hoiles got one, and John Hunt, a former policeman who commentates now for Radio 5 Live and who was on duty when I visited Chelmsford City, got the other.

When he was starting out, racecourses mostly employed their own commentators, and were not especially hospitable to Hoiles and his colleagues. The racecourse commentators got access to the commentary boxes, while the SIS team had to find the best spots they could – sometimes an upturned crate next to a bookmaker's pitch. In his first year, Hoiles was at the races almost every other day. After a while, he began making regular appearances on *Channel 4 Racing*, where he became the number two to the broadcaster's lead commentator, Simon Holt. Racing coverage switched to ITV in 2017, with Hoiles taking over the top job (reported to have been declined by Hunt). It was a surprise appointment – not because Hoiles is not superbly skilful, but because Holt, unlike some members of the Channel 4 team, did not obviously need replacing. Perhaps ITV thought that viewers would appreciate a change: Holt had been the principal Channel 4 commentator for more than fifteen years.

The BBC had not come to that conclusion about the legendary Peter O'Sullevan ('the Voice of Racing') until he had been in the job for fifty years – but it was a different era.

Hoiles, like his fellow commentators, is freelance. When not on ITV duty, he is one of about eighteen colleagues on a rota organised by RaceTech, supplier of broadcasting and other technical services to racecourses.* He lives near Reading, but makes himself available to work at far-flung courses when the need arises. The deal is that you get a standard fee, whether you're commentating on Gold Cup day at Cheltenham or a Thursday evening card at Chelmsford City. 'We believe it's the same job,' Hoiles says. 'If anything, it's harder at the smaller tracks than it is at the bigger tracks.' The commentaries are transmitted on course, to viewers of the racing subscription services Sky Sports Racing and Racing TV, to betting shops in the UK and overseas, and to bookmakers' streaming services. When Hoiles comes to the end of his introduction of the runners for the racecourse and for the broadcasters, he carries on talking into the microphone: this is for the bookmakers' sites and apps. A humdrum afternoon at Exeter has a broad reach.

As racecourses indirectly pay his wages, I don't ask him to name his least favourite ones. 'Which courses are the most challenging?' is the way I put it. The commentary positions at Perth and Kelso are quite low, he replies, so you cannot get a proper perspective. 'I defy anyone to watch races from the Perth box and be sure who is in the lead at the second-last fence.' Figure-of-eight Windsor is also tricky, because the horses come at you from an angle. At the Devon National meeting at Exeter last year, the weather was so bad that the commentator – John Blance – couldn't see further than about seventy-five yards. But sunshine can be a problem in this glass-sided box too, glaring off the monitor. It's alarming to find that the person who is supposed to be informing the spectators what's happening can see less than they can. 'Whereas at Cartmel, you can see and most other people there can't – that's fantastic, because it makes me sound good.' Where else is he happy? 'Goodwood,' he says. 'The colours stand out, it's green, it's archetypal England. You look beyond

* None of these commentators is female. Race-calling has been even harder for women to break into than football commentary. In April 2022, Newbury announced that it was employing Dani Jackson to call the charity races at the course – a total during the summer of four. It's a start.

the stands, and you can see only two other buildings.'

Which races are the most challenging? The contests for two-year-olds at Royal Ascot, Hoiles says, are not much fun: twenty-plus horses you've never seen before charging down the straight at you. You wouldn't know it from listening to these commentaries, though. Hoiles is able to carry on thinking clearly when the rest of us would be in a panic.

'The thing with commentating is just to have fun with it and relax,' he says, perhaps not realising that, while the rest of us can appreciate that point in theory, we would never be able to put it into practice. 'When I started, I went around with various people to see how they did it. The two biggest influences were Simon Holt and Ian Bartlett (then with the BBC), because they were always themselves – they were never fazed by the job. I remember Ian saying to me: "Don't worry that there are things you won't know, because there will be – the important thing is how you get out of it."'

There are little tricks. Don't say: 'The last three are . . .', because that obliges you to name them all; say: 'The back-markers include', and if you can name only two of them, it doesn't matter. As I've mentioned, Hoiles rarely misses an incident; but what does he do if a horse falls and his attention was elsewhere? Unlike some commentators, he never uses 'spotters', whose job is to plug such gaps. Instead, he will consult his mental map, fixed as early as possible in the race, of where each horse is in the field, and then look to see what's missing; or a member of the production team may shout something through his headphones, even if it's only, 'It had red and gold colours.'

What you must avoid is naming a horse in a rush out of desperation and then finding you've got it wrong: these days, substantial amounts of money are traded on racing in-running (that is, once the race has started, and sometimes when the horses are just yards from the finishing post), and an incorrect commentary can have serious financial implications. People with public profiles get enough flak as it is. On the horseracing online forums, the busiest threads are the ones in which the users slag off racing broadcasters. When he and John Hunt started out, Hoiles says, they did not have to deal with social media trolls; young people at the starts of their careers today face confidence-sapping scrutiny. It's not all bad, though: he appreciates it when people point out if he's over-using certain phrases. 'There are only so many ways of saying things in a racing commentary, and in thirty years I've probably said them all.'

Most of my working life has involved reading books, and I am puzzled when people ask me, as they often do, whether I have been able to enjoy reading under these circumstances. Hoiles feels the same way about commentating on racing. 'I'm very fortunate to have got the opportunity to do this job, in the sport I love,' he says. 'I never forget that. If you can't enjoy it, what's the point?'

CHELTENHAM

Jumps

10–13 March 2020

Going: not

A selfish consideration clinched the debate. Our day at Cheltenham, concluding with a curry on our arrival back in London, is a delightful, thrilling break from working life. But this year, my friend Geoff and I stayed at home.

When the 2020 Cheltenham Festival opened on Tuesday 10 March, there had been 373 reported cases of coronavirus in the UK. The government was in the 'containment' phase of its response to the disease, and said that there was no reason to cancel large public events such as race meetings and football matches. But phase two, which we all knew was on the way, arrived with alarming rapidity. On Friday 13 March, all the next day's football league matches were called off, while in Cheltenham, apparently another world, Al Boum Photo won the Gold Cup in front of stands crammed with 69,000 people. The Midlands National meeting at Uttoxeter went ahead on Saturday 14, but at Kelso on Monday 16 and at Wetherby and Taunton on Tuesday 17 racing took place behind closed doors, and the following day horseracing in Britain was suspended. The lockdown would be imposed until, according to the official announcements, early May.

Geoff and I, opting out in spite of having long since bought our tickets for Cheltenham's Thursday card (12 March), were in the minority. More than 251,000 people attended the four days of the festival, only about 15,000 fewer than had been there the year before. It would have taken dire warnings to keep them away. Cheltenham for the regulars is, in the words of Greg Wood of the *Guardian*, 'Christmas for grown-ups' – an event at which racegoers 'cram a year's worth of fevered anticipation into just four days'. The broadcaster, writer and former jockey Brough Scott, who rode a horse to finish third in the 1968 Champion Hurdle, wrote on the eve of the festival: 'This year, more than ever, we need the Cheltenham Festival, not just as a race meeting but as a rite of spring.' It's also a sacramental occasion for the *Racing Post* journalist Alastair Down, who opened his pre-Cheltenham piece with an adaptation of a carol: ('O come ye, o come ye, to Cheltenham') and concluded: 'For 45 years this has been the pilgrimage that faith in the marvellous compels me to undertake. May it ever be thus with you all.'

Phew. So much for the 'great triviality'. (Though I suppose Phil Bull's point may have been that trivial things could matter a great deal.) The festival to these writers, and perhaps to the 251,000 who defied coronavirus to attend, seems to be what football was to the Liverpool manager Bill Shankly (not a matter of life and death – more important than that, to paraphrase the famous quote). So intense was the speculation about the viability of Cheltenham 2020 that a market on whether it would take place generated £4 million in bets. The year before, these four days had staged twenty-five races that appeared among Ladbrokes' list of the forty most gambled on races of the year. Cheltenham is, except to racing followers interested only in the flat, the highlight of the racing calendar, and it contributes £100 million to the local economy. Royal Ascot is splendid; but it is an event that foregrounds wealth and breeding (of spectators and horses), keeping most of us at a distance. Derby Day is no longer a date-defining spectacle. The Grand National is a distinctive epic, but is a handicap rather than a championship race run at level weights.

Come February, and fans think of little else. Between mid-February and the festival there are some fifty Cheltenham preview evenings in Britain, and twenty in Ireland. Five days before the festival, and little more than a week before the packing of more than a hundred people into a hotel meeting room will be unthinkable, I go to the London Racing Club's preview evening at the Holiday Inn near Gloucester Road, with panellists including the racing broadcaster Lydia Hislop and Phil Smith, former senior handicapper at the British Horseracing Authority. The audience has not, largely, come to secure a list of horses to back, but to enjoy the exchanges of opinion that are an essential part of any big sporting occasion – indeed, some relish the anticipation and the speculation more than they do the events themselves. In any case, following these experts will not be profitable. Asked to give their 'best bets' of the meeting, they all name horses who will turn out to be losers.

Even while Cheltenham is taking place, bookmakers are quoting prices for races at the festival the following year. Will the novice hurdle winners graduate to the line-up for next year's Champion Hurdle, or will they switch to jumping fences? Will the Brown Advisory Novices' Chase winner be a serious contender for the Gold Cup? What price the Gold Cup winner taking the race again (or, in the case of the 2020 winner Al Boum Photo, for a third time)? Trainers set out their charges' campaigns with Cheltenham as the goal, and run their best horses sparingly, for fear of over-taxing them before the days that matter the most. In each of the seasons leading up to his 2019 and 2020 Gold Cup wins, Al Boum Photo raced only once. Epatante, the 2020 Champion Hurdle winner, had not run since engagements at Newbury and Kempton at the end of the previous year.

This is a relatively recent phenomenon. Desert Orchid, winning the Gold Cup in 1989, was racing for the sixth time that season; Beech Road, the 1989 Champion Hurdle winner, was racing for the seventh time. One of the prices we have paid for the transformation of Cheltenham into an annual Olympic Games of horseracing is rarer sightings of exciting animals such as these. Another, which some people regret, is that the rest of the season can seem like a series of staging posts on the road to the main event – though British flat racing, which a few years ago instituted a Champions Day with nothing like the same status, would be grateful for such a problem. (The Breeders Cup, introduced in the US in the mid-1980s as a climax to the season there, has been a success.)

The place suits the occasion. The racecourse site of Prestbury Park is a natural amphitheatre, with the backdrop of Cleeve Hill, the highest point in the Cotswolds, lending an epic quality to the action that takes place in its shadow. It is a breath-catching experience to emerge from the stands and have this scene open up in front of you; and then, as you try to get your bearings, it can also be somewhat confusing, as you notice the jumble of running rails on the park. It's a jumble because what you are looking at is not one course, but three. The Old Course is the outer track on the circuit; at its highest point at the end of the back straight it turns sharply left, descends, and turns left again for home.

After the last fence or hurdle, the runners must negotiate the 'Chelten-ham Hill', a gruelling trial that has altered fortunes in many races. The New Course runs inside the Old, crossing it at the high point of the back straight before making a more sweeping turn and descending. Horses in two-mile-four-furlong races start in the middle of the course, make for the far end of the park, turn, and come up a straight before joining the relevant circuit. Then, also in the middle, is the Cross Country Course, presenting the runners with a series of banks, ditches and other idio-syncratic obstacles. Watching cross country races at Cheltenham or on TV, I have never understood the layout; but a map on the racecourse website shows me that it consists of a figure-of-eight first circuit; inside it, a figure-of-eight second circuit; and then an ordinary circuit that feeds into the home straight of the main racecourse. There is no vantage point, except perhaps high up in one of the boxes or in the commentary position, that will enable you to keep track of this itinerary.

Racing is first recorded as having taken place here, on the hill itself, in 1818. It was controversial. An influx of people to take the waters at the spa town was all very well, but the crowd that horseracing attracted was another, most regrettable phenomenon, according to certain locals. 'I verily believe that, in the day of judgment, thousands of that vast multi-tude who have served the world, the flesh and the devil, will trace up all the guilt and misery which has fallen on them either to the racecourse or the theatre,' preached the Reverend Francis Close. An anti-racing tract warned: 'The Heathen festivals of Venus and the Bacchus are exceeded on a Christian race ground.' The noise you hear in the town's cemeteries each March is that of the spinning skeletons of the pious.

The Grand Annual Steeplechase, the oldest race in the National Hunt calendar (the first Grand National took place two years later according to some accounts, and five according to others), was run nearby in 1834. But it was not until 1911, when a race called the National Hunt Steeple-chase – these names are highly confusable – moved to Prestbury Park, that the Cheltenham Festival proper began. In 1924, the Cheltenham chairman Frederick Cathcart founded the Gold Cup, and three years later he founded the Champion Hurdle.

Though it was a race that, in theory, the best horse won, while the Grand National might instead be decided by weight burdens rather than ability, the Gold Cup was regarded for many years as a Grand

National warm-up. The only horse to have won both races in the same season is Golden Miller, who on completing the double at Aintree in 1934 received from his owner, the moneyed and wilful Dorothy Paget, an appreciative kiss – he was, it was rumoured, the only member of his sex on whom she ever bestowed such a favour. Paget lived with an all-female staff, rarely rose before nightfall, placed bets on races that had already taken place – which her bookmaker accepted – on the grounds that she had been asleep at the time, owned many fine horses and drove their trainers mad, and died in 1960, at the age of fifty-four. Golden Miller remained her most prized horse, going on to win the Gold Cup in five consecutive years, an unequalled record.

It was a triple Gold Cup winner who was in part responsible for sparking the Irish invasion that contributes so ebulliently to the Cheltenham atmosphere. Cottage Rake (1948, 1949, 1950) was trained by Vincent O'Brien, who saddled another hat-trick horse in Hatton's Grace (Champion Hurdle 1949, 1950, 1951), and scored a further hat-trick by training consecutive winners of the Grand National (Early Mist, 1953; Royal Tan, 1954; Quare Times, 1955). Switching to the flat, O'Brien was no less masterful, managing the careers of great horses including Sir Ivor and Nijinsky. *Racing Post* readers voted him the most influential person in racing in the twentieth century.

Another great Irish horse – the greatest, in fact – lit up the 1960s. Arkle announced his arrival to the British (he was already the talk of Ireland) by winning the 1963 Broadway Chase for novices (now the Brown Advisory) by twenty lengths. But two days later at Cheltenham a giant English-trained horse, Mill House, won the Gold Cup by twelve lengths, convincing all observers apart from Irish ones that he was the best they'd seen. The debate between fans of the two was vigorous, with national pride as an intensifier.

Arkle and Mill House first met in November that year, in the Hennessy Gold Cup at Newbury. Mill House won; but Arkle, unnoticed by the TV cameras and out of sight of the spectators in the foggy conditions, had lost his chance when he slipped after jumping the third fence from home. The Irish still insisted he was the superior, and he proved it in the 1964 Cheltenham Gold Cup – the Race of the Century (among a number of races so designated). There were two other horses in the race, and though they were not untalented they were left a long way behind as Arkle and Mill House began racing against each other seriously from the third-last fence. As the rivals turned for home, Arkle – who had been four lengths behind just a few yards earlier – loomed up on Mill House's outside. 'This is it!' cried the BBC's commentator, Peter O'Sullevan – the race, unlike so many hyped contests, had become exactly the clean head-to-head that everyone had been waiting at least a year to see. And there was nothing questionable about the result. Arkle surged into the lead, maintained it at the last, and a few yards later accelerated to the line to win by five lengths. 'This is the champion!' O'Sullevan announced. 'This is the best we've seen for a long time.' He knew what he had seen. Arkle won two further Gold Cups. He met Mill House in three further races, winning each time.

To the Irish, Arkle had always been 'Himself', peerless. His bearing was commanding without arrogance: upright neck, alert head, pricked ears. He seemed to skim along the ground. He was by all accounts a gentle creature. My favourite Arkle story concerns the time when the trainer's young daughter was playing with a ball that rolled into Arkle's box. She went in, looked for it, but couldn't see it. On her way out, she felt a nudge. She turned round. Arkle dropped the ball at her feet.

Growing up, I learned on several painful occasions that sporting heroes who had seemed invincible could be beaten. I was at Kempton on 27 December 1966 when Arkle ran his last race, injuring a cannon bone and slowing almost to a standstill on the run-in, to be overtaken by Dormant, a horse far his inferior. There were similar heartbreaks to come. England lost to Germany 3-2 in the 1970 World Cup quarter-final, after being two goals up. My schoolfriends and I spent a day in stunned disappointment after waking up to the news that Muhammad Ali ('Float like a butterfly, sting like a bee') had been beaten on points by Joe Frazier; 'The broken butterfly' was the headline in one paper, above a picture of Ali lying on the canvas in the fifteenth round. Even friends with no interest in horseracing joined me in watching the 1970 Prix de l'Arc de Triomphe, which was supposed to be the triumphant climax of the Triple Crown winner Nijinksy's career, but ended in defeat. And another Cheltenham hat-trick hero, Persian War, was beaten in the 1971 Champion Hurdle.

In truth, I hadn't been paying attention: Persian War was far from invincible. In 1970, the Champion Hurdle – his third in a row – was the only race he won all season; in 1971, his loss to Bula, the rising star of the division, surprised neither pundits nor punters. Still, he was an all-time great, at the start of a golden period in hurdling, with Champion Hurdle winners who are legendary among aficionados: Bula, Comedy of Errors, Lanzarote, Night Nurse, Monksfield, Sea Pigeon.

Three remarkable Gold Cups are, I think, what most racing fans would pick out as highlights from the 1980s. In 1983, the driven and eccentric Yorkshire trainer Michael Dickinson, who had taken out his licence only three years earlier, saddled the first five horses home in the race. In 1986, the Irish mare Dawn Run, winner of the Champion Hurdle two years earlier, became the first horse ever to achieve the Champion Hurdle/Gold Cup double; she had looked beaten at the last fence, but, with Peter O'Sullevan crying 'The mare's beginning to get up!' some time before most spectators had taken on board that it was happening, dragged herself back in front by the line. In the late eighties, the grey Desert Orchid became the most famous and the most popular racehorse since Red Rum; but he seemed to have an aversion to Cheltenham, and was in danger of being remembered as are tennis players who never won Grand Slams, golfers who never won Majors, or athletes who never won Olympic Golds. Rain poured down on Prestbury Park on the day of the 1989 Gold Cup, creating the muddy ground that Desert Orchid detested; but he overcame the disadvantages of course and going, after what *Racing Post* readers later voted the Race of the Century. (Another one.)

In 2004, Best Mate emulated Arkle and won his third Gold Cup in a row. I was there to see all three of his victories, as a freeloading journalist enjoying the hospitality of a publisher – these were the days when publishers would blithely spend thousands of pounds on entertaining media folk and booksellers in boxes at racecourses. Pan Macmillan was promoting the thrillers of Jenny Pitman, reputed to be as demanding as an author as she had been as a trainer of horses such as the Gold Cup-winning Borough Hill Lad. She was always amiable enough to me, though no more amiable than the occasions required. We would gather in a glass-fronted, balconied box some three furlongs from the winning post: the balcony offered a grand view of the course, but we had to rush inside to catch the climaxes of the races on TV.

Arkle, Persian War and his successors, Dawn Run, Desert Orchid, Best Mate: these and other equine heroes brought accumulating lustre and prestige to the festival, and in 2005, the organisers introduced an extra day to the event. (As I write this there is even talk of adding a fifth day.*) I preferred it when the top-class action was packed into three days, but that is a lost position.

In 2005, after three years of freebies, I decided it was about time I paid my way. So began the first of what have become annual outings for me and a group of friends. If you know a bit about racing and have ever been to a racecourse in the company of people who know very little, you'll guess what happened. My friend Adam filled out the Placepot card as if grappling with advanced algebra, made a mistake on one line but let it stand, and went on to win £450. I won nothing.

I had a great day, however, for non-financial reasons. My favourite horse at the time was a two-mile chaser (that is, he specialised in races two miles in length; the Gold Cup distance is three miles, two furlongs) called Moscow Flyer, trained in Ireland by Jessica Harrington (whom we'll meet later). His races tended to go one of two ways: he would suffer a lapse of concentration and fall, or stay upright and win. In the 2004 Champion Chase, defending his crown, he had fallen. The winner was a horse called Azertyuiop, the assertive celebrations of whose owner John Hales, wealthy thanks to the manufacture of Teletubbies dolls, I resented. In December that year, the two met again in the Tingle Creek Chase at Sandown, with Moscow Flyer prevailing after the most thrilling race I have seen on a racecourse. Hales suggested that Azertyuiop's jockey, Ruby Walsh, had got the tactics wrong. The 2005 Champion Chase was billed as the decider. 'They shall not pass,' Hales was quoted as predicting; but Azertyuiop dropped his hind legs in the water at the water jump, lost momentum, and that was the end of his challenge. The roar as Moscow Flyer jumped into the lead at the third last, and held off his closest rival Well Chief at the last, was of such force that you felt it might lift you off your feet. I loved it.

The moment when the crowd foresees the victory of a favourite – favoured either in the betting market or in their affections – is the most spine-tingling. It happened as the field turned for home in the 2016

---

* The proposal was largely unpopular, and was dropped.

Champion Chase: everyone suddenly realised that the magnificent Sprinter Sacre – winner of the race three years earlier, out of action the next year, and a shadow of his former self in 2015 – was going to win. Most of them had backed Un de Sceaux, but that did not temper their delight as Sprinter Sacre rediscovered his best form. 'One of the great comebacks . . . what an amazing horse!' yelled commentator Simon Holt, as Sprinter Sacre beat the market leader by three and a half lengths. My only regret is that I didn't back him when I noticed that his price had drifted to an insulting 5/1; but really, you shouldn't need a financial involvement to be thrilled by such a spectacle.

This is what Cheltenham gives you, in more intense form than any other meeting: the communal excitement, the shifting emotions of the crowd as it – it is a unified force – responds to the action, the celebration of magnificent animals and their brave partners. The victors return to the paddock and winners' enclosure via a long, narrow path that runs in front of the stands; they are cheered and applauded the whole way, whether the cheerers have backed them or not. If you're on the club enclosure lawn, you have time to witness their progress as well as to make your way to the rear of the paddock before horse and jockey get there, and to cheer and applaud again. In these moments, joy is pure.

The Rachael Blackmore show

16–19 March 2021

A year ago, I didn't expect or even suspect that the only way to enjoy the 2021 Cheltenham Festival as a shared experience would be to run a tipping competition with my friends, and to watch the big race each day on a shared Zoom link. I had never heard of Zoom, for one thing. For another, I didn't allow myself to entertain the notion that – except for a very brief period in the autumn – well over a year might pass before we were able to visit racecourses again.

It has probably always been true, and is not just a phenomenon of the social media era, that it is how a story comes across rather than the facts involved that lingers in the popular memory. King Canute may have been trying to demonstrate to his courtiers that there were limits to his powers, but what endured was the image of a monarch making a futile attempt to get the tide to retreat. Perhaps the Canute analogy does not quite fit the verdict on the 2020 festival, the staging of which was damned both by the evidence and by widespread opinion. My point is, though, that while the *Racing Post* was questioning the robustness of statistics about apparent clusters of Covid-19 cases and deaths in the Cheltenham area following the 2020 festival, the argument was already lost: what clinched it was the picture of 69,000 people in packed stands the day after the World Health Organisation had declared a global pandemic. Now, when we have lived in the shadow of the virus for more than a year, the photos from Cheltenham 2020 look more grotesque still.

ITV, despite its role as a cheerleader for racing, could not ignore the issue. Its short film about Cheltenham 2020, shown on day one of the 2021 festival, included an interview with the television presenter Piers Morgan, who confuses the many people who find him an irritant by being right from time to time; he had argued for cancellation. Nick Rust, former head of the British Horseracing Authority, conceded that 'absolutely' the festival should not have taken place, but insisted that this was a question of hindsight. The government's chief medical officer Chris Whitty and chief scientific officer Sir Patrick Vallance had both advised that the event was safe; on Gold Cup day, Sir Patrick declared in a radio interview that the chances of contracting Covid-19 at a mass outdoor gathering were 'slim'. It would have been 'the easiest thing in the world' to cancel, Rust said – a disingenuous claim, given the significance of the festival to the racing world and to the local community.

Some racing people were unhappy about this film, in effect saying to ITV: 'You shouldn't have tried to give a balanced report of this subject, because it has made us look bad.' Perhaps they were so defensive because racing was dealing with the fallout from another PR disaster, caused by the appearance on social media a few weeks earlier of a photograph of leading Irish trainer Gordon Elliott sitting astride a prostrate mare who had just collapsed and died on his gallops. A friend of mine, notoriously unsentimental (he's a doctor), thought that the Elliott affair was a lot of fuss about nothing: here was an industry, was his argument, that compels animals to risk injury and death for our entertainment, that is a playground for Middle Eastern despots, and that depends on a gambling industry responsible for ruining people's lives – and yet a picture of a man behaving crassly is what causes the greatest outrage? Again, though, it's the image. What does it tell us about the attitude of Gordon Elliott to the animals in his care?

For many, it was evidence that what critics say of racing people was true: that protestations of love for horses are humbug, and that horses unlucky enough to be bred for racing are, to the industry, fodder. Elliott was banned from racing for twelve months, six of them suspended. Denise Foster, who enjoys the nickname 'Sneezy', took over the yard during his sentence, and ran his horses – the ones whose owners had not moved them elsewhere – at Cheltenham. She had three winners; three horses who had left the Elliott stable for other yards were victorious too. If he had not been banned, Elliott would have been the 2021 festival's leading trainer.

Despite unpromising circumstances, however, Cheltenham 2021 became a feelgood festival. What made it so was Rachael Blackmore, the superb Irish jockey who, as I was starting work on this book at Wetherby, was at Leopardstown adding to her already impressive tally of Grade 1 victories. On Cheltenham day one she triumphed on Honeysuckle in the Champion Hurdle; she went on to ride the winners at the meeting of the Ballymore Novices' Hurdle (Grade 1), Champion Bumper (Grade 1), Ryanair Chase (Grade 1), Mares Novices' Hurdle (Grade 2), and JCB Triumph Hurdle (Grade 1). Less happily, she came second in the Gold Cup, chasing home Jack Kennedy on Minella Indo, a horse she could have ridden but had rejected in favour of A Plus Tard; and she had four fallers. Such are the dangers of jump racing that if everything went *too* well you'd start to worry.

On TV, AP McCoy and Ruby Walsh – the two finest jump jockeys of recent years – enthused. 'She's incredible,' Walsh said; McCoy commented: 'She keeps everything simple – she's brilliant at simplicity.' Blackmore herself was modest, and she certainly was uninterested in the question of whether she was riding on behalf of her sex. She's a jockey, and she's riding good horses, end of, is her view. The sport will have moved on still further when commentators agree, and no longer feel the need to be quite so emphatic in their praise.

Three weeks later, at Aintree, Blackmore becomes the first woman to ride a Grand National winner (Minella Times). At Cheltenham 2022, she again rides Honeysuckle to victory in the Champion Hurdle; and this time, she and A Plus Tard come home first in the Gold Cup.

NEWMARKET

Flat

5–7 June 2020

The heath behind closed doors
A photographer, from a vantage point overlooking the Newmarket track as well as the entire members' enclosure in front of the stands, captures the moment when Kameko, at 10/1, hits the winning post in the 2000 Guineas of 2020. Close to the rails, a groom has her arms aloft in triumph. She does not need to worry about social distancing: only three other people, well away from her, are visible. Together, they comprise a substantial percentage of the total number of spectators for one of the most important flat races of the year. Welcome to racing at Newmarket during lockdown.

Among the current rules of lockdown racing – they will become more flexible as time goes on – are these. A few people connected with each runner, including the trainer but not including the owner or owners, are allowed on course, provided they pass a screening process involving questionnaires and temperature checks. There is monitoring to ensure that everyone sticks to the two-metre social distancing rule; in places where distancing may be difficult to maintain, such as the paddock when jockeys are being legged up to their mounts, and the start when handlers are shoving the horses into the stalls, wearing masks is compulsory. The jockeys wear masks all the time, and cannot use the shower or sauna.

The only ITV Racing presenter at the course is Rishi Persad, sports broadcasting utility player. With the aid of an extendable microphone, Persad has the task of interviewing jockeys and trainers. Just to make him feel even more lonely, rain showers give him an occasional drenching. His colleagues are broadcasting from their respective homes, relying on their broadband connections. 'I hope the neighbours aren't on their Xbox,' lead presenter Ed Chamberlin says. The atmosphere, no doubt for those on course and even for us viewers, is subdued; but we're all relieved that racing is back. 'Racing can be a force for good, bringing hope and joy to people's lives,' is Chamberlin's line. An upbeat manner is part of a TV presenter's job description; Chamberlin has the tricky task of fulfilling that requirement while not seeming to say: 'Who cares about ill people? Let's go racing!' He does it well.

The shortage of spectators certainly compromises the sense of occasion at what is supposed to be one of the most prestigious meetings of the flat racing season; but I find the races themselves as exciting as ever. Later, when football returns, I conclude that of the two sports, racing is better adapted to these conditions. A crowdless football match is like a training exercise. Without fans, the action seems neither urgent nor consequential; a vital ingredient, akin to oxygen, is missing, and the canned crowd noises that broadcasters soon introduce don't supply it. Whereas on the racecourse, one's focus narrows to the purity of the contest of magnificent thoroughbreds and their jockeys. The TV viewing figures, for this meeting and for Royal Ascot ten days later, suggest that the public – albeit desperate for any live sport after enforced abstinence – agrees.

The plot of the 2000 Guineas is absorbing enough. Indeed, it's the ideal plot, with the previous episode having ended on a cliffhanger. This is an important race: founded in 1809 and usually held on the first Saturday in May, it is the first classic of the season, run over a mile and open to three-year-old colts and fillies (though no filly has run in it for a while). The two hundred and twelfth running has an odds-on favourite, Pinatubo, who last year raced six times undefeated, earning the highest rating given to a two-year-old for twenty-five years – higher even than the one given at the same stage in his career to Frankel, probably the best flat racehorse of my lifetime. Pinatubo ended the season here at Newmarket with victory in the Dewhurst Stakes, which is the most important two-year-olds' race in Europe. Being the champion two-year-old is nice, but what really matters is how you get on at three, in this and the other classics as well as in top races at Royal Ascot and elsewhere. Is Pinatubo as good as his rating advertises? He was a lot better than his rivals last year, but has he retained that supremacy over the winter? Racing fans and racing professionals have been asking themselves these questions for the past seven months. Frankel, in the 2000 Guineas of 2011, had answered them by the time the race was half over: he was already ten lengths clear of the field.

Covid-19 denied us another plot point, involving Pinatubo's owner. In March, the High Court in London found that Sheikh Mohammed, leader of Dubai, had sanctioned the abduction to the emirate of two of his daughters after they had tried to escape his rule, and that he had waged a campaign of intimidation against his estranged wife, Princess Haya. Would he show his face at Newmarket to see Pinatubo run? Would he make his usual visits to Royal Ascot and to the Derby at Epsom, where his box is next to that occupied by the royal family, following reports that the Queen would 'distance herself' from him? We were not to find out.

The sheikh would have had a disappointing afternoon. Pinatubo, on this evidence, is no Frankel, finishing third after possibly finding the mile trip a bit too far. Kameko, who overtakes him in the final furlong, is a first winner of the race for Qatar Racing, subsidiary of race sponsor Qipco and fronted by Sheikh Fahad, a member of Qatar's ruling family.

Qatar is an increasing presence here, as owner and sponsor, bankrolling what is known as the Champions Series, as well as the Glorious Goodwood festival and other important races. We've all read stories about the alleged corruption involved in securing the 2022 World Cup for the country, and about the appalling conditions under which migrants have been working on the stadia for the tournament. Amnesty International reports Qatar to be a place where freedom of expression is 'unduly restricted' and where there is discrimination against women as well as against lesbian, gay, bisexual, transgender and intersex individuals. Oh, and Qatar has also been accused of turning a blind eye while powerful individuals in the country have sponsored terrorist organisations.

Another alleged source of terrorist funding has been Saudi Arabia, also notorious for being one of the execution capitals of the world. The owner of Frankel and many other outstanding racehorses, as well as of the significant breeding operation Juddmonte Farms, is Khalid Abdullah, a member – though apparently not involved in government – of the House of Saud. (Abdullah dies in January 2021.)

As for the United Arab Emirates, of which Dubai is a part, migrant workers are 'vulnerable to labour abuses and exploitation' here too, according to Amnesty; detainees, including foreign nationals, have been subjected to 'arbitrary arrest and detention, torture and enforced disappearance'; critics of the government have been held 'in dire conditions'.

You don't hear much talk in racing about such matters. (You don't hear it either in football – Manchester City is in the ownership of the Abu Dhabi royal family, and the Qataris own Paris St Germain.) The money means too much. Sheikh Mohammed has invested more in British racing than any other individual, and is the largest employer in Newmarket. His legacy is apparent round the world in training complexes, stud farms, houses, educational programmes, and thoroughbred bloodlines. So there was a good deal of disquiet in racing circles when in 2013 Mahmood al-Zarooni, the trainer at one of the two Newmarket yards the sheikh owns, was found to have twenty-two doped horses in his care. The scandal was bad; but much more alarming was the possibility that it might cause the sheikh to terminate his British thoroughbred operations. Fortunately, the British Horseracing Authority (BHA) and the sheikh's own investigation concluded that al-Zarooni and a few colleagues had been rogue agents, acting without anyone else at Godolphin (the sheikh's racing operation) knowing what they were doing. The BHA found al-Zarooni guilty at a tribunal, but could not interview him further, because within a couple of days he was out of the country. The *Guardian* reported: 'There was concern . . . about the astonishing speed with which the Zarooni case was processed; from samples being taken to publication of the verdict took a fortnight, whereas other BHA cases commonly take years. Most of the BHA's investigation took place after the hearing, with very few details ever being released.'

Perhaps while writing this book I'll meet someone who has trained for a controversial owner, and ask whether he or she wonders about the morality of such associations; or perhaps I'll chicken out of it. After all, I can predict the answers. The government and other industries do business with all sorts of people and regimes; why should racing observe different rules? International trade and co-operation are good, and can promote liberal values. Leading literary figures, many of them left-leaning, seem happy enough to attend the Emirates Airline Festival of Literature. Sport is one thing, politics another. And so on. Still, I do feel a bit queasy when I see ITV Racing interviews with Sheikh Fahad, helping him to promote himself as just a charming and easy-going guy.

Such thoughts, and the excellent sport, keep me absorbed during the lockdown Guineas meeting. In some ways, the circumstances suit the venue. Newmarket heath appears bleak now, and it is not much less bleak when there are 20,000 people in the stand. As you drive towards town on the A1304 and look left, you get a view of an expanse of countryside with a grandstand plonked for no apparent purpose in it; arriving at the course and seeing the running rails stretching away for over a mile across open heathland does not dispel the notion that this is some ad hoc arrangement, and that humans are temporary interlopers here.

For horse people, it is heaven – the best kind of heaven, because it offers earthly delights. James I, by reputation more enthusiastic than accomplished in the saddle, first spotted the potential of what until then had been an obscure village, though he was more interested in hawking and hunting than in racing. He built a palace here that collapsed, and commissioned Inigo Jones to design a second, where he, and his doomed successor Charles I, confirmed their reputations for profligacy, as well as for carelessness about their official obligations. 'There were daily in [Charles'] court 86 tables, well-furnished [with 500 dishes] each meal,' an observer noted.

It was Charles II who did more than anyone else to establish Newmarket as the Headquarters – that is how it is known, with a capital 'H' – of racing. He arrived in 1666, restoring the palace, and thereafter setting up his court for extended stays during the spring and autumn race meetings. He rode, and in 1671 was victorious in a race commonly thought to have been the Newmarket Town Plate, which he had been responsible for establishing six years earlier – 'I do assure the King won by good horsemanship,' a courtier insisted, as if anyone could have suspected otherwise. He acted as an adjudicator in racing disputes. He amused himself, bringing to town his queen and one or two mistresses; there was thought to be an underground passage linking the palace to Nell Gwyn's lodgings over the road. (Epsom also claims to have offered the king this facility.) Part of the palace site is now the home of the National Heritage Centre for Horseracing and Sporting Art.

Everyone spent prodigious amounts of money gambling. The king's mistress Barbara Castlemaine lost £25,000 one night, Samuel Pepys noted. Another disapproving diarist, John Evelyn, found at Newmarket 'the jolly blades racing, dancing, feasting, and revelling, more resembling a luxurious and abandon'd rout, than a Christian court'. Later, Alexander Pope wrote:

> Then Peers grew proud in Horsemanship t'excel
> Newmarket's Glory rose, as Britain's fell.

Charles's priorities became apparent when he wasted no time after his return from exile in 1660 in appointing James Darcy, proprietor of Sedbury stud, as master of the studs. Some years later, the second Duke of Buckingham, who had come to ownership of the Helmsley stud by marrying into the Fairfax family, became master of the horse. It was to these and other Yorkshire studs that horsemen began a concerted campaign of importing Eastern stallions, which came to be known by names such as Darcy's White Turk and Fairfax's Morocco Barb. The horsemen mated the stallions with their mares, and bred what would evolve into the first thoroughbred racehorses.

The best known of these stallions are the three whose male lines endure, because despite genetic science we tend to give male lines special significance. (This is not true in the Arab world, where mares are specially valued.) They are the Byerley Turk, the Darley Arabian, and the Godolphin Arabian. The male line of the Darley Arabian is dominant, though the Godolphin Arabian has a larger presence in modern pedigrees.

The Darley Arabian's son Flying Childers (1714–41) – you pronounce it with a short 'i', and not as in 'child' – was the first great racehorse of the new era, thrashing any opposition that came his way, when not simply walking over the Newmarket course after his rivals had pulled out of the challenge. Flying Childers had a brother called Bartlett's Childers, who never raced but nevertheless enjoyed stud duties and became the great-grandfather of the second great horse of the era, Eclipse.

Eclipse raced three times at Newmarket, and walked over the course once (no opponent having turned up), during his unbeaten, eighteen-race career. Two of the races were on the Beacon course, nearly four miles distant, if you follow the dog-leg layout from the winning post that Kameko passes. A portrait of Eclipse by George Stubbs in the Jockey Club Rooms at Newmarket shows the great horse at the Four-Mile

Stables before one of these races, a match against a reputedly formidable opponent called Bucephalus. The rivals raced for more than two
miles before negotiating a right turn and heading up what is known as
the Rowley Mile, in memory of Charles II's hack Old Rowley; after they
had passed today's winning post they forked left, still with about six
furlongs to go. Here Bucephalus mounted his challenge, forcing Eclipse
into the most effortful gallop of his career. Bucephalus could not go the
pace, was well in arrears at the post, and never raced again.

Eclipse, however, was out again two days later. If from the grandstand you look up the Rowley Mile course to the left, you see, running
parallel to it, the Devil's Dyke, a defensive earthwork once claimed to
have been constructed by Boadicea's Iceni but more reliably dated to
the seventh century. On the other side of the dyke is the Newmarket
July Course and the Round Course, both probably laid out or revamped
at Charles's instigation. The July course, leafier and more intimate than
the Rowley Mile, stages racing in July and August – though the diary
is altered in this year of the pandemic. The Round Course, now in use
only for modern runnings of Charles's Town Plate, was then the stage
for racing run in heats, sometimes four of them of four miles each in one
day. Such contests were trials of 'bottom', a quality they admired very
much in that era, whether possessed by men or by horses: it implied
stamina, courage and soundness. Eclipse possessed bottom in spades,
demonstrating it in this contest by seeing off two of his four rivals after
the first heat, and eliminating the third, Pensioner, by finishing more
than a distance – 240 yards – ahead of him in heat two.

His bottom notwithstanding, Eclipse at stud – along with his leading contemporaries – sired horses who, as well as possessing stamina,
were speedy. The racing programme began to change to accommodate
them. Lord Derby and chums set up the Oaks, a mile-and-a-half race
for three-year-old fillies, at Epsom in 1779; a year later, they introduced
the Derby, a mile race, extended to a mile and a half in 1784, for three-
year-old colts and fillies, with sons of Eclipse winning three of the first
five runnings.

The story of Eclipse intersects with another important development
in racing history. The Jockey Club set up a base at Newmarket in 1752,
and soon became the ruling body of racing in the town – and, later, in
the country. (Some historians believe the club to have been active earlier

than this.) It never admitted Eclipse's owner, Dennis O'Kelly, to membership: a former debtor, the partner of a brothel madam, and a ruthless gambler, O'Kelly wasn't quite the thing. Today, as mentioned above, the Jockey Club Rooms at Newmarket have on display a Stubbs portrait of Eclipse, as well as a mounted hoof of the great horse and a whip into which are reputedly woven hairs from Eclipse's tail. The club instituted the 2000 and 1000 Guineas.

World wars have failed to interrupt the classics programme. There have been adjustments: the Derby and Oaks moved from Epsom to the Newmarket July Course during the Second World War, and this year Covid-19 has delayed the two Guineas races and the Derby by a month each. The atmosphere is weird, with furiously contested and exciting sport taking place to the accompaniment of less noise than you'd hear at curtain call for an experimental play in a pub theatre. Some things never change, though – such as speculation about the next important race as soon as this one is over. Kameko looks rather good, but boasts a family tree suggesting he may not have inherited a great deal of stamina: will he be able to cope with the extra half-mile of the Derby? A day later, a filly called Love wins the 1000 Guineas for trainer Aidan O'Brien, who is not at Newmarket to witness it because if he were he'd have to go into quarantine on returning to Ireland: Love does have stamina in her pedigree, and immediately is quoted at short prices for the Oaks. On we go.

ASCOT

Flat (also stages jumps racing)

16–20 June 2020

The show goes on

I wouldn't have gone anyway. The Royal Enclosure is not my scene, and the grandstand, known as the Queen Anne Enclosure, is intolerably packed and rowdy. I sound like a snob with a chip on my shoulder, I know.

Why is it fun to be at Epsom on Oaks day and to mingle with 70,000 others at Cheltenham, and torture to be at a crowded meeting at Ascot? The Epsom enclosures are on a more human scale: that's one factor. At Cheltenham, you can find placid spots: in the back corner of the parade ring, for example, or on the lawn in front of the stands. At both courses, it's possible to watch the races undisturbed. At Ascot, in my experience, the grandstand spectators move about like commuters rushing for a train; you're just in their way, and if you've found a good viewing spot and they decide to plant themselves directly in front of you, too bad. I sound like an apoplectic contributor to the *Daily Telegraph* letters page, I know.

On a quiet day, it's delightful. You get the run of the place: Ascot drops its distinction between the King Edward VII Enclosure (the name of the Royal Enclosure at other meetings) and Queen Anne Enclosure,* allowing anyone to visit, say, the coffee shop with its widely spaced tables and shaded terrace. I went on a very hot Friday in July. Occasions arise from time to time when lager is the ideal beverage, and this was one of those days, after a fifty-minute train journey in a sweaty carriage

---

* A recent visit suggests that the distinction has been reinstated. But a King Edward ticket was only £5 more expensive.

and a walk from the station. On the top floor of the impressive Ascot stand, opened in 2006 and with an ambiance reminiscent of airport terminals, is the Stella bar.* I had a half, expecting to be charged as if it were champagne, but was amazed to find that the cost was reasonable – I've paid almost as much for a bottle of water at other race meetings. Then I had another half. Now I sound like a timid fusspot.

I would rather have been among the 500-odd people who were inside the Ascot grounds for Royal Ascot 2020, even if the coffee shops and bars were closed, than among the 60,000 to 70,000 people who would have been there without the Covid-19 lockdown. But I don't think many others felt this way. Not the Queen, who missed the meeting for the first time in her 58-year reign. She was watching on TV in Windsor Castle down the road, confided her racing manager John Warren: 'Every day of her life, she follows racing one way or another when she can, so she would have read the *Racing Post* in great detail and built up to this week, and known very well the important fancied horses.' Not the Royal Enclosure members, for whom Ascot, whether they are interested in racing or not, is as fixed in their calendars as public holidays. Not the other racegoers, almost all of them far less bothered by minor inconveniences than I am. Not the owners, barred from the course (the Queen was in this category too), and receiving only half of the original prize budget of more than £8 million.

The horses probably didn't mind. Some of them may have benefited from the conditions: the champion sprinter Battaash, inclined to get agitated amid a crowd and twice defeated at previous royal meetings, remained calm this year, and scored a brilliant victory in the King's Stand Stakes, a highlight on day one.

The Queen had a third reason for regretting the diminished Ascot: she owned the place. The racecourse is part of the Crown Estates, and is leased by the Ascot Authority, over which Her Majesty had ultimate control. Her predecessor Queen Anne founded the course in 1711; it was enclosed and came into Crown ownership in 1813. George IV ('Prinny') and Edward VII ('Bertie') were the previous most enthusiastic royal promoters of the meeting, the latter to the alarm of his mother, Queen

---

* Now Peroni.

Victoria, whose request that he stay away from Ascot for a couple of days provoked him to rebellion: 'As I am past 28 and have some considerable knowledge of the world and society, you will, I am sure, at least I trust, allow me to use my discretion in matters of this kind,' Bertie insisted. In 1897 Bertie's horse Persimmon, the Derby and St Leger victor the year before, won the Gold Cup, the most prestigious race of the meeting. The late Queen won the Gold Cup in 2013 – she was the first reigning monarch to do so – with Estimate.

Ascot cannot be badly off, one imagines. Still, the loss of crowds at the royal meeting – they usually generate 70 per cent of the turnover from the five days – is a big blow. Three hundred thousand tickets unsold. All that food not eaten and champagne not drunk, at prices for hospitality packages rising to about £2000 per person. There was a 'communicable disease' insurance policy for Royal Ascot, as there was for the Grand National and the Derby; but one suspects that the payout fell some way short of matching all the expected income – and Ascot incurred a good number of the costs of staging a five-day meeting anyway, with only media rights and Levy payments from the betting industry in return. The course lost three racedays before the royal meeting, will have to stage another important raceday, featuring the King George VI and Queen Elizabeth Diamond Stakes, behind closed doors, and must be doubtful – with good reason, it transpires – about bringing spectators back in significant numbers for its autumn highlight, Champions Day. It all adds up to a £20 million loss.

I talk to Nick Smith, Ascot's director of racing and public affairs, a month after the royal meeting, and he's not entirely confident of returning to normal even in time for the royal meeting in 2021.* 'It's going to be really tough going forward, there's no question,' he says. 'I mean, it's a robust business and we'll be fine, but we'll have to do a complete remodelling for the next two years to gradually bring us back to where we were – and that's assuming that there's a solution to the social distancing requirements. If there's no vaccine, it might just be that like all sports venues – and places like theatres and cinemas, which are in an even worse position – we're going to have to find a new way of doing

---

* It went ahead with 12,000 spectators a day. For 2022, Ascot announced that its maximum capacity would be reduced, to provide 'an enhanced experience for all our racegoers'.

things, and to cut our costs. At Royal Ascot, you have lavish entertaining – well, there won't be any lavish entertaining.'

One of Smith's usual tasks is to travel round the world schmoozing owners and trainers, in order to persuade them to come to Ascot with their best horses. From mid-March this year onwards, he was grounded. He and his colleagues set about planning the centrepiece of their year without knowing whether it would take place, let alone whether any overseas competitors would join in. By mid-May, Smith and other members of what had become known as the Resumption of Racing group began drawing up a nationwide fixture list, on the assumption, then unconfirmed, that the sport would return at the beginning of June. Then Ascot framed its own programme, rearranging its usual schedule to co-ordinate with the emergency fixtures. For example, the St James's Palace Stakes is normally a highlight on day one, which this year fell only ten days after some of the potential competitors had run in the 2000 Guineas; it moved to day five. Other races, usually regarded as consolation events for also-rans in the Derby and the Oaks in early June, were transformed into trials for those classics, due to be run on 4 July. Owners would receive personalised racecards, and a 360-degree camera in the parade ring would enable them to focus on their own horses before the races. Confirmation that all this planning had not been futile did not arrive until the evening of Saturday 30 May.

Four members of the Ascot ground staff had been maintaining the track. Towards the end of May, the whole team got to work, not only on the racing surface, but on every area of the course, and on floral arrangements that, poignantly, were as immaculate as if prepared to beguile tens of thousands of visitors. After the meeting, Ascot donated its plants to local care homes. Markers and signs giving social distancing instructions were installed. Food for the people on course each day was ordered. 'For an organisation that's used to doing 12,000 lunches and teas a day, 500 take-away packets of lunch wasn't a massive job,' Smith observes. But he was as busy as he has ever been answering questions from the media. The day before the meeting, film and radio crews got access to the grounds, at intervals; for the next five days, they would have to park themselves outside the gates.

During the meeting, he wasn't so busy. 'Normally, I'd be in the parade ring and the winners' enclosure for most of the time, making sure the

programme is up to speed, talking to owners, taking winning owners
and guests to the room we have for them. Or I'd be rushing from one
enclosure to another – something's wrong in the grandstand, a window
has fallen in – that sort of thing. And there's a bombardment of media
queries, mostly about stuff like whether we're being strict about short
skirts, or who's in the royal procession.' This year, Smith and his fellow
Ascot directors had the time to watch each race from the stands, and then
to make their way to the parade ring viewing area – they weren't allowed
in the ring itself – to ensure the winners got at least some applause.

It was all a bit surreal, he found. 'Watching a horse race without a
crowd is a pretty strange experience. As Frankie Dettori said, you
needed an espresso to pick yourself up a bit.' But Dettori and his fellow
jockeys were committed to the cause. Ryan Moore, sometimes uncomfortable in front of a microphone, was statesmanlike when interviewed
after winning race two, the Queen Anne Stakes, on Circus Maxmimus,
after a tremendous tussle with Dettori's mount Terebellum: 'We're very
happy that we're here and racing. Obviously it's not the same, and [the
lack of a crowd] detracts from it all, but that's the world we're in at the
moment and we'll just have to make the best of it and keep going and
putting on the best show that we can.' Watching from home, I was rather
moved that a sportsman at the top of his profession should acknowledge
his and his fellow jockeys' role in entertaining the public.

The ITV racing frontline presenters are, by design or not, a human
illustration of the class distinctions suggested by the three Ascot enclosures (Royal, Queen Anne and, about a quarter of a mile distant from
the winning post, Windsor): at podia set apart at medically approved
distances are Francesca Cumani, racing royalty as the daughter of
trainer Luca Cumani; Ed Chamberlin, sports broadcaster, regular guy;
and Jason Weaver, former jockey and once an apprentice at the Cumani
yard. In the centre of the pre-parade ring, penned in, is another former
jockey, Mick Fitzgerald, famous for declaring of his Grand National
victory aboard Rough Quest: 'After that . . . even sex is an anti-climax.'
Hoping for similarly memorable quotes at the winners' podium, and
armed with an extendable microphone, is Matt Chapman, who dials
down his usual bludgeoning manner and conducts thoughtful and interesting interviews with victorious jockeys and trainers. Oli Bell, member
of another elite racing family, is at home fielding social media comments

for a segment called the Social Stable, which before the lockdown had seemed to me to be painfully trivial and unnecessary, but has found its place since.

Richard Hoiles is in his usual commentator's perch at the top of the stands, about twenty yards along from his old chum Ian Bartlett, appointed to deliver the commentary for the racecourse. Bartlett is not there simply to inform the few spectators at Ascot: his words will be streamed to bookmakers' sites and apps as well as, should they want it, to more than a hundred countries with broadcasting rights to the meeting. When Hoiles's delivery intensifies towards the climax of each race, so does Bartlett's, distinctly audible to the TV audience as a contrapuntal voice undampened by crowd noise.

Soon, the unusual circumstances recede from one's attention, and the racing comes to the fore. After getting touched off in the Queen Anne Stakes, Frankie Dettori wins the next race on board the pleasingly named Frankly Darling, who is immediately quoted at short prices for the Oaks (in which she is to finish third). Pyledriver's victory in the next race means that he becomes a contender of interest in the Derby (in which he will finish eleventh). Then comes the five-furlong sprint, the King's Stand Stakes, with the nervy odds-on favourite Battaash. The cameras focus on Battaash as he leaves the paddock with his groom, Bob Grace – no sprinter himself, with his burly physique and limping gait. But the horse, with Grace's familiar figure at his side, remains calm. After Battaash has sped past the post two lengths clear of his nearest rival, Grace, who has never previously led up a winner at the royal meeting, gets the main TV interview – normally, he would have faded into the background by this point.

Further stories emerge. On day two, the Queen has a winner: Tactical, trained by Andrew Balding, brother of broadcaster Clare. On Saturday, Frankie Dettori rides three winners, dismaying bookmakers (because punters like backing him) and overtaking Jim Crowley to become the leading rider at the meeting, for the seventh time. After pundits state that the Coventry Stakes, the most prestigious race for two-year-olds at the meeting, usually goes to a horse prominent in the betting, Nando Parrado wins it. He has run once before, finishing fifth of eleven in an apparently minor race at Newmarket, and is priced at 150/1 – the longest odds ever returned by a Royal Ascot winner.

Royal Ascot's flagship day is the Thursday of the meeting, Gold Cup day, also known unofficially as Ladies' Day. But the Gold Cup is not the race it was when the likes of Persimmon were winning it. You won't find a Derby winner in the field now. Horseracing, in common with other sports, has become more specialised, and horses no longer switch easily between mile races, mile-and-a-half races (the Derby distance), and races over two and a half miles (the Gold Cup distance). Moreover, there is little demand for 'stayers', as horses who race over distances of two miles and beyond are known, as stallions, except perhaps to breed racers over jumps: flat breeders value speed. The ultimate prize from contesting most championship flat races – a lucrative career in the breeding shed – is no longer part of the Gold Cup offering. In some years, the Gold Cup crowd gets the unexciting spectacle of a race between horses whose principal qualification is that they were too slow to compete at more fashionable distances.

Not this year. Stradivarius, who has won the past two Gold Cups and is going for the hat-trick, boasts a combination of stamina and a turn of foot: he would be competitive at much shorter distances. The mount of Frankie Dettori, he is odds-on favourite. But there is a cloud over him today, and not a metaphorical one: it is pouring with rain, and according to his trainer John Gosden, Stradivarius is not happy on soft ground.

Perhaps Stradivarius's tastes have changed; or perhaps he has decided to make an exception of this occasion; or perhaps he doesn't mind this sort of soft ground, loose rather than stickily muddy; or perhaps his opponents like the ground even less than he does: anyway, Stradivarius cruises up to the leader as the field enters the short Ascot straight, and when Dettori asks him to accelerate, whizzes a distance clear. The others look as though they'd been galloping through soft ground for two and a half miles, and he looks as though he's sprinted for one and a half furlongs. 'I was worried about the rain, and he actually really surprised me because he went like a hot knife through butter,' Dettori said. 'I had everybody covered by the four [furlong marker], then was surprised that I didn't have anyone to challenge me. There is always a scary moment when you get to the furlong marker, whether you will pick up or not, but he did and stretched away by ten [lengths].'

Just over a month later, Stradivarius wins his fourth Goodwood Cup (two miles) in a row; after the field dawdles for two-thirds of the distance, Stradivarius, locked in by his rivals, escapes just in time, and has enough speed to overtake them, prompting his owner to commit him to the most prestigious middle-distance race in Europe, the Prix de l'Arc de Triomphe in October (one and a half miles). The Goodwood evidence suggests that this is a plausible ambition; the profiles of past Arc winners indicate otherwise, and turn out to be the better guide (he finishes seventh).

Apart from the not-making-any-money thing, Royal Ascot at Home, as it is branded, is a success. TV viewing figures, despite the absence of frocks and hats to goggle at, are up. Ascot's #StyledWithThanks promotion, encouraging people to dress up just to watch the racing on TV, post pictures of themselves on social media, and donate to frontline charities, raises £166,000; the photos submitted will become a 'giant rainbow mosaic image tribute' installed at the course. Total contributions for charity from the meeting, with bookmakers and jockeys also making donations, are £400,000. Frankie Dettori gives a signed saddle-cloth on which he rode his seventieth Royal Ascot winner, and someone bids £30,000 for it. All the jockeys donate the riding fees they would have received on the final day.

So there have been good things. The decision to go ahead with the Cheltenham Festival in March attracted mostly bad publicity for horseracing, despite the organisers' protests that they were acting on government advice; but racing since the easing of lockdown has been well received, and generates more coverage for the sport than it had enjoyed for some time. 'I'm not saying,' Nick Smith qualifies, 'that coronavirus has been a good thing – it has been absolutely horrendous for everyone, and it will take the industry years and years to recover. But we haven't panicked. We've learned a lot, and there are positives we can take forward.'

The next big challenge for the sport is to take the positives from an empty Epsom Downs on Derby Day.

EPSOM

Flat

4 July 2020

56,000/1

'The most disappointing finish since the *Game of Thrones* finale' was one social media verdict on the 2020 Derby, won by the 25/1 shot Serpentine.

There's a swimming pool I know in Normandy with a giant water slide. You start on a gentle incline, and may have to push yourself forward. Then the tunnel goes dark, so that you don't see, and are not ready for, the sudden drop, and you plummet helplessly for the rest of the descent, eventually being fired, arms and legs flailing, into the water below. A similar challenge faces the runners in the Epsom Derby as they hit the sharp incline to Tattenham Corner, at the entrance to the Epsom home straight: some horses gallop down happily, while others lose control. Serpentine, in the former camp, freewheeled, while his opponents had to apply the brakes, and a lead that had been a couple of lengths at the top of the hill turned into twelve lengths. 'Will they catch him?' asked racecourse commentator Simon Holt; but by then, he and everyone else watching could see what the answer was. Serpentine was still five and a half lengths clear at the winning post. In second place was Khalifa Sat, at 50/1; third was Amhran Na Bhfiann, at 66/1. The result of the Derby is not supposed to look as if it has been randomly generated.

This 1/2/3 is what you call a Placepot buster. Of the total Derby Day Placepot pool of £135,759, only £24.56 was wagered by backers whose cards listed Serpentine, Khalifa Sat, or Amhran Na Bhfiann. For each £1 bet into the pool, the payout was £5527.60. The tricast – predicting the first three in the correct order – paid, for a £1 stake, £55,977.83.

A good many punters and serious racing fans were disgruntled. You look forward to the Derby for months, you study the form, you endure the fear that Covid-19 will enforce the first ever cancellation of the world's most famous horserace, you enjoy the qualified relief of learning that it will be staged behind closed doors, you wonder if there'll be a winner fit to join racing immortals such as Nijinsky and Shergar; and then a 25/1 outsider steals the race. Theft is the metaphor that observers use: Serpentine's opponents were like patsies who realise only in hindsight how their pockets have been picked. The colt's little-known jockey, Emmet McNamara, set only a steady gallop, lulled his rivals into thinking that they had him in their sights, and escaped from them before they had time to react. Khalifa Sat and Amhran Na Bhfiann were in the first three throughout. If McNamara had set off too quickly, as his fellow jockeys appear to have thought he had done, the front three would all have been caught and overtaken.

For some, an anomalous result spoils what should be a test of greatness. For the rest of us, it's a good story. For trainer Aidan O'Brien, it's a record eighth win. 'Incredible really, Ed,' he tells ITV frontman Ed Chamberlin via Skype from the Ballydoyle stables in County Tipperary; but then earlier in the afternoon he had described the definitely deserved and highly impressive Oaks victory of his filly Love as 'Unbelievable really, Ed.' In any O'Brien interview, you can predict at least half of what he will say.

Racing fans tend to smile wryly when they listen to O'Brien, pointing out that he trains for the powerful Coolmore bloodstock operation, and that his first duty is to enhance the value of the business rather than to say anything that might interest the public. Cynics are also suspicious about O'Brien's policy of entering up to half a dozen horses in top races such as the Derby, suggesting that most of his runners are there to diminish the chances of the others rather than to aim for victory themselves. But I have come round to a different view. Serpentine, as we have noted, was a 25/1 shot. In 2017, O'Brien saddled Wings of Eagles to win the Derby at 40/1. His 2013 winner, Ruler of the World, was a shorter price at 7/1, but beat the more fancied runner from the stable, Battle of Marengo, ridden by O'Brien's son Joseph. If Aidan O'Brien has been attempting to manipulate the running of the Derby in favour of his fancied runners, he's been making a hash of it.

We should be grateful to O'Brien and Coolmore, because in targeting the Derby they have done more than anyone to shore up the prestige of the race. Their 2001 winner Galileo was, until his death in 2021, the dominant stallion in the European breeding industry, siring a record five horses who followed in his footsteps at Epsom, Serpentine being the latest; O'Brien's three further Derby winners were also sons of Coolmore stallions. Coolmore may be the only contemporary conduit of the spirit of the remark by the Italian breeder Federico Tesio (1869–1954): 'The Thoroughbred exists because its selection has depended, not on experts, technicians or zoologists, but on a piece of wood: the winning post of the Epsom Derby.'

Despite Coolmore's contribution, the Derby is not as momentous as it once was – when Tesio made his remark, or when the Victorian parliament went into recess during the week of the race. You could not now translate into twenty-first-century idiom the words of the painter and journalist Ben Marshall, who in 1830 described the Derby as of 'extraordinary excitement and interest to the sportsman, and to millions of others in every part of England, from the manufacturers of twelve stories high to the Yorkshire ploughman; from the cockney behind his counter to the cellarman at Hatchett's'. (Hatchett's was a hotel and coffee bar in Piccadilly.) From dawn onwards, the roads from London to Epsom, seventeen miles distant, were congested with conveyances ranging from grand carriages to costermongers' carts, and with racegoers trudging along on foot. William Powell Frith's painting *The Derby Day* (1858) captures the scene on the Hill, the common land in the centre of the course (not far from the place where, in 1913, women's suffrage campaigner Emily Davison was to throw herself, fatally, at the King's Derby runner Anmer): here are top-hatted members of the Reform Club, thimble-riggers out to rob them (the unwitting spectator would try to identify which thimble concealed a pea), pickpockets, circus performers, musicians, society ladies and gentlemen drinking champagne, and beggars; on the left of the painting is a society courtesan, and on the right is a bare-footed young girl offering flowers for sale to an arrogant young buck. Half a mile away is the grandstand, and only a small patch of the course is visible. Derby Day, for most of the teeming crowd, was a jamboree with a horserace attached; and Frith was interested in the jamboree.

As on the Hill, there was a good deal of skulduggery in the race. One trainer was reported to have confessed that he twice won the Derby – a contest for three-year-old colts and fillies – with horses who were four years old. The first past the post in the notorious Derby of 1844 was certainly four, as was demonstrated in a subsequent court case: entered as Running Rein, he was in fact called Maccabaeus. (More about 'the dirtiest Derby in history' in a later chapter.)

Such shenanigans did not compromise the reputation of the Derby as, in the words of Benjamin Disraeli – though no racing man himself, he was talking to a man who was, and who was devastated after seeing the Derby won by a horse he had sold – 'the blue ribbon of the Turf' (again, more about this later). Nor did the apparent inappropriateness of the venue.

It is typical of the British that they should stage a race of this importance on a weirdly configured course over rolling downland; the term 'flat racing' seems misapplied. As the runners leave the stalls, they face a climb of about forty metres in half a mile. At the top of the hill, they turn and start a descent that is at first gradual, then steep – a tipster once predicted that a tall horse among the contenders that year would negotiate this section 'like a giraffe on a helter-skelter – without a mat'. Entering the home straight at Tattenham Corner, they have about three and a half furlongs to run, and continue to descend, but more gradually, until the course levels a furlong from the winning post; for the entire straight, they also have to negotiate a pronounced camber towards the far rail.

If you were designing a fair championship course by committee, you would not come up with this. But, somehow, it works. I can think of only one horse in my lifetime who should have won the Derby but who was defeated by the Epsom contours: the brilliant Dancing Brave (1986), who didn't enjoy running downhill, came into the home straight last, struggled to regain his balance, and then overtook the entire field – save a horse called Shahrastani. Dancing Brave's jockey, Greville Starkey, never lived it down, but was probably not to blame. Dancing Brave went on to win the Eclipse Stakes, the King George VI and Queen Elizabeth Stakes, and the Prix de l'Arc de Triomphe, and in the last two put Shahrastani in his proper place, some distance behind him.

The Derby is run here because the 12th Lord Derby lived nearby, at a house called The Oaks, where he enjoyed entertaining lavishly. In 1778, he and his houseguests, among them the author of *The School for Scandal* Richard Sheridan, decided to apply the house name to a new race, to be run over a mile and a half by three-year-old fillies. The first Oaks took place on 14 May 1779, and was won, satisfactorily, by Bridget – owned by Lord Derby. He and his guests decided to build on this success with another new race. Legend has it that Derby and Sir Charles Bunbury, the 'perpetual president' of the Jockey Club, tossed a coin to decide naming rights; but as this story first appeared in print a hundred years later, it may not be reliable. Anyway, the Derby it was; and other racing jurisdictions adopted the name for their own championship races, such as the Kentucky Derby at Churchill Downs (which, like all American courses, is a flat oval). The Bunbury Cup is a seven-furlong handicap at Newmarket.

The Epsom card on 4 May 1780 featured, as well as the races, a round of cockfighting, about which Lord Derby was as enthusiastic as he was about horseracing: he used to stage fights in the drawing room at The Oaks until his second wife, the actress Eliza Farren, put a stop to them. Race one on the card was the Derby Stakes, a mile contest for three-year-old colts and fillies, and compensation, if such were needed, for Bunbury: his horse Diomed won, at 6/4. Second came Budrow, the charge of the roguish Dennis O'Kelly, finding Bunbury his nemesis here as well as in his doomed ambition to become a member of the Jockey Club. O'Kelly, whose Eclipse was the greatest horse of the era, returned the following year to win the Derby with Eclipse's son Young Eclipse. At Eclipse's racecourse debut, at Epsom twelve years earlier, O'Kelly had made the most famous prediction in racing: 'Eclipse first, and the rest nowhere.'

In 1784, the Derby distance was extended to a mile and a half. The race took a while to achieve its pre-eminent position in the calendar, and was only halfway there in 1801 when the trainer Cox, mortally ill and sharing his last words with the local parson, managed to utter: 'Depend on it, that Eleanor is the hell of a mare.' A short while later, Eleanor became the first filly to win the Derby, and the following day she won the Oaks as well. Five further fillies have been Derby winners: Blink Bonny (1857), Shotover (1882), Signorinetta (1908), and Tagalie (1912). But it doesn't appear likely to happen again any time soon. The last filly even to take part was Cape Verdi (1998), who started as the favourite but finished unplaced, perhaps discouraging trainers from entering their female charges ever since. That is not to say that fillies could not win the Derby: any racing fan, given the benefit of hindsight, would have backed the 2017 Oaks winner Enable, for example, to beat that year's Derby winner Wings of Eagles.

In the nineteenth century and for a good part of the twentieth, winning the Derby meant the world, and being on the wrong end of the result was devastating. 'Hermit's Derby broke my heart, but I didn't show it, did I?' said the Marquess of Hastings, having lost £120,000 on the 1867 race by betting against Hermit, owned by the husband of his mistress. Hastings was to die the following year, at the age of twenty-six. The man whom Disraeli had found in a state of misery after the Derby victory of a horse he had sold was Lord George Bentinck, who told the future prime minister: 'All my life I have been trying for this, and for what have I sacrificed it?' The answer was politics, clearly a lesser matter. Bentinck died a few months later, at forty-six. I don't really suppose that the Derby results were the fatal blow in these cases; but they indicate the level of obsession that the race inspired.

Another Victorian aristocrat, Archibald Primrose (the Earl of Rosebery), indicated his priorities when he chose to be sent down from Oxford rather than give up his racing interests. 'Dear Mother,' he wrote, 'I have left Oxford. I have secured a house in Berkeley Square; and I have bought a horse to win the Derby. Your affectionate Archie.' He was wrong about this horse, but did not miss out on his ambitions, reportedly stated at the time, to win the Derby, marry an heiress, and become prime minister – unlike Lord George Bentinck, he never regarded political and sporting aims as incompatible. In 1878, he married banking heiress Hannah de Rothschild, the wealthiest woman in Britain; he became prime minister in March 1894; and he saw his horse Ladas win the Derby in early June that year. He won the Derby again, with Sir Visto, in late May 1895, just a few weeks before his brief premiership came to an end.

Prinny, the future George IV, won the 1788 Derby with Sir Thomas. Another Prince of Wales, Bertie (the future Edward VII), won in 1896 with Persimmon and in 1900 with the topically named Diamond Jubilee (his mother Victoria celebrated the sixtieth anniversary of her reign in the year of the horse's birth), and in 1909 enjoyed the unique achievement of winning the race as monarch, with Minoru. Queen Elizabeth's Aureole, in coronation week in 1953, finished second, and in 2011 her horse Carlton House started favourite but finished third. She had two Oaks victories, thanks to Carrozza (1957) and Dunfermline, who triumphed in the silver jubilee year, 1977.

The victory of Lord Rosebery's Ladas caused a scene of 'happy pandemonium' at Epsom, according to racing historian Roger Mortimer. Two years later, when Persimmon won, 'the downs echoed from one end to another with cheers that were renewed again and again'. A film of the finish set a new vogue for newsreels when it was shown in London theatres the following day; audiences stood, demanded encores, and shouted 'God bless the Prince of Wales!'

One cannot imagine similar acclaim for a horse owned by any recent prime minister, or by the king and his consort. We might be happy enough for them, but we would not experience the feeling that apparently animated the Victorian celebrants: that this was a victory that we shared. The Derby is no longer a public jamboree.

The change in perception of the Derby took place gradually, over the second half of the twentieth century. There have been various contributing factors. One, in our mass media era, has been increased competition from other sporting events, and from other horseraces that have assumed significance in the racing calendar. Racing people sometimes fear that this constitutes an existential crisis – but we should remind them that it is a phenomenon that has affected sports events that are not otherwise thought to be in danger of decline – for example the FA Cup, which, particularly since the creation of the Premier League, has a much lower profile than it once enjoyed.

The second factor is the modern predilection for speed. As I have suggested, a Derby winner would not command a high fee among breeders unless he had top-class form at shorter distances. When Galileo won the 2001 Derby, Aidan O'Brien reported that the horse's future engagements would include the Queen Elizabeth II Stakes (over a mile) and the Breeders Cup Classic (over a mile and a quarter, on American dirt): he was giving the message to breeders, 'Whatever kind of racehorse you want, Galileo's sperm will impart those attributes.' In the end, Galileo stuck to a mile and a half and a mile and a quarter; his best advertisements as a stallion were his offspring.

I have a theory that the retirement in 1995 of Lester Piggott also has something to do with it. Piggott rode a record nine Derby winners, and his presence in the race encouraged thousands of occasional punters to back his mounts, just as the Victorian public happily backed anything ridden by the brilliant but doomed Fred Archer ('Archer's up!' – Archer rode the last and greatest of his five Derby winners, Ormonde, in 1886, just over five months before, in a delirium caused in part by his brutal weight-reducing regime, he shot himself). Frankie Dettori is pretty well known, but not by comparison with these two. (Though when I was at school, a friend asked me whether Lester Piggott was a man or a horse.)

In the year of Piggott's retirement, Epsom acknowledged these trends by switching the Derby from its traditional Wednesday slot to Saturday, hoping to attract the larger audience that attends or watches sports at the weekends. The special Derby atmosphere, of a carnival that is all the more joyous for taking place on a day that would otherwise be devoted to work, is lost, critics argued – and still argue. They are right; but it had gone anyway, and could never be recreated. A good deal endures. Viewing figures are up, both in this country and round the world; the total audience for the race is reckoned to be upwards of 150 million. The ratio of outstanding horses the Derby reveals does not appear to have declined: in this century, they have included Galileo, High Chapparal, Sea the Stars, Camelot and Golden Horn – not all of them trained by Aidan O'Brien.

Epsom is my favourite among the premier league racecourses. I haven't tested this affection with a recent visit to the Derby: accounts of an overcrowded and edgy atmosphere have made me cautious, and there lingers in my mind the experience of my father and his chums, who discontinued their annual outings to Epsom after the year when a gang of youths stole their picnic. I go on Oaks day, Epsom's 'Ladies' Day', and it's a highlight in my calendar. There's a pleasant walk over the downs from Epsom Downs station, but I usually go for the more frequent service to Epsom station in the town, and instead of taking one of the racecourse buses I set out on foot to the course, forty minutes away. I've never seen another racegoer on the route. I pass the University of the Creative Arts, then a stretch of handsome villas of the type in which spa towns specialise, an extensive cemetery, and a wood. The road turns and rises, the wood ends, and it is as if a curtain opens on a big sky, fluttering flags and banners, and directly ahead the Rubbing House pub, on the site where Eclipse took refreshment as Dennis O'Kelly bet that the great horse would leave his opponents a distance behind. The entrance to the course is chock-a-block with young men in tight suits and young women in tight dresses; at a time when one fears that racing is losing its place in the sports mainstream, it's good to see them here. Long gone is the splendidly attired tipster Prince Monolulu (real name: Peter Carl Mackay), once a conspicuous feature of the Epsom scene with his cries of – as the title of his memoirs had it – 'I gotta horse!', but there are still Romany women selling 'lucky' heather; I weave past them like a slippery fly-half.

I walk through the betting hall to the grandstand. I look left towards Tattenham Corner, and the infamous slope down which the runners hurtle as they approach the home straight – a sight evoking races past and fuelling anticipation of those to come. On the Hill there's a fun-fair; lining the rails are open-top buses hosting stag and hen parties. Through the trees straight ahead, beyond the back straight, is another reminder of Eclipse: Downs House, where the horse was stabled during his all-conquering racing career in 1769 and 1770. South, to the right, there's a view over a decent chunk of Surrey. Sometimes, the weather makes a telling contribution to the atmosphere, as it did in 2017, when Enable established her place among the greatest Oaks winners as the scene darkened, thunder resounded, lightning forked across the sky, and rain sheeted down; by the time she was being mobbed in the winner's enclosure, the sun was out again.

History is part of the present in racing to an extent that no other sport matches. Follow back Serpentine's pedigree in the male line and you find that he has emulated ancestors including, seventeen generations back, the Derby winner Whalebone (1810) and before him Whalebone's sire Waxy (1793); Waxy's grandsire was Eclipse. And of course other lines of Serpentine's pedigree, no less significant genetically, are rich in Derby winners, Kentucky Derby winners, and other racing greats.

The heritage must be maintained, and carried forward. World wars did not interrupt the Derby, which, while Epsom racecourse was claimed by the military, moved to Newmarket from 1915 to 1918 and from 1940 to 1945. This year, racing resumed on the first day that any sports were allowed to take place again, and Epsom staged the Derby despite being ill-suited – it normally allows free public access to the common ground in the centre of the course and beyond the running rails – to keeping people out. The organisers erected three and a half miles of temporary fencing, hiring stewards to patrol the length of it. The Derby was run, and produced a result in keeping with the extraordinary circumstances of the event. It need not fear comparison with TV fantasies.

WINDSOR

Flat

17 May 2021

Swan on the track

It is not how a celebratory occasion should have ended. The rain is falling in torrents when the stalls open for the 7.20 at Royal Windsor, on the first card with spectators present at the course in almost two years. As the runners come within yards of the finishing post, the favourite Aplomb, running third, loses his footing, and instead of galloping past the line skids past it on his side, his momentum propelling him a good few yards further along the slippery ground, with his jockey Ryan Moore doing somersaults beside him. Both get to their feet unscathed. After his groom has led Aplomb away and the mud-covered and disgruntled Moore has trudged back to the weighing room, officials rush to the site of the mishap, prod the ground, call a consultation with some of the jockeys and trainers, and decide that the next race may go ahead. The horses in Aplomb's race had all kept to the far rail; in the 7.50, the jockeys steer their mounts down the near, stands rail. The rain is remorseless. Further deliberation ensues. Eventually, half an hour after it had been scheduled to take place, the 8.20 is abandoned, and our first evening back at the racecourse is over.

Even in normal times, it would take more than this inconvenience (with respect to the unfortunate Aplomb and Ryan Moore, who suffered no injuries, and had not been going to win anyway) to spoil a Monday evening meeting at Windsor – or Royal Windsor, as it styles itself, in reference to the associations of the area. At a venue populated by enthusiasts, most of whom have not been able to go racing for more than a year, the mood resists deflation.

You feel as if you're in a haven, perhaps because you're on an island,

80

surrounded by the Thames on one side and a mill stream on the other. Arriving by train at Windsor & Eton Riverside, in the shadow of the castle, you can get to the course by walking down to the promenade and catching a river bus, with a return ticket priced at £7.50 (at the time of writing). It's a journey of about fifteen minutes and a pleasantly calming experience for me. I travel early, the sun is sparkling on the water, the trees are displaying their vibrant spring greenery, and there are only a few other passengers. Having arrived later, another racegoer tells the *Racing Post* that there had been 'a lot of effing and blinding' on the boat she took, 'but it was still good fun'.

The course is very green. The car park and spacious paddock are fringed by limes, unusually shaped into columns, like Italian poplars. There are careful little touches, such as a small, triangular flower bed, by the stairs leading to the club stand, full of pansies. Here, as at most racecourses, only members and club ticket holders tend to gain access to grass, and those with grandstand and silver ring tickets mostly tread on asphalt. This evening, as social distancing regulations remain in place, tickets are limited (1500 sold, when there would normally be about 5000 people here – and more than that when there are post-racing concerts), and we can all enjoy the paddock lawn, with its open-sided marquee, gourmet grill huts, champagne bars and restaurants. (A year later, the racecourse causes anger by barring the paddock area to anyone not holding a premier ticket, costing £35 – a policy soon rescinded.)

Certain facilities have not reopened. The grandstand restaurant, better suited to social distancing than the proper weighing room, is occupied by jockeys and clerks. A group of Chinese hat marquees, designed for corporate hospitality, is unpopulated. The caterer First Cafes has staffed its burger hut and bakery van, reserving its pizza concession and 'roti shack' for another, busier fixture. You are supposed to be seated while eating and drinking, but I forget this rule as I munch my burger – not a rival to the superb offering at Plumpton, but perfectly pleasant – by the paddock, and no one rugby-tackles me. The silver ring has a stall selling fish and chips that, judging by my nosy survey of diners at the nearby benches, are rather good.

The ground-floor interior of the club grandstand has dark wood floors, with a staircase and banisters constructed from the same dark wood; it suggests – though I'm guessing here – a house at a long-established though minor public school. On top of the steeply angled roof is a commentator's hut, home this evening to Richard Hoiles. If you're standing underneath the roof, his voice over the tannoy is muffled – a shame, because spectators here could use all the help they can get.

Windsor is one of only two courses in Britain – the other is Fontwell – to be laid out as a figure of eight. The runners in the back straight race diagonally to the home straight, crossing it about two and a half furlongs up, before disappearing out of sight of the stands. They turn round a sharp bend before joining the straight at about the five-furlong marker. But it isn't a straight straight: for two and a half furlongs the horses race at a slight angle to the stands, and are partially visible at best, before they bear right at the crossing point and gallop towards you. The only place that offers a complete view of the action is the centre of the course – but that is closed this evening. The viewing experience, then, is not so different from that at Chelmsford, where the stand is on the inside of the course and the horses come into view only when they round the home turn.

Spectating on a French mountainside during the Tour de France, you catch a glimpse of the cyclists as they grind their way past you, and that's your lot. If you go to the Open Championship, you have a choice of following one group of golfers or parking yourself at one hole. Racegoers' views of the action, while more informative than this, are often partial too. Short circuits such as Fakenham and Plumpton, and park courses such as Sandown and Kempton, offer all-round views, while other courses, Chelmsford and Windsor being examples, have less helpful layouts. Why do we go? For the sense of occasion, for the communal excitement, for the thrill of seeing these splendid creatures in the flesh. And also to be in a place that offers some insulation from other concerns – a haven, as I've mentioned.

Since the introduction of big screens, the layout of some of our more eccentric courses is of less concern. Until the runners get to the final couple of furlongs, the screen gives you a better sense of what's going on than your eyes or even binoculars can detect. You may feel that it's a bit odd to rely on a screen to convey the best part of the action at a live event; still, that's what I'd recommend.

There had been race meetings round here for at least two hundred years by the time a Mr John Frail drew up plans for a course on land that was known as Rays Meadows, which hosted its first meeting in 1866. Henry VIII had maintained a stud at Windsor Castle. Charles II, though favouring Newmarket, is known to have attended meetings at nearby Datchet Ferry.

Windsor offered both jumps and flat meetings until 1998, when the management concluded that it was impossible to maintain decent ground if National Hunt horses pounded it throughout the winter, and went flat-only. (Jumps racing returned for one season in 2004/2005, when Windsor took over some fixtures from Ascot, which was being redeveloped.)

The standard of racing at Windsor is decent but not stellar, and spectators at the course have not witnessed many notable contributions to turf histories. One such did occur, however, in 1926, after Winston Churchill, who was Chancellor of the Exchequer at the time, introduced a betting tax. At Windsor, bookmakers refused to trade, with the result that, according to reports that may be apocryphal, 'the bewildered crowd [watched] the racing in silence' (James Gill, *Racecourses of Great Britain*). The tax did not stay on the statute book for very long. Two years later, Churchill founded the Tote, and in 1949 – his reputation considerably enhanced in the interim – dared visit the course, to be awarded 'a rapturous reception' on the victory of his horse Colonist II.

Windsor, Salisbury and Newmarket were the three southern courses allowed to hold meetings during the Second World War. A doodlebug fell nearby during a Windsor meeting in 1944, injuring no one and failing to halt proceedings.

On an eight-race card here late in the 2012 season, the jockey Richard Hughes rode seven winners; he was on the 2/1 favourite in the other race, but could finish only third. Hughes shares the record for the most winners ridden at a meeting with Frankie Dettori, who achieved his 'Magnificent Seven' at Ascot in 1996.

There are clear risks in putting a racecourse on flat land adjoining the Thames. In 1947, a year of dreadful weather, the course and stands were flooded to a depth of three feet, causing £10,000-worth of damage – the equivalent of £400,000-worth now, the internet tells me. If you walk up the course, you'll see and hear on your right one of the weirs that have been constructed to alleviate the problem. Nevertheless, there was standing water on the track in 2014 and 2018, and the rain on this Monday evening, on top of a soggy fortnight, quickly causes the ground to deteriorate.

At 4 p.m., as I step off the river boat, the blue sky and fluffy clouds belie the raindrop symbols on my weather app. 'Are you getting soaked?' my wife, consulting the same app at home, asks later in a text. 'No!' I'm still able to reply, though as I press send I hear a rumble of thunder.

How does it feel to be back? It's the popular question. As I sit down with the bookmaker John Hooper to ask him how it feels, a journalist from the *Mirror* approaches us to ask how it feels, and, reporting for Sky Sports nearby, Matt Chapman is poking his microphone in race-goers' faces to ask them how it feels. 'Evenin',' greets jockey-turned-TV pundit Jason Weaver as I walk past the Sky Sports pitch near the pad-dock – friendly of him. 'Good to be here,' I observe. '*Great* to be here,' he replies. Later, I spot Lee Mottershead of the *Racing Post* asking people how they feel, and being rewarded with a kiss from one of his interviewees, Susie Huxley, an owner with the Elite Racing Club – she feels good, clearly.

How it really feels to me is *normal*. True, there are the Covid regu-lations: masks to be worn indoors; a green zone on the course for professionals, and an amber zone for us punters; no racecards, because distribution of printed material is considered unsafe. Nevertheless, it's that experience of arriving again at a familiar place: despite the period of absence, you settle in as if you've hardly been away. Back to the routine: fill out the Placepot card (doomed this evening to go down in the fourth), check out the pre-parade ring, on to the pad-dock, from there to the grandstand; and repeat, with breaks for food and drink.

The Prince of Wales and the Duchess of Cornwall have a runner in the first, the Fitzdares Welcomes Back Spectators to Racing Handicap. Dark Motive, a son of the 2005 Derby winner Motivator, falls behind the leaders at halfway, and continuing to gallop at what the form book later describes as 'one pace', stays there; he finishes fifth of eight. Charles and Camilla are owners on a modest scale, certainly by comparison with Charles's racing-mad mother and late grandmother. The *Racing Post* database records that horses in their colours have competed in twenty-five races in the past five years, recording just one victory. Total earnings:

£36,144. Once their Royal Highnesses have settled the training fees, they'd have to raid another kitty to afford even a celebratory bottle of Duchy Originals Organic Elderflower Cordial.

I head off to explore the far end of the course. Past the enclosures, a flotilla of Canada geese and their chicks swims gently by. The only other frequenters of this area are the ground staff, among whose tasks, in addition to replacing divots, is shooing the geese and the occasional swan from the track; a swan has been nesting at the stream, and gets somewhat tetchy with the groundsman who tries to encourage her to get out of the way of the fillies racing in the 7.50. There's a marina here, and a waterside restaurant, both at present uninhabited. I walk further on round the bottom bend, and pee behind a bush, ready to claim, if anyone shouts at me, that I'm doing the socially responsible thing, taking care of the matter at a social distance – two furlongs from the nearest by-stander – rather than in the more virally hazardous surroundings of an indoor lavatory.

Back at the paddock lawn, there's an eager queue at the burger shack. First Cafes, which has concessions at some half-dozen courses and provides catering services for other venues and occasions, has been in-active for fourteen months, so must be grateful for this return to trading, modest though it is. But the weather apps keep telling us it's raining, and the clouds say that we're still dry only on sufferance. At seven o'clock, they hold back no longer; it's the kind of deluge that soaks you to the skin within seconds. The queues at the food stalls vanish. 'First Covid, now this,' the woman who sold me a burger says.

There remain a few undaunted punters at the bookmakers' pitches. Here is another sector in which there has been no business for fourteen months. John Hooper, who trades under the Sid Hooper name and has pitches all round the country, tells me: 'I'm very fortunate in life in that I have enough funds to survive. But for others it's been dreadful – as it has for people in lots of industries, and I feel very sad for those people who have been on the breadline.' He did operate at a few earlier meetings when owners were allowed to attend, but at a loss. 'We were paying to go to work.'

Windsor has four pitches – two of them Hooper's – next to the pad-dock. This evening, there are some dozen further pitches in front of the grandstand, and half a dozen on the rails separating the grandstand from the members' area. 'Probably too many for the attendance,' Hooper observes. 'But people like to get out, don't they?'

At the end of the evening, Hooper is pleased. The firm has taken some sizeable bets, by which he means three-figure and four-figure sums (though surely not the £50,000 wager that the *Racing Post* reports), and has finished ahead.

For Sophie Candy, clerk of the course, things will get worse before they get better. The morning after this meeting, she looks at the weather forecast, sees a good many more rain symbols and no lifting of the unseasonal chill, and can already predict that the meeting on the forthcoming Monday, 24 May, will be called off. But in the last week of May, the weather improves, and by the first week of June the Windsor ground is good, good to firm in places; Candy and her colleagues are turning on the sprinklers. Come 21 June, and the ground is waterlogged again – another meeting lost.

Maintaining the ground at racecourses is a tricky and high-pressured business. One nightmare is when you get too much rain, as happens at Windsor on Monday 17. Another is when you get too little, and the ground becomes so hard that horses running on it risk injury. You can turn on the taps; but what if the forecasts tell you that you might soon get water from the skies? Sprinkler-softened ground on which rain falls tends to get very soft, quickly. Meanwhile, trainers of horses that like firm ground and trainers of horses who like ease in the ground want you, and sometimes lobby you, to provide conditions in their favour. As Candy and I talk, in Derby week, Epsom clerk of the course Andrew Cooper is watering the ground on which the Derby runners will race, to some trainers' displeasure. True, the forecast predicts showers; but no one can be sure whether they will fall on Epsom or miss it. Cooper ends up unlucky: the course is hit by rain on Friday, Oaks day, and the ground softens. The trainer William Haggas withdraws from the Derby his fancied horse Mohaafeth, a 9/1 shot: 'I have never felt he would be comfortable on soft or dead ground,' he explains.

No weather expert could have guaranteed that Cooper would make the right decision. On the afternoon Candy and I talk, the Met Office reports that it should be raining in Windsor. She is looking out of her office window at a few puffy clouds and bright sunshine. All racecourses employ their own forecasters, but accept that even forecasts tailored just for them are fallible.

There are not only trainers, owners and jockeys to please. There are spectators, broadcasters, and the British Horseracing Authority, which has to be satisfied that the meetings you stage are conducted within its rules.

It's a demanding job, for which Candy has two qualifications before she even gets down to the technicalities: she is a racing insider, and she is used to getting up early. Her father is the trainer Henry Candy, for whose stable she 'rode out' – rode the horses at morning exercise – from the age of thirteen. While studying law in Cambridge she rode out for the nearby Newmarket yard of Sir Michael Stoute, and now, during the winter months and on quieter days in the summer, she rides out for jumps trainer Nicky Henderson; one of her regular mounts is the mare Epatante, winner of the 2020 Champion Hurdle ('I love her').

At 6 p.m. each Friday before a Monday meeting, she and Windsor's head groundsman walk the course, making their own assessment of the ground (the 'going'), and prodding it at various points with an instrument called a GoingStick, provided by sports data company Turftrax. The stick gives a reading in the range 0–15, with 0 indicating that the surface consists of more water than soil, and 15 indicating that it is as hard as the adjacent A308. The clerk and the groundsman will also make their own assessments, ranging from 'heavy' to 'firm'. Neither extreme is welcome, and racecourses usually employ watering to ensure that good to firm is as hard – or fast, as racing people would say – as the going gets.

By 7 a.m., Candy contacts by text all the trainers with preliminary entries. An example might be: 'Windsor going is good to firm; GoingStick reading 7.2 [not contradictory information: readings above 10 are very rare]; dry weekend expected; showers possible on Monday; temperature 22 degrees.' Using this information, the trainers have until 10 a.m. on Saturday to confirm that their horses will run. (The rule is known as '48-hour declarations'.)

Candy and the groundsman are back on the track at 6 a.m. on Monday, going through the routine again. Perhaps the forecast was wrong and there was a deluge at the weekend, softening the ground: there's still time for a trainer to decide against loading the horsebox and driving to Windsor with a horse who runs well only on fast surfaces.

Then it's paperwork. The printouts include microchip lists: details, sent in advance by the BHA, of the microchips that all today's runners carry, and that are scanned when they arrive at the racecourse stables. There's a list for the stable manager of the times when the runners are due to arrive. There's a list of the jockeys with rides at the meeting, and information for the jockeys about today's conditions.

Candy walks the course again two hours before the first race, this time with the chair of the stewards' panel. (More about stewards in a later chapter.) Is the steward happy with the going description? Have the rails been moved? (This matters, because it can alter the distance of a race, and therefore affect the time it takes to run – information that must be transparent if punters, whose money partly funds the sport, are to believe in the integrity of racing statistics.)

There's just time for a change into smarter clothes. Then there are radio checks with the ground staff and veterinary team. A trainer wants a couple of extra badges for owners. Another wants her horse to be allowed to leave the paddock early and canter to the start alone. You must make sure that the horses enter and leave the paddock when they are supposed to, and that the races start on time.

There's a problem at the stables, and you must explain what's happened to the stewards. Or, as happens on this Monday, several jockeys say that the rain has caused the ground to be unsafe. Or: you must ask a member of the ground staff to shoo a touchy and territorial swan from the track.

BRIGHTON

Flat

1 June 2021

In the ring

If Porterinthejungle (number 4 on the card) had won or finished in the first three in the 3.20 at Brighton, he would have ruined bookmaker Mark Pariser's day.

The sun is out, the English Channel is sparkling blue, and a good many of the small crowd are here for a pleasant excursion. Bets of £1 each way (£1 to win, and £1 to be placed) – which, at a busy Royal Ascot or Epsom, Pariser would turn down – are popular. Then along comes a punter and asks for £500 each way on number 4, at 9/1. Pariser lays the bet. The punter also places a £200 win bet on Porterinthejungle at the next board, Bob Stock's.

A bookmaker must be fearless on these occasions. But maybe Pariser cannot help thinking, as he takes the punter's money and contemplates paying him back £5400 (£4500 for the win, plus a fifth of that amount for the place), 'He must know something.' It turns out, however, that he doesn't. Porterinthejungle finishes fifth of nine, 'outpaced final two furlongs', as the form book puts it. He makes Pariser's day.

It's far from a bonanza. Pariser's turnover from the seven races on the card is about £5000. He took three times that amount at the bank holiday meeting at Brighton ten days earlier. 'Unfortunately,' he says, 'that was a well-informed crowd.' While Pariser managed to lay (take bets on) quite a few losers, he paid out a fair amount as well, and later discovered that one punter had handed him a bundle of notes containing two fake £20s. It's a ruse sounding a faint echo of the dodgy and dangerous Brighton that Graham Greene evoked in his 1938 novel *Brighton Rock* – a work that you cannot avoid mentioning in any portrait of the seaside town and its racecourse.

The race meeting in *Brighton Rock* is like Derby Day: 'It was as if the whole road [to the course] moved upwards like an Underground stair- case in the dusty sunlight, a creaking, shouting, jostling crowd of cars moving with it.' This is not the scene on a Tuesday morning as I take my quiet walk, up past low terraced houses painted in seaside colours – yellow, teal, sky blue – to Whitehawk Hill, 400 feet above sea level. Nor is there, when you get to the course, a half crown enclosure – favoured playground of the razor gangs – across the track from the grandstand; instead, a narrow strip of land hosts a car park and a row of cypresses, shielding a view of the housing estate in the valley below. Gangs such as the one that assaults Greene's anti-hero Pinkie are long gone – the course website, no doubt aiming to dispel the images that 'Brighton racecourse' will prompt among readers of the novel, emphasises that gang warfare was rife in many other towns too, and not confined to racecourses. But the official history does confirm that there were once enclosures on both sides of the rails, and that meetings in the pre- and post-war years would attract up to 20,000 spectators.

It's like arriving at Epsom, except with less imposing edifices. As you make your way upwards to the course, you see a grandstand with only sky behind it. From the other side of the stand, there are commanding views: at Epsom, of the Surrey countryside; here, of the Channel to your right, beyond the winning post, and of the South Downs to your left. Both courses are horseshoe-shaped, and about one mile four furlongs in length. Both rise from the 1m 4f marker, then fall as the horses turn left (with a gradual turn at Brighton by contrast with the sharp one at Epsom's Tattenham Corner); at Brighton, the horses must negotiate a rise for the last two furlongs. The finish is the highest point of the track. Staging the 'Brighton Derby Trial' seemed like a good idea, once; but no horses who ever ran in it went on to win the Derby (though two won the St Leger), and the race was discontinued in 1967.

Racing was one of the many pleasures that George – Prince of Wales, later Prince Regent, later George IV – enjoyed at Brighton. He had abandoned Newmarket after a furore over his horse Escape: he and his retained jockey, Samuel Chifney, had been accused of deliberately caus- ing Escape to lose one day in order that they could back him at better odds when he won the day after. George was miffed to be told by Sir Charles Bunbury, who as chief steward of the Jockey Club felt no awe before royalty, that unless he sacked Chifney, 'no gentleman would start against him'. Some years later Bunbury visited Brighton races and co-authored a letter to George begging him to grace Newmarket again with his presence; but George, not inclined to forget the earlier reprimand, was unmoved.

The racing here since those days of prestige has been moderate: for regulars, that is part of the appeal. Horses with abilities in the mid to low ranges tend to run frequently, often at the same few courses, and punters get to know them. They win, and their handicap marks, determining the weights they have to carry, go up; they lose, and their marks fall, until arriving at a level at which the horses can be competitive again. And so it goes on. Pour La Victoire, running in the 4.25 today, is eleven years old, and has 116 starts under his belt; he has won ten times at Brighton. His official handicap mark has yo-yoed, ranging from 48 to 84; he runs today off 57. (I attempt to explain elsewhere what such figures mean.) He's a character: he insists on heading down to the start early, away from his competitors, and on walking there rather than cantering, with his jockey leading him. He finishes seventh of eleven.

One apparently unremarkable race here did later acquire significance: the 1977 Bevendean Stakes was won by a horse called Hatta, who was the first winner on British soil in the colours of Sheikh Mohammed, soon to become the most powerful owner on the racing scene.

Unremarkable racing and a lack of investment from municipal owners were a recipe for decline at Brighton until Northern Racing took over in 1998, investing £4 million in upgrading the venue. In 2012, Northern merged with Arena Leisure to create the Arena Racing Company (ARC), which owns Brighton as well as Bath, Chepstow, Doncaster, Fontwell, Ffos Las, Great Yarmouth, Hereford, Lingfield, Newcastle, Sedgefield, Southwell, Uttoxeter, Windsor, Wolverhampton and Worcester.

Mark Pariser wishes that ARC – owned by David and Simon Reuben, ranked second on the 2021 Sunday Times Rich List, with assets of £21.465 billion – would spend a few quid on decent anchors for the bookmakers' 'joints' (metal stands). Even while the English Channel is flat calm, there's enough wind on Whitehawk Hill to blow over a joint worth some £2500, along with the attached electronic display board worth another £6000 or so. These aren't the only expensive pieces of kit that a bookie needs: there's the card reader (and you have to pay fees for card transactions); a printer for the tickets; a laptop; bookmaking software; a battery capable of running the laptop all day long. Then there's the cost of the pick (also called a pitch) – the position you occupy in the ring; the *Racing Post* has reported that at the top of this market, a prominent pick at Cheltenham would set you back £250,000. You have to buy various licences. There's the cost of travelling to courses; and sometimes the cost of hiring someone to transport the heavy equipment. There's the cost of getting in: five or more times the entrance fee for the main betting badge holder, and just below the entrance fee for assistants (who will also cost you money in wages). Oh, and you'll need a strong umbrella. And to get something to eat and drink. And if you're betting at the Cheltenham Festival, you'll need to stay in the town or nearby for the four days. Bets of £1 each way aren't going to cover it.

In the early days of racing, the betting market comprised gentlemen – many ladies gambled heavily too, but mostly at the gaming tables – placing bets with each other. A man called Harry Cobden has been labelled the first racecourse bookmaker, having set up his pitch at Newmarket in the mid-1790s, though the racing historian Roger Longrigg says that the true origin of the betting 'ring' – the collective term for racecourse bookies as well as the name of the place on the course they occupy – was the subscription rooms at the bloodstock auctioneers Tattersalls near Hyde Park Corner. (The area of the racecourse housing the main grandstand and bookmakers' pitches is still referred to as 'Tattersalls' at some courses.) Anyway, it was in the early years of the nineteenth century that layers began offering prices – making a book, in other words – about all the runners in a race.

Let's imagine a match race between Eclipse and Nijinsky, and assume that they possess equal abilities. In theory, each should be even money (1/1), with a 50 per cent chance of winning. Let's imagine further that a bookmaker, offers to lay – to sell bets, in other words – Eclipse and Nijinsky at those odds. The bookmaker lays five £1 bets on Eclipse, and five £1 bets on Nijinsky, receiving £10 in total. Eclipse wins. Each of the five holders of winning tickets gets back £2 – £1 for the win and £1 returned stake. That makes the total payout five times two pounds, equals £10. So: £10 received, £10 paid out. Profit, nil. In this situation, therefore, the bookmaker wouldn't offer even money about each horse, but odds-on: 4/5 (0.8/1), say. These odds, in percentage terms, are 55.5

recurring, making the total odds percentage 111. Of course, the true total should be 100: the chance of something happening – one of the horses winning the race – cannot be greater than that. (But what if two horses finish side by side in a dead heat? See below.) The 11 per cent extra is the 'overround': the bookmaker's margin, what in the US they call the 'vig' (short for vigorish, a Yiddish slang word for winnings). In our example, the bookmaker pays out £9 (80p each to holders of the five winning tickets, plus their £1 stakes). Total paid out, £9; total takings, £10. Result happiness, as Dickens' Mr Micawber would note.

(Prices expressed in numerals, such as at the Tote or on the Betfair betting exchange, refer to the total sum returned. So even money in the ring is the same as 2 on the Tote: the placer of a £1 winning bet in each example gets in return £1 in winnings and £1 in returned stake. To convert Tote odds to fractional odds, subtract 1: for example, 5 is 4/1. These odds suggest that a horse's chance of winning is 1 in 5, or 20 per cent.)

Of course, bookmakers in real life will never have the same liabilities about every horse in a race. Some horses will be more popular, and their prices will contract, while others, less highly rated by the market, will be available to back at longer odds. Perfectly balanced books, guaranteed to make a margin whatever the result, are almost impossible to achieve; in each race, there will be a few horses about which the liabilities – the sums to be paid out should the horses win or be placed – will be greater than the total amount received in wagers. As Pariser's colleague Lynn takes the Brighton punters' money and prints out their tickets, he enters the bets on his laptop software, which shows whether each horse is a winner or loser for the firm, and which updates the odds accordingly. Winning favourites tend to be unwelcome, but long-priced winners can be bad news too, if you happen to have taken bets on them. Pariser bears the scars from having laid a 100/1 winner at Lingfield.

Bookmakers can override their software. At the bigger meetings, they will have studied the form, looking in particular for favourites that may be vulnerable, and about whom they may try to attract punters by offering 100/30, say, while the rest of the ring is showing 3/1. But Pariser, who has home-schooled his daughter during lockdown, rarely has time for detailed form study; at the smaller meetings, these judgements are mostly a matter of maths. So in race two, he decides that he'll make more money if he can lay the favourite, because no other horse is showing much potential profit for him. While the rest of the ring is offering Arabic Charm at 3/1, he goes 100/30, and attracts a flurry of interest. Uh-oh: Arabic Charm wins. What might have been a £300 profit, had he left well alone, turns into a £100 loss.

The punters come to collect. Lynn scans the winning tickets, and pays out, unless the payment was by card, in which case the card will be credited. Someone whose ticket is lost will have to wait until the end of the afternoon; if the ticket hasn't been scanned by then, Pariser will honour the bet.

The £1000 losing bet that arrives later makes up for the disappointment of Arabic Charm's success. The horse's victory gives one an inkling of what a scary business bookmaking can be. At Cheltenham and Ascot, hefty wads of money are bandied about, and the payouts can be massive. The late 'Fearless' Freddie Williams, celebrated for never ducking large bets, lost more than £1 million in one day at the 2006 Cheltenham Festival to Irish punter and racehorse owner J.P. Mc-Manus (and then lost another £70,000 when armed robbers ambushed him and his daughter on their way back to their hotel). Stories such as this, along with an assessment of bookies' day-to-day expenses, suggest that commonly heard phrases – 'You never see a poor bookmaker', 'The bookies always win' – may need revision.

The business has got tougher. The ring is a changed place. Not so long ago, a bookie would arrive at the course and start pricing up on his board with chalk or, more recently, a marker pen, using odds that he (it was a very masculine calling – much less so now) had compiled, or that he had paid someone to compile. Colleagues would broadcast the prices across the ring using the specialist sign language known as 'tic-tac'; Pariser's colleague Lynn was one of the last of the tic-tac signers. Now, the bookies can base their opening shows on what is on offer online at Betfair, William Hill, Bet365 and other operators, and via their laptops keep tabs on the online markets throughout.

It sounds convenient. The problem is that the online bookies are competition: even at the racecourse, there are many people betting via their phones rather than in the ring or at the Tote windows. Above the Brighton track today, four drones hover: Pariser says they are there to transmit to professional punters live pictures that are not subject to the delays in the feeds through broadcasting channels, enabling the punters to be a step ahead when betting in-running. On the betting exchanges, punters can be layers or backers. If I, watching TV with a several-second delay, see a horse cruising up to the leaders with a furlong to run, I might be tempted to back him; if you, with the benefit of a real-time feed, have already seen that the horse's challenge has fizzled out, you'll take my money. Terrifying sums are gambled and lost at the clicks of mouses in these brief moments.

A related problem is that competition in the betting market has compressed prices. For some races, the market is 'overbroke', far from adding up to 111 per cent, the combined odds add up to less than 100 per cent, meaning that it's theoretically possible for a punter to back every horse in the race and make a profit. Going back to our example, let's price up Eclipse at even money (50 per cent) and Nijinksy at 2/1 (33.33 per cent): combined odds in percentage terms of 83.33 per cent. I place £2 on Eclipse to win and £1.50 on Nijinsky to win. I've gambled £3.50. If Eclipse wins, I get back £4: 2 x £1, plus my £2 stake. Profit: 50p. If Nijinsky wins, I get back £4.50: 2 x £1.50, plus my £1.50 stake. Profit: £1. Result for the bookmaker: to quote Micawber, misery.

Pariser says that his firm, which trades under the Sam Harris banner, is in better shape than most. This is what John Hooper, whom we met at Windsor, says too; and he must be an optimistic sort, because in recent years he has bought the racecourse pitches of Ladbrokes, William Hill and Coral as those established firms have left the ring. Here's another change: not only have the firms given up laying bets on racecourses, but placing them too. You used to see their representatives moving up and down the ring, backing the horses about which they had the biggest liabilities, in order to shorten those horses' starting prices – the odds at which the majority of bets were settled. They had moved away from this practice before the pandemic, and since then have had no need to continue it, because starting prices are no longer a reflection of those generally on offer in the ring: they are 'industry prices', determined off course.

Hooper argues that racecourse bookies offer a unique service. Bet with an off-course firm and show any expertise at the game, and you'll soon find your account shut down. 'I have . . . had twelve accounts closed or restricted to the point of worthlessness inside two years,' a self-described 'small stakes punter' reported to the Racing Forum message board, echoing the experiences of many. If you're at Cheltenham and want to wager £50,000 on a horse, Hooper may well take you on. If you're a customer of one of the big firms and seem to know what you're doing, you may find yourself barred if you venture £10 each way. The firms would be very happy, though, if you wanted to gamble any amount, online or in their shops, on fixed-odds games, because the results of these games will always go in their favour. In 2019, much to the firms' annoyance, the government introduced a £2 stake limit on notorious fixed-odds betting terminals, on which until then you could have wagered up to £100 a go. Problem gamblers, estimated to comprise 14 per cent of users of the machines, were losing thousands of pounds within minutes of entering the bookmakers' premises. Now, they lose their money more slowly.

No doubt some problem gamblers bet with racecourse bookies too. But Pariser's customers appear to be mostly serious racing fans or people enjoying 'a bit of a flutter' on a sunny day out. The atmosphere is impressively amicable, given that each party is scheming to take money off the other; Pariser and his Brighton regulars enjoy chats and a few laughs, and occasionally he obliges one of them by laying a bet at slightly more rewarding odds than the board shows. He does this for me, giving me 6/1 about the 11/2 shot Little Sunflower in the first. I oblige him by having picked a loser: Little Sunflower finishes eighth, 'well beaten' as the form book reports.

It is not only among the horsey set that involvement in the sport passes down the generations. Many bookmaking names have been around for a while too. Mark Pariser's great-grandfather founded the Sam Harris business, and Adrian Pariser, Mark's father, is still a director. Mark started out in the building trade, and would often work on site in the morning and at the racecourse in the afternoon, until one day on a building job he fell two storeys and was left unable to walk for three years. At Brighton today, several visitors to his pitch note the absence of his surgical boot, recently discarded.

There's drama in the 3.55. The favourite, Kendergarten Kop ridden by Tom Queally, leads inside the final furlong, but Nicola Currie galvanises her mount, Batchelor Boy, who comes roaring up the outside. They flash past the line together. Standing opposite the winning post, I think Kendergarten Kop has held on; but no announcement comes from the judge. Eventually, the tannoy alert sounds and the verdict comes: a dead heat. What happens here is that backers of each horse get half of what they would have got had the horse scored a clear victory. Groans at the Sam Harris pitch: after you've waited five minutes for the result, it's disappointing to hear that Kendergarten Kop, a loser in the book, hasn't been beaten. But the payout would have been twice as much had he got his nose in front. There's a 17/2 winner in the last race, the 4.25, so that compensates somewhat too.

The Sam Harris team enjoy their job, are relieved to be able to do it again, and have more than covered their costs. But a racing programme consisting of meetings like this is not going to support a business indefinitely. Next week, it's Epsom, with the Oaks on Friday and the Derby on Saturday. There will be 4000 spectators on course each day, rather than the 35,000 who would be there in normal times. Although lockdown restrictions are due, according to the government 'roadmap', to end in England in twenty days, they may, owing to a resurgence in cases of the virus, be kept in place for longer. Bookmakers are among many who need normality to return soon.

RIPON

Flat

17 June 2021

Thoroughbreds in the garden

Ripon is the Garden Racecourse. More significantly for racing, it sits in the middle of what might be called the Birthplace of the Thoroughbred – a less catchy brand, I can see. What is a thoroughbred, and in what sense can the breed be said to have been born?

In any event, Garden Racecourse works. The team here put a lot of care into their floral displays, which seem splendid to me despite being, I am told, at an intermediate stage: there will be many more blooms in a month or so. The plants and shrubs add to the attractions of a setting that features, in the paddock and throughout the enclosures, mature maples, horse chestnuts, limes and a weeping willow. The buildings are unexciting, but the scenery is grand. VisitEngland's selection of Ripon as one of the top eleven racecourses for visitors in the country is surely uncontroversial.

The Ripon circuit is an elongated oval. When the horses enter the home straight, they still have five furlongs to run – more than twice the length of the straight at Ascot. The ground undulates; MD and clerk of the course James Hutchinson sometimes wonders if he'd attract more runners if he provided a level surface, but feels that idiosyncrasy is a selling point too.

In the centre of the circuit is a lake, rented out to jet-skiers and anglers, though not, one guesses, at the same time. In common with other courses, Ripon is available for conferences, weddings, car boot sales, dog shows, as a film set, or for anything else that's feasible and might bring in some extra revenue; but non-raceday activities are not essential parts of the commercial model. During the pandemic, the non-raceday activity has been non-commercial: the course has been a vaccination centre.

The hit from the pandemic on a privately owned racecourse has not been quite as damaging as Hutchinson and his colleagues had feared. Between mid-March and the beginning of June 2020, when no sporting events took place in Britain, Ripon lost six of the seventeen meetings it stages each year. For the next eleven and a half months, all horseracing took place behind closed doors. No spectators, no bookmakers, no caterers; but at least there were Levy and media rights contributions, and this income, in a normal year, accounts for about 75 per cent of Ripon's turnover. 'We will get through relatively unscathed at the end of it,' Hutchinson says.

The rule as we speak is that Ripon can sell up to 4000 tickets each raceday. On the busiest days in normal times, there would be some 9000 spectators, and it's those extra people who would provide the Ripon Race Company's profit. Today is Ripon's Ladies' Day – while, not coincidentally, the Royal Ascot Ladies' Day is taking place down south. The skies above Ascot are grey, and tomorrow they will disgorge so much rain that racing comes close to being abandoned; here, the sun is out, there's a light breeze, and it's a very pleasant 20°C. But the advance ticket sales have been a little disappointing, with only 1700 spectators expected. There have been two inhibiting factors, Hutchinson believes: the weather forecast, which until the day before the meeting told us we would get soaked, and possibly struck by lightning; and continuing uncertainty about the pandemic rules. 'After eighteen months in which people may have been isolating or shielding, there is going to be a reluctance among some to start mixing in bigger crowds,' he says. 'And knowledge that they can now come may be lacking. We've done as much as possible to promote the meeting, but we still get calls: "Are we able to go racing yet?"'

Hutchinson, in common with so many in the sport, is from a racing dynasty. His grandfather Charles conceived the 'Garden Racecourse' idea, and began planting up the Ripon enclosures in the fifties and sixties. His father Michael – like Charles, a solicitor and businessman, with interests ranging from concrete to hotels – ran the course from 1977 to 2007, which is when James took over. James had previously worked as clerk of the course or deputy clerk at Beverley, Sedgefield and York.

He has learned to play to his strengths. Today, Ripon is staging three Class 6 races, two Class 5s, a Class 4, and a Class 3. The horses with the highest official ratings, in the Class 3 race, are Highwaygrey and Benadalid, both on official handicap marks of 89. The scale is 0–140. Down at Ascot, the Gold Cup favourite Stradivarius (who will be beaten), races off 125.

No doubt Hutchinson and his customers would be thrilled to see Stradivarius running round Ripon's tight bends and up and down its undulations, just as the local rep company would be delighted if Sir Ian McKellen were to star in one of its productions. But it's a matter of what your business, and trainers and owners, will support.

'Sometimes, we do over-stretch ourselves,' Hutchinson concedes. 'We had a Saturday earlier this year with four Class 2 races. The ground was very quick, and we got disappointing field sizes for what we considered to be reasonably good prize money.' (The total pot for the day was over £100,000.) Two of the races attracted three runners each, and there were only thirty-five runners in total for all seven races. Small fields mean less betting, which means a lower book-makers' profit going towards the Levy, which in part funds prize money.

There's a dissenting view of this shortfall, and it comes from the combative trainer Mark Johnston, who has a blog called 'Bletherings'. In a post before the meeting, he blethered: 'I have two of the three runners in the two-mile handicap, but, I have to say, I wouldn't be running two and might not have been running any at all if I'd had to take on more rivals. The prize money [£11,338.80 to the winner] is so appalling that it simply doesn't make sense to risk horses of this calibre for such poor rewards.' Johnston recognised that racecourses had to cut their prize money during the pandemic, but pointed out that the pot for this handicap had been declining anyway: his winner of the race in 2019 took home less than did the winners in 2014 and 2015. (I shouldn't imply that no horse of Gold Cup standard has ever trod the Ripon turf. Trip to Paris, Johnston's 2015 winner, went on that year to win the Ascot showpiece.)

Ripon is by no means the only racecourse to have received such criticism. The Arena Racing Company courses, among them my most recent destinations Windsor and Brighton, come in for particular stick, perhaps because they are part of a group, and perhaps because their owners are multi-billionaires. But it is a problem throughout British racing: prize money is considerably lower here than in any other comparable country.

The disagreement seems not to have caused a breakdown in relations. Johnston sends four runners to Ripon today, and has a winner (£3606) and two seconds (£2540, £1003). The owner and breeder of one of the second-placed horses, Aletoile, is Kirsten Rausing, who is not short of a bob or two. One wonders though whether even someone as dedicated to the sport as Rausing, and clearly prepared to lose money on it, might one day decide that the financial rewards are so low as not to be worth competing for.

Aletoile is a daughter of Sea the Stars, winner in 2009 of the 2000 Guineas, Derby and Prix de l'Arc de Triomphe. Sea the Stars' other offspring have included 2016 Epsom and Irish Derby winner Harzand, along with winners of the Oaks and the Irish Oaks, as well as the above-mentioned Stradivarius. So when Kirsten Rausing chose him as a mate for her mare Alamode, she probably hoped for grander achievements than second place in a Class 6 handicap at Ripon. Harzand is the sire of a filly in the 2.15, a Class 4 handicap; another Derby winner, Camelot, has a son in the race; and the sire of the winner, the Mark Johnston-trained Harlem Soul, is Frankel, the greatest racehorse of this century, and possibly of other centuries too. Harlem Soul, admirably though he performs, is not another Frankel.

The leading sires are particularly effective at fathering talented offspring. But, covering more than 100 and in some cases more than 200 mares a year, even they get many more horses of average abilities than they do notable ones. It follows that average horses in training outnumber notable ones. Here is another reason why Ripon may get smaller fields if it tries to attract better horses – there aren't enough of them to go round.

The course does stage two races of national significance. The Great St Wilfrid, named after the city's patron saint and run in August, is one of the big sprint handicaps of the season, with total prize money of about £75,000; later in the month, a field of promising horses contests the Two Year Old Trophy.

*

For generations, breeders have been following the adage, 'Breed the best to the best, and hope for the best.' Since medieval times, Britain has imported Eastern stallions, aiming to improve the native stock. (In the Arab world, the female line is what counts, and owners are reluctant to give up their mares.) What happened to upgrade English 'running horses' in the late seventeenth and early eighteenth centuries to 'thoroughbreds' – as they became known in the nineteenth century – has been the subject of myths, half-baked theories, and special pleading.

Anyone with a smattering of knowledge of racing history can tell you that today's racehorses are all descended in their male lines ('tail male') from one of three Eastern stallions: the Byerley Turk, the Darley Arabian and the Godolphin Arabian. We know that Thomas Darley bought his Arabian in Aleppo and shipped him back to the family estate in Yorkshire; what we cannot verify are the widely told stories that the Byerley Turk was captured at the Siege of Buda and later took part in the Battle of the Boyne, and that the Godolphin Arabian was discovered pulling a milk cart in Paris. We're not sure whether the Byerley Turk was Turkoman; some say the Godolphin Arabian was a Barb, but we're not sure about that either.

Still, we do know that these horses existed. The 'foundation mares' with whom they and other imported stallions mated are more mysterious still, in part because the first systematic attempt to document them, James Weatherby and his researcher William Sidney Towers *An Introduction to a General Stud Book*, did not appear until 1791. Weatherby (see the Perth chapter) identified seventy-two such mares, assigning to some of them uninformative monikers such as 'royal mare'. Researchers have found genetic traces of just thirty foundation mares in the thoroughbreds they tested. They have also found that, contrary to the beliefs of dogmatic early twentieth-century writers who insisted on the purity of Arabian blood in racehorses, the mares largely belonged to European breeds. (DNA testing has produced similar news of racial diversity for people who have believed that they were pure English or pure Celts, or pure anything else.)

We also know that many of these these mares lived in Yorkshire, with a concentration of them not too far from Ripon. For some reason their matings with imported stallions produced horses with speed and stamina surpassing anything that had been seen on a racecourse before. Locals believe it must have had something to do with the outstanding qualities of the Yorkshire environment. The theory is not far-fetched: environmental factors do appear to make significant contributions to racehorses' development. Diomed, in 1780 the first winner of the Epsom Derby, was a flop at stud in England, with his sons and daughters failing to excel on the racecourse; exported to the US, he suddenly turned into a stallion superstar, siring winner after winner. I go to PedigreeQuery.com and check on the family tree of one of today's Ripon runners, Impulsive One, whose racecard entry reads 'Impulsive One (USA)', meaning he was foaled in the US; tracing back all the (USA) lines in the pedigree, I always get back to Diomed.

There was racing at Ripon before all this happened. Henry VIII had a stud here. The first recorded race meeting in the town took place soon after the Restoration, in 1664. A new course opened on the High Common in the early eighteenth century, with a family called Aislabie providing support, including a plate for the first ever ladies' race to be held in Britain.

The common was enclosed in 1826. After a ten-year gap, a course opened on the north bank of the River Ure; in 1865 it made way for another new course, on what was known as Redbank. When this course closed in turn, the grandstand there morphed into the main building of the Cathedral Choir School, while the current course opened in 1900.

I've seen Sea the Stars, Enable and other equine greats race, and have lasting memories from doing so. Those horses had physical attributes and talents as racers, such as dramatic turns of foot, that are not on show at Ripon today. But it's a snobbish racing fan for whom racing at this lower level holds no appeal. The horses may not be world beaters, but they're still beautiful, and impressive. Many of them have numerous runs on their CVs, and you get some sense, just by watching them in the paddock and reading their racecard profiles, of their personalities. It's fun to try to work out whether today might be one of their better days.

I risk a fiver on a new theory. Joshua R, in the six-furlong handicap, has form figures reading 000006, meaning that sixth, in his most recent race, has been his only finishing position worth noting in his past six races – and that was out of eight runners. But he's quite prominent in the betting. My theory is that if his shortish odds cannot be justified by his form, they must have been influenced by people in the know who believe that he'll perform better today. But guess what: I haven't invented a brilliant new betting system, and Joshua R finishes twelfth, gaining another zero in the form book. The first three home were drawn 4, 3 and 2, while Joshua R was in stall 15, on the stands' side, suggesting that he had more than lack of form to overcome. But there are no excuses really: the field split into two groups, and of his group of ten he was the eighth to cross the line. Back to the drawing board.

I reflect further on the appeal of the unpretentious as I have my lunch. I'm a fan of the great Motown artists, but I also very much enjoy the performance in the Ripon bandstand of mother and daughter singing duo The Cherrytones, whose light, somewhat fragile voices give a touching quality to 'Can't Hurry Love', 'Walk on By' and other sixties hits. I listen to them from a sparsely populated spot while tackling a pepperoni pizza from the 'Knead 'N' Feed' van. The fewer people who witness me trying to eat, by hand, this stringy mozzarella-topped foodstuff, the better.

I never learn, and finish my lunch with an Americano that is the colour of weak tea and as flavourless as the liquids passed off as coffee at most courses. I can sympathise with racecourses that, rather than hiring trained baristas, use machines that require only the pressing of a few buttons. I just shouldn't expect to enjoy what the machines emit.

When it comes to the Ladies' Day best-dressed competition, we're dealing with high street rather than the designer outfits on display down south. And again, nothing wrong with that. An enthusiastic crowd gathers.

First prize goes to Jasmine Padinske, from Harrogate and originally from California, sporting a midnight blue, floral, chiffon dress, and a hat with dark blue swirls. She goes forward to compete with winners at other Yorkshire courses for a two-night stay at Country Huts on the Wolds.

I stay to watch the Ladies' Derby Handicap Stakes, in which Serena Brotherton, who has won the race four times previously, sets off in front on Whitwell and sees off all challengers. Then I head for home. Cab to Thirsk; Transpennine Express, which runs hourly, to York; York to King's Cross. The ticket to the races cost £13; the train and taxi journeys cost about £250. That's not an attractive ratio for a day's excursion. But if you're in Yorkshire, do go.

GREAT YARMOUTH

Flat

1 July 2021

Ground concerns

On a grey, chilly, mizzly day, Yarmouth racecourse presents a somewhat bleak face to the visitor. The staff are so friendly, however, that I'm inclined to discount that impression. If I had dressed appropriately like the locals, who arrive wrapped in quilted and waterproof coats while I shiver in jacket and open-necked shirt, I might have found the venue more attractive; if the sun had been shining, I certainly would.

Perhaps I had expected the whole town to be bleak. In the 2016 referendum, Yarmouth earned the title of 'Brexit capital of Norfolk' and recorded the fifth highest percentage of votes in the UK in favour of leaving the European Community – a reflection, one may theorise, of the economic hardships it and many seaside areas have been suffering. But I don't see too much evidence of blight on the half-hour walk from the station to the course. I pass the Leaf Park Dementia Village and The Lawns care homes before the road broadens into a dual carriageway, with mock-Tudor detached houses on one side and pebble-dashed semis on the other; almost all have several cars on their paved forecourts, and at only one is the forecourt serving as a junkyard. There is a single flag of St George, probably signifying support for the England football team in the European Championship.

I arrive at Freemantle Road. On my left is an estate of red-brick bungalows; on the right, behind a wall that one can imagine topped with spikes or barbed wire, is the racecourse.

With Covid restrictions still in place, everyone enters the course at the far end. You pass through a green hut and find a scene that in fair weather would look very attractive; a lawn, of a breadth not usually on

106

offer in cheaper enclosures, with an open-sided marquee and a generous collection of tables and chairs. The two nearest grandstands, one of them reported to have been transferred after the First World War from an earlier course in the town, have the dispiriting appearance of all aged and weatherworn municipal constructions, but next to them is the smart, white Horatio Nelson stand, also bearing the title of Horatio Nelson Conference Centre. It is usually home to members and club ticket holders, but today is open only as a jockeys' changing room. Nelson was a local: 'I am a Norfolk man, and glory in being so,' he boasted. Yarmouth's landmarks include, as well as the racecourse tribute to the naval hero, a 144-foot Nelson's Monument, and the Norfolk Nelson Museum.

Not a great deal of indoor space is open in the stands apart from a couple of dimly lit bars. A lawn behind the grandstand features various food concessions: fish and chips; hot dogs; free-range hog roast; sweets and chocolates; an ice cream van. I go for the hog roast, delicious in a bap with stuffing. Then, having at last taken on board that I almost certainly won't enjoy the racecourse coffee, I get a cup of tea; it has a curious flavour, somewhere between tea and gunpowder. (I don't mean gunpowder green tea; I mean the stuff that propels bullets.)

Another lawn separates a long, brick Tote building from the paddock, which boasts a couple of dark-leaved trees. Herring gulls circle overhead; their cries, evoking the lure of the sea on sunny days, sound desolate in this weather. There are also swallows, who must be a bit disappointed with the conditions after flying here all the way from Africa. On the far side, across the track, is a caravan site; as at Fakenham, the central enclosure also functions as part of a golf course. Go out to the stands, and the view takes in the Seashore Holiday Park, a packed collection of cream and grey constructions. Beyond the far rail, the judge's hut resembles a dovecote, or a spaceship in a low-budget, 1950s sci-fi movie. A few wind turbines are the only evidence of the North Sea lying just out of sight.

This area is the North Denes. The previous course, closed in 1920, was on the South Denes. It opened in 1715; because it staged donkey races and chase-the-pig contests alongside the races for horses, it did not gain official recognition until the early nineteenth century. A handbill for an 1810 meeting warned: 'It is requested no person will bring dogs as they may be destroyed.' Most courses apply this rule, though not the sanction, today – Fakenham being a notable exception. Another rule, briefly in place, was a ban imposed by magistrates on betting; 'Fortunately,' James Gill writes in *Racecourses of Great Britain*, 'their worships soon came to their senses.'

A day at Yarmouth races was a grand occasion, with affluent racegoers arriving in landaus or other carriages, or by ferry from quays on the River Yare to a landing stage next to the course. The track, laid out in a figure of eight, had a tight turn near the harbour mouth, and jockeys who failed to control their charges would find themselves jumping the rail and tumbling into the water. In the evenings, the mayor and town corporation would entertain the gentry at the Bear Inn, and there were plays at the Theatre Royal or cockfighting at the taverns.

The configuration of the current track is like Ripon's: a narrow oval, with the horses rounding the home turn and entering the straight five furlongs from the finishing post. There are three differences from the Yorkshire venue: the runners at Yarmouth race left-handed (anticlockwise); the straight, going beyond the home turn, stretches for a mile rather than six furlongs; Ripon has undulations, while Yarmouth is flat. Yarmouth has, though, suffered from ridges, which compelled the racecourse executive to resurface the entire straight in 2015.

Richard Aldous, clerk of the course, first came to work here in 2005, had spells at Brighton and Fontwell, and returned in 2010. He is affable and forthright – qualities that must be useful when answering to the racing community on what must be one of the most difficult tracks to maintain in the country. The Yarmouth soil is sandy and dries out fast; if rain falls on the hard surface, conditions get slippery.

Being the nearest turf course to Newmarket (apart from Newmarket's own two), Yarmouth attracts runners from the Newmarket yards, and is known as a schooling track for two-year-olds. But the leading trainers did not relish the prospect of running their precious charges on ridged ground, and were staying away.

'I was one of the people asking for the resurfacing to be done,' Aldous says, speaking to me in his rather dark office tucked into the side of the middle grandstand. 'So we had the track surveyed, and head office gave me the money to relevel it from the mile up to the crossing here.' Head office is Arena Racing; the budget was £300,000.

Work started in September 2014 – in hindsight, Aldous says that this was too late in the year. In October and November there was a lot of rain, and the track was left uncovered throughout the winter. 'It was like the Somme out there.' Reseeding did not take place until the spring, and the reopening was delayed until the end of August 2015; again in hindsight, Aldous says that they should have waited until spring 2016. At the three-day September 2015 meeting, racing on the middle day was abandoned and the following day's card was postponed after a runner fell near the finishing post. This may have had nothing to do with the new surface: there had been torrential rain on top of firm ground. But it brought unhelpful publicity. Such incidents can take place anywhere from time to time: Yarmouth endured another in August 2020, when a horse suffered a fatal injury during a race. A hole in the ground was blamed, but no holes have disrupted meetings since then. Yarmouth stages twenty-three meetings during the flat season. 'It's a lovely, flat galloping course now,' Aldous says. 'The jockeys enjoy it, and I think the best horse on the day wins.'

Aldous and his team water the Yarmouth track daily. The nature of the soil, the summer warmth (sometimes), and the coastal winds demand it. 'You can be inland and enjoying a nice breeze, while here we've got 25- to 30-mile-per-hour winds,' Aldous says. 'We can dry out in a morning from good ground to the quick side of good to firm.' With changeable weather around and a meeting imminent, he'll check the forecast every hour. 'If there's rain coming from the west, the chances are we're not going to get it here. If it comes up from the south there's a fair chance we'll get something, and if it comes in off the continent there's a very good chance we'll get it.' From the evidence of the forecast, and from what he feels underfoot as he walks the course, he may alter his watering instructions. 'I can upset my staff very quickly,' he acknowledges. 'But as far as they're concerned, they're watering seven days a week unless they hear otherwise.'

Some courses have sprinkler systems. But if it's windy, sprinkled water will not land on the track; the horse you backed may be drawn to race where the ground is slower. Aldous has a machine called a Briggs Boom Irrigator. It consists of a reel holding 200 metres of piping, one end of which is attached to a boom – a metal frame that may be opened out to stretch across the whole track, and with taps that distribute water out of the back. The ground staff drive the boom on a tractor to the start of the mile straight, extend it to cross the track above the rails on either side, drive forward 200 metres with the pipe stretching along the track behind, and connect the reel to a hydrant. (Yarmouth's water comes from a borehole and from the mains.) They set the machine according to the amount of water they want to distribute: the equivalent of 7mm of rainfall, say. The reel then pulls in the pipe, dragging along the boom, at the appropriate speed.

If there's a wind, they have to adapt the boom to compensate; otherwise, water intended for one part of the track will be blown on to another. The wind can change direction, too. 'They have to be on the lookout all the time,' Aldous says. 'That's the way I train them. They all have at least six years' experience now – they know their jobs.' But there was one occasion – Aldous says he was away – when a failure to open the appropriate extension resulted in a 'golden highway' – a stretch of ground that gave a huge advantage to the horses drawn to race on it. 'That's the last thing you want.'

Watering the entire straight can take from five in the morning to nine at night – if all goes well. 'They're temperamental beasts, irrigators. They can break down the day before racing.' The next day, the ground staff will water the back straight. Then back to the home straight; and so on.

All this effort takes place because Aldous and his fellow clerks at other courses are under pressure to serve up going descriptions containing the word 'good'. Thirty years ago, clerks of the course were inclined to let the weather gods dictate the ground conditions. Perhaps today's thoroughbreds are more fragile, or perhaps today's trainers are more careful; anyway, if trainers see the word 'firm' on its own, they will most likely withdraw their entries. (At the Cheltenham National Hunt festival, the clerk aims to provide good to soft ground on the first of the four days.) This does not mean that trainers can lobby to get the ground conditions that their horses favour, although no doubt they try to do so from time to time. 'If Mr Gosden rings up and says, "I want good ground", I'm not going to do that. You get what you get,' Aldous says. One can imagine his robust response. (He's not saying that the trainer John Gosden is one of those who try it on; he's saying that no matter how eminent you are, you won't get special treatment.)

Various further machines are essential. The ground, subjected to pressure from horses' hooves and indeed from the irrigator, gets compacted: to alleviate the effect, Yarmouth employs a Verti-Drain aerator, which when driven at about 2mph digs tines into the soil, heaves it, and withdraws, as you might do with a pitchfork. It also has three kinds of slitter: again driven over the course, they have tines that cut into the ground and encourage root growth and moisture absorption. Then of course there's a mowing machine, operated so that it maintains the blades of grass at four inches height, as stipulated by the British Horseracing Authority. The ground staff feed the grass at the beginning of winter and at the start of spring. They also use a wetting agent, which lengthens the time in which moisture stays in the ground.

Such are the efforts required to maintain turf on which horses can safely race.* They are paying off, Aldous says. Now that the newly laid straight has bedded in, the leading trainers are returning with some of their more promising two-year-olds. Perhaps we'll again see at Yarmouth newcomers of the calibre of Dubai Millennium, who made his debut here and went on to win top races including the Dubai World Cup, and Ouija Board, owned by the current Lord Derby and winner of the English and Irish Oaks.

The two-year-old Maglev, who today comes home first in the British Stallion Studs EBF Novice Stakes (Class 4), may not match those achievements, and the rest of the card consists of Class 4, 5 and 6 handicaps. They offer some intriguing little plots, however. In the first, the favourite is Genesius, trained by Sir Mark Prescott, of whose well-fancied runners the bookmakers tend to be wary. Having been forecast by the *Racing Post* to be odds against, Genesius shortens in the betting to odds-on. Sir Mark is here, surrounded in the paddock by an enthusiastic group from the owning syndicate – surely a sign that we're looking at a 'plot horse', trained and raced specially with this day in mind. But no plot is proof against the vagaries of horseracing. Genesius is beaten into second by Toora Loora, a filly who has failed until now to get her nose in front in all eleven of her previous starts.

There's a plot horse in the seventh race too, and this one comes good.

---

* The UK is world leader in sports turf management. The *Guardian* reports that the English grounds management sector is valued at £1 billion and employs more than 27,000 people.

Rectory Road, trained in Newmarket by Alice Haynes, is forecast at 10/1 in the *Racing Post* and dismissed in the racecard with the phrase 'Others more persuasive.' Some people appear to have access to conflicting evidence, and in the betting ring Rectory Road is advertised as 11/4 favourite. These people are proved right. Rectory Road – who has previously run eighteen times without winning, and who a week ago was 'below form' in finishing fourth of nine at Leicester – comes home in front by half a length. How mysterious, misleading even, the form book can be. Still, well done, Alice Haynes. One of the jobs of a trainer at this level of the sport is to help your owners land the odd gamble, and she has done the business here.

Well done too, jockey Marco Ghiani, who a few weeks earlier rode a winner at Royal Ascot and who today 'rides out' his 3lb apprentice's claim on Surprise Picture. What this means is that Ghiani has hit the ninety-five winners mark and will no longer be able to 'claim' 3lb off his mounts' allotted weights. Apprentices start their careers on 7lb claims; when they reach twenty winners, the claim goes down to 5lb, and when they reach fifty winners, to 3lb. Trainers like to take advantage of this system in handicaps: if the apprentice is competent, the advantage of a lower weight will be worth more than the disadvantage of inexperience; and trainers get percentages of their apprentices' riding fees and prize money. Two races today go to 5lb claimers, Alex Jary (on Toora Loora) and Laura Pearson (Electric Love). The problem with riding out your claim is that trainers can lose interest in you once you no longer offer them the weight concession; but this is unlikely to be the fate of Ghiani, widely noted as an up-and-coming talent.

Placepot watch: reports of my consistent failure to land this bet are getting repetitive. No closer to a winning strategy, I have given up donating my money to the Tote in this way and am doing notional Placepots, on paper only, instead.

Today, my notional Placepot comes up! I would have received £6.02 in return for my £6.40 stake, so I am not too disappointed.

SANDOWN PARK

Flat (also stages jumps racing)

21 July 2021

Paddock watching

The Waterloo–Esher train deposits racegoers alongside Sandown Park. At most meetings, a gate at the top of the platform leads us to a tree-lined path, and then to a turnstile by the back straight; we cross the centre of the course, past the Go-Kart track and nine-hole 'Eclipse' golf course, to the grandstand. But this evening, when Sandown stages a low-key meeting, we are frustrated to find the gate closed. It is hard to see why, because station staff are out in force, rivalling in numbers the alighting passengers – although I have seen solitary inspectors at the gate helpless to prevent crowds, shouting claims such as 'Oyster Card, mate' (the card is not valid here), from surging past. The closure of the gate and path means that the Sandown busker, a specialist in raucous folk music who has been a regular here for years, must entertain us on another day, and that we must walk the longer route by road.

At this early time, an hour and a half before the first race, there are only a few dozen of us, soon spread out at intervals. I miss the overheard snatches of conversation you catch as a crowd makes its way across the course: the swapping of opinions; the 'upspeak' of young City types encountered the last time I was here:

'Charlotte's coming later?'

'Oh my God, Charlotte! She's gonna, like, drop a hundred on every race? Just because she's Charlotte?'

Sandown has had quite a makeover. The hall in the grandstand that dominates the course was once a dim, echoey space, with grey paint peeling from exposed piping and air vents. Now it's all wood and cream and glass. The loos are smarter too, boasting dispensers of upmarket soap and moisturiser. But there are still those annoying taps: you press one, and a torrent of scalding water emerges, at tremendous force; you release it, and the flow stops. You cannot soap and moisten your hands at the same time; and if you hold your hands at the wrong angle, you deflect the torrent on to your shirt and trousers. Grrr.

I wait too long before visiting the food hall at the far end of the stand, and find a massive queue. I've tried the fish and chips from here and didn't find them so amazing; but maybe everyone is after the 'Esher Spice' curry, which I had missed out on last time and which I shall have to forego again. I double back to the Racing Pie Company, just securing the last steak and ale pie, on its own next to a pile of apparently less popular vegan offerings. It's good, with pastry that is crispy in parts and gooey in others – a dream combo, slightly let down by the mini roast potatoes, which are dry.

Behind the stand is the parade ring, lovingly mown in a circular pattern. Beyond, you come to a statue of the late Queen Mother's steeplechaser Special Cargo, who won the Whitbread Gold Cup here in 1984. (Sandown is a 'dual-purpose' course, staging jumps races in the winter.) Special Cargo overlooks the winners' enclosure, behind which are the weighing room and racecourse offices. Further on, shaded by maple trees, there is the pre-parade ring, an area of quiet and calm that was once a favourite spot, but that is now hardly worth visiting. 'It's the worst pre-parade ring in the country,' says my contact this evening, renowned paddock judge Ken Pitterson. The problem is that the racecourse stables are nearby: it's convenient for trainers to saddle horses there, bypassing the pre-parade and its saddling stalls, which for some reason they regard as 'not horse-friendly'. A group of racegoers has complained to the Sandown executive, arguing that the pre-parade offers an informative experience for racegoers, but without effect. This evening, only two or three horses circulate here before each race; before race five, not one horse appears.

My education from Pitterson, therefore, takes place mainly at the regular paddock. I have a lot to learn. When I'm at the races, I always dutifully examine the horses as they walk round with their grooms, and conclude that they all look good. What am I failing to notice? Pitterson, with thirty years' experience of judging horseflesh, can tell me.

Before the encounter that was to change his life, Pitterson was a pastry chef in London, taking days off to enjoy trips with friends to race meetings up and down the country, and overseas too. They knew little about the sport; they simply loved the raceday experience. But gradually the friends developed other preoccupations, and Pitterson, at the races on his own, began to feel exposed: 'I realised that I was the only Black geezer on the track,' he recalled for the Oddscrackers podcast. 'I thought: "I don't know what I'm doing, and I don't know anyone."' But he did come across someone he knew at a Cheltenham meeting one day, and this person introduced him to Gerald Delamere, analyst for the *Racing Post*. 'It's thanks to Gerry that I'm in the position I'm in now,' he tells me.

Delamere took Pitterson under his wing, teaching him what to look for: how to tell if the horse was fit; if the horse needed more 'work' (exercise); if the horse's coat suggested well-being; if the horse seemed unlikely to be on best form. The tyro began to fill in as the *Racing Post Weekender* paddock-watcher when Delamere was away, eventually taking over the column; now, he also works for William Hill and Sky Sports, and at top meetings gives his expert assessments for ITV Racing.

Racing people have been largely welcoming, as he told Oddscrackers. True, he gets the occasional 'Oi, Pitterson, you're the worst judge on the racecourse!' – but then every tipster has had abuse of that nature. Other punters come up and thank him for pointing them towards winners, and the trainer Nicky Henderson has congratulated him for his emphasis on horses' well-being. As Pitterson and I stand by the tree-lined horsewalk between the Sandown paddock and the track, several jockeys give him cheery greetings as they go past. He recalls only three upsetting incidents: being told 'You shouldn't be here' as he made his way to the Fontwell press room; being stopped by a Windsor steward every time he approached a gate that his press colleagues were passing through unchallenged; and, at another press room, finding a desk and watching someone – still active, apparently – pointedly move his laptop, keys, wallet and phone away from the desk next door.

Pitterson goes racing four or five times a week, and before each meeting he puts in a good two to three hours' preparation, studying every runner: the horse's form, ground preferences and breeding (which may be relevant in deciding whether a horse will like firm or soft ground, or whether the horse is likely to be suited by the race distance). Is the trainer enjoying a good run? A trainer's horses often come good at the same time; at other times, they can all be out of sorts. The favourite in race 1, C'mon Kenny, is trained by Ian Williams, whose last thirty-plus runners have all lost. C'mon Kenny wins. There's another point to consider: no one piece of information is an infallible guide – not even the apparent state of the horse.

'Horses can do things out of character and still win,' Pitterson says. 'A prime example was Starman at Newmarket last week [in the paddock before the July Cup, one of the big sprint races of the season]. He's a horse that generally stays nice and calm. But this time, when he walked into the paddock, he was coltish [a racing euphemism sometimes meaning, 'He had an erection'], he was sweating – he looked as if the whole thing was getting to him. But it didn't stop him winning – he won really well.'

Are you talking yourself out of a job, Ken? Not at all. Even the most astute punter in the world is going to be wrong most of the time. Horses such as Starman behaving out of character and still winning may account for some of the losses. But for every Starman, there will be plenty of sweaty and coltish horses who lose. This is why in the past bookmakers have employed Pitterson to advise them on horses that look below par and that are worth laying – offering apparently generous odds in order to attract bets. It's a scary job, doing this in a betting cauldron such as Cheltenham and knowing that a misjudgement could cost your employer tens of thousands of pounds. He once advised bookmaker Victor Chandler to lay Denman, an equine superstar who, in the paddock before one race, looked to Pitterson's eyes to be a bit peaky. Never mind the horse: it was Pitterson who was sweating up for the next fifteen minutes, before Denman suffered one of his rare defeats.

What else should we look for? Pitterson, as the horses in the first race parade, directs my attention to Coverham, the top weight, and therefore judged by the handicapper to be the best horse in the field. Coverham is a darker bay colour at his neck and belly than he is at his hindquarters, indicating that he has not yet 'come in his coat' – the darker patches are woollier, whereas the summer coat is fine and smooth. Coverham finishes out of the places. Some horses on this warm evening are looking a bit overheated, which may or may not be a bad sign: I recall a famously sweaty horse called Benny the Dip, unkindly nicknamed 'Benny the

Drip' – and winner of the 1997 Derby. Before race two, for two-year-olds, Pitterson points out a horse showing some of his ribcage: you want your runner to be fit, but not to have been subjected to such a rigorous regime that the ribs seem to be covered with very little flesh. This horse is also 'unfurnished'. What does that mean? 'He hasn't got much of a body yet; he's leggy,' Pitterson explains. He adds, as the horses go past: 'You want a horse that looks tight under its girth. Eight's coat is not great [he means Dawn View, number eight on the racecard], five is not too bad; that one looks well, and is quite small, and that one is a bit warm.'

Decide on the best-looking horse in the paddock, and use it for comparisons, Pitterson advises. Some horses are 'close-coupled', a phrase meaning that they are compact, and possibly best suited to sprint distances. Does your horse have a defining line before the hindquarters, indicating taut muscles?

We make our way to the front of the grandstand, seeking further clues as the horses canter to the start. Some raise their knees quite high, a trait that would help them were the ground soft but that is a drawback on the firm ground underfoot this evening. One horse is 'scratchy', a term I haven't understood until now, when I see him flapping his legs about in an uncoordinated way. We want horses with 'daisy-cutter' actions. One of the daisy cutters is the filly Porsche Cavalier, who comes home first at 11/2.

The form book says of Porsche Cavalier's run: 'Made virtually all, hard pressed throughout, ridden and led clearly 1f out, kept on well final 110yds.' No mention of how she looked, and Pitterson feels that we're missing out on the complete picture of her performance. But he will have this picture, at home: after every meeting, he adds the information he has gleaned to his database. If Porsche Cavalier doesn't look so well before her next race, he'll notice, while others may not. He likes to have the odd bet, and successful betting requires getting an edge not only on the bookmakers but also on other punters.

Does he have a favourite course? 'Salisbury – but because I back more winners there than anywhere else.' I don't know whether he has backed Just Fine in the fifth race, but he does tell me that he thinks the horse, owned by the Queen, has a good chance: Just Fine's unplaced run last time out was in a Royal Ascot handicap, and this is a much less daunting

race. I, less sophisticated, ignored Just Fine because of the form figures
'00'. Just Fine romps home.

You'd think there were a good many successful punters here this
evening, to judge by the number of young men sloshing around lager as
they wave their arms in the air and chant victoriously. It was in part to
protect sensitive ladies from such scenes that Sandown became, in 1875,
the first 'park' course in Britain, restricting admission to those who paid
at the gate; its 'club' or members' enclosure spared grander folk from
proximity to common people and offered reassurance that 'a man could
take his ladies without any fear of their hearing coarse language or un-
couth behaviour'.

The enterprising owners set up the course on land that was once
chosen by Henry II as the site for a priory, later transformed into a hospital after all the priory residents had fallen victim to the Black Death;
later still, the land belonged to a farm. In the early years of the racecourse, a man called Hwfa Williams, who was chairman and clerk of
the course here for fifty years, masterminded the Eclipse Stakes, named
after the paragon of racehorses and, with £10,000 going to the winner,
the most valuable race in the country at the time. Run over one mile
two furlongs in early July, it is the first important race in the calendar in
which three-year-olds – the 'classic' generation – meet their elders.

In 1903, Sandown staged what was to be known as 'the race of the
century' – an accolade that, despite other claimants, still seems plausible from our twenty-first-century perspective. The three principals
were Rock Sand, who had won the 2000 Guineas and Derby and who
was to go on to win the third leg of the Triple Crown, the St Leger; the
filly Sceptre, the most popular horse of the time and winner the previous
season of four classics – 1000 Guineas, 2000 Guineas, Oaks, St Leger;
and Ard Patrick, who had won the 1902 Derby, with Sceptre, below her
best, in fourth. 'All the rings were packed to suffocation, and everybody
was keyed up to the highest pitch of excitement,' a report enthused.
Rock Sand was the favourite and Sceptre the sentimental choice; but it
was Ard Patrick, comparatively unfancied at 5/1, who prevailed by a
neck after a tremendous battle with Sceptre over the final furlong.

I was at Sandown in 1988, for the launch of my friend Sean Magee's
The Channel 4 Book of Racing and for an Eclipse Stakes that was billed

as a rival to the Rock Sand/Sceptre/Ard Patrick running. There were again three principals: Nashwan, winner of the 2000 Guineas and Derby; the filly Indian Skimmer, unbeaten that season; and the crack miler Warning, stepping up in distance for the first time. It was an odd race. A 200/1 outsider called Opening Verse suddenly surged clear at the halfway mark, and as the field entered the home straight was showing no signs of stopping. Indian Skimmer and Warning could not cope with this change of pace – older readers may recall that the athlete Steve Ovett had been defeated by a similar tactic in the 1980 Olympic 1500 metres final. But Willie Carson on Nashwan was alert to the danger, and sent his mount in pursuit; in the end, Nashwan won by five lengths. 'That's the trouble with races of the century,' Sean said, lowering his binoculars. 'They usually aren't.' (Sean is a little older than I, but had missed the 1903 race.) Nashwan returned to the winner's enclosure exhausted, and although he scraped home a month later in the King George VI and Queen Elizabeth Stakes at Ascot, was never the same horse again.

My favourite running of the Eclipse was in 2009, in part because I was publicising my book *Eclipse* and was a guest for the day of the friendly team at Channel 4 Racing, but also because the winner was Sea the Stars, who matched Nashwan's achievement in adding victory here to his 2000 Guineas and Derby successes, and who was to surpass it in taking three further Group 1s, among them the Prix de l'Arc de Triomphe. Sea the Stars' undemonstrative trainer John Oxx was part of the appeal – you wanted him to do well. The race was a proper contest. As Sea the Stars led into the final furlong, Rip Van Winkle, from the powerful Ballydoyle/Coolmore team, loomed up ominously on the outside; I, with my head-on view from the lawn in front of the grandstand, went through a bad few moments, taking a while to realise, thanks at first to the renewed surge of cheering from the crowd, that Sea the Stars had found an extra reserve of stamina. He drew away again to win by a length.

The Sandown jumps course was the scene of two of the greatest performances by the great Arkle: at the 1965 Whitbread Gold Cup, which he won with two and a half stone more on his back than his nearest rival carried; and, in November that year, the Gallaher Gold Cup, when he swept past his great rival Mill House – carrying more than a stone less

– as if Mill House were in first gear and he in fourth. And Sandown staged the most exciting race I have ever seen live: the 2004 Tingle Creek Chase showdown between Moscow Flyer, Azertyuiop and Well Chief (see the Cheltenham chapter). Do watch the video. The noise of the crowd!

There are two finishing posts at Sandown: one for the jumps track, and one for the hurdle and flat track. It has caused more confusion than you would expect to occur at a Grade 1 racecourse. At a hurdle race in 2019, the judge called One for Rosie, a 12/1 shot, the winner – and yes, One for Rosie had been in front at the first winning post. But it was the second winning post that should have counted, and Third Wind (13/2) had overtaken by the time they reached it. Ten minutes had passed, One for Rosie had entered the winner's enclosure, trainer Nigel Twiston-Davies had told reporters how delighted he was with the victory, and bookmakers had paid out, when the stewards announced the revised result. The bookies found themselves having to pay out on Third Wind too. The outspoken Barry Dennis was quoted in the *Guardian* as saying that the mistake had cost him £10,000.

There have been other cock-ups here. Bookmakers also had to pay out twice following a five-furlong handicap the previous year, when the judge, having studied the photographic evidence, announced that Rio Ronaldo (13/2) had won, only for the stewards to overrule him in favour of Vibrant Chords (6/1). On the Eclipse card in 2021, another five-furlong handicap was announced as having gone the way of Phoenix Star (6/1), but later ruled a dead heat between Phoenix Star and Hurricane Ivor (11/1): the photo that might have separated them had been compromised by a wonky mirror. (The judge makes a decision based on both a direct image and a mirror image.)

Such matters do not compromise my liking for Sandown. If you're a Londoner, it's the easiest racecourse to get to; it's an excellent course for the spectator; it hosts top-class racing; and the facilities rate a solid 8/10. Now it's on to a course that should be a favourite, but somehow isn't.

GOODWOOD

Flat

28 July 2021

Garden party

Goodwood: by common consent, the most beautiful racecourse in the UK, if not the world. From the stands, you get a northwards view over miles of Sussex downland, with scarcely a building visible, and only the occasional car passing on one of the minor roads nearby. Then there's Goodwood-plus: five days of the Glorious Goodwood festival, with men in pale linen suits and panamas, and women in light summer dresses – it's so much more relaxed, don't you think, than Royal Ascot, where men sweat in morning dress and women compete in designer outfits. And there are free strawberries!

Why do I not love it? As someone said of the First World War front, or possibly of the retreat to Dunkirk: 'My dear, the noise! And the *people!*' The noise here comes from the Earl's Lawn, where a DJ plays, very loudly and all afternoon, a succession of beat-heavy R&B tracks, occasionally with a saxophonist or trumpeter joining in. Sure, it's not artillery fire, but it is torturesome. It's the accompaniment as the horses circulate in the pre-parade and parade rings, and on the lawn itself it dominates the aural landscape, to headache-inducing effect. Mine is no doubt a minority reaction: I must concede that plenty of people are happily reclining here on the low, white-cushioned loungers, and chatting away almost as if they can hear each other.

The people: to an inhabitant of a North London borough, they're a bit white. I see more ethnic diversity among the staff than among the spectators. It's not that everyone is posh. It's that Ascot and Goodwood – but not Cheltenham, where the horses are at the centre of the occasion – attract a certain kind of spectator, or rather enough of this

121

kind to create a different, less congenial atmosphere than you'd enjoy on a normal raceday. Someone I encounter on the way home exemplifies what I mean. This man, standing behind me in the queue to get on the train at Chichester, pushes me in the back in his impatience to grab a seat, ruling that I've given the elderly lady trying to get off more than enough opportunity to do so. Time's up, old person; now get out of our way! On the train, he shares with his friend and the rest of the carriage his definitive selections for the next British Lions test match, describes his holidays in Barbados, gives a high score to the food and bubbly on offer in his marquee, and reveals that he is not heading straight home, because he wants to avoid seeing his young children, with whom he can't get out of spending a large part of the following day. My guess is that he hasn't visited Goodwood to enjoy the spectacle, or a day out in beautiful surroundings: he has collected a VIP experience that he can boast about.

I think most of us can agree that this man is an arse, but I realise that my reaction to Goodwood, possibly influenced by a chip on my shoulder, may not be yours. There are other, less subjective irritants.

I've seen smarter loos, and one I visit has several taps running permanently, because the mechanism supposed to release them to the off position has failed. Then I make the mistake of taking my lunch at the canteen in the Gordon enclosure. (I should have tried the Goodwood Organic Food stall in the cheap, Lennox enclosure, or – if I could have wolfed down my meal before the disco unhinged me – a falafel wrap on the Earl's Lawn.) The canteen is in the Sussex Grandstand, which was opened in 1990 and won a commendation from the Royal Fine Arts Commission. The architects have gone for a sort of chic cellar effect in this basement room, with a brown and white colour scheme, central pillars, strip lights hanging from the ceiling at odd angles, and tables arranged against one sloping wall. At the table where I settle with my box of fish and chips (very average, and pricey, £12), I notice a damp surface on my right. Then I notice that, from an invisible source, fine drops of water are spraying my right hand. In short, I'm not witnessing the 'insatiable appetite to get it 100 per cent right' and 'meticulous attention to detail' of which Goodwood owner the Duke of Richmond and his colleagues boast on the estate website. Sort it out, your grace!

I may be chippy because I don't have access to the premier, Richmond enclosure, reserved for Goodwood members. I am in Gordon (£40).

This brings me to another point, before I move on: in Gordon, you're at least half a furlong from the winning post, and as the horses flash past, you must focus again on the (not generously sized) screen sited opposite the Richmond enclosure to find out who won, the commentary having been drowned out. There's another screen opposite Lennox, but for some reason today it's removed halfway through the afternoon. Even in Richmond, in my experience, you require a high perch to get a clear notion of what's happening: something to do with the upwards slope in the final furlong means that at ground level it's hard to get a perspective on the runners. I learn later that commentators also have to resort to a screen at the climax of races: the racecourse commentary position is fifty yards ahead of the post.

Even in a country of oddly shaped racecourses, Goodwood is odd. It has a six-furlong straight. The six-furlong marker is hidden from the stands behind a hillock. The runners crest the hillock at the five-furlong marker, and race downhill until they have about a furlong to go, when the track rises again. To this course is attached a loop, descending the hillside before arriving at a small chute from which horses in one-mile-four-furlong races start; it turns right, ascends the hill, and meets the straight just below the five-furlong marker. In some races, the horses start on the far, upper side of the loop, cross over, and enter the straight from the lower side; in others, they start in the lower part, cross over, and enter the straight from the upper part (the 'top bend'). Confused? You may not be less so after a visit to the course, because the far points of the loop are a long way from the stands, and parts of the track are obscured. But jockeys seem to know where they're going.

It was the third Duke of Richmond, grandson of an illegitimate son of Charles II, who laid out this course, later improved with the approval of the fifth Duke by one of the great figures in racing history: Lord George Bentinck.

Bentinck was an energetic reformer and scourge of the corrupt who was himself guilty of all sorts of sharp practices: he had a rumbustious ego of the type that enables a man to believe that he is the arbiter of whether rules apply to him. One of the trainers of his racehorses wrote: 'What a humbug it all is, and if everybody knew all that I know of his tricks and artifices, what a rogue he would be thought . . . He has made for himself a peculiar code of morality and honour, and what he has done, he thinks he has a right to do, that the game at which he plays warrants deceit and falsehood to a certain extent and in a certain manner.' Perhaps we can think of modern counterparts.

After starting out in the army, Bentinck became an MP in 1826. He was already on the path to becoming, in the words of the racing historian Roger Longrigg, 'easily the heaviest bettor in Britain'. He lost £26,000 on the 1826 St Leger, and was bailed out by his mother and sister; his father, the Duke of Portland, 'gave him a firm lecture and an estate in Ayrshire'* – not the kind of mortification usually meted out to gamblers.

The attractions of south-west Scotland could not keep Bentinck from the turf. He had such a large string of racehorses that he needed to win substantial sums of money by gambling to stay solvent, and he was not above disguising a horse's ability, or faking an injury, in order to profit from better odds. Such practices and worse were widespread in the sport, and led to many disputes. When Bentinck believed himself to be the injured party, at the hands of a sportsman called George Osbaldeston, he declined to pay Osbaldeston's winnings. Some months later, Osbaldeston caught up with him. Bentinck asked: 'Can you count?', to which Osbaldeston gave the splendidly haughty reply: 'I could at Eton.' Bentinck handed over the £200 debt in notes, one by one. This insult could have only one outcome.

Accounts of the duel differ. Some say Osbaldeston missed, and Bentinck shot in the air. Some say Bentinck missed, and Osbaldeston shot in the air. Some say Bentinck missed, and Osbaldeston, a crack marksman, emphasised his superior skills by shooting a hole in Bentinck's hat. Who knows? Anyway, no one died.

Racing in the first half of the nineteenth century was hugely corrupt. Horses were poisoned, or nobbled; jockeys, starters and judges were bribed. Bentinck, acknowledging no hypocrisy, was a rigorous pursuer of wrongdoers, achieving his most notable triumph in the exposure of the owners of Maccabaeus, who as a four-year-old disguised as a three-year-old called Running Rein came first past the post in the Derby of 1844. It was 'the dirtiest Derby in history': the rider of the favourite, Ugly Buck, was bribed to make sure his mount did not win, as was

---

* *Biographical Encyclopaedia of British Flat Racing.*

the rider of Ratan, the second favourite; Ratan, thanks to a belt-and-braces approach by conspirators, was drugged as well; and a German entry called Leander, put down as a result of an inoperable injury, was examined and declared also to have been four – though his smarting German owner, furious with the British authorities, later declared that they were so incompetent that they could not get the horse's age right – he had been six. But it was Bentinck's relentless pursuit of Running Rein's (and Maccabaeus's) owner Goodman Levy and Levy's cohorts, who were eventually routed at a sensational court case, that earned him widespread acclaim and a Jockey Club award. With the award, he set up the Bentinck Benevolent Fund, for dependants of trainers and jockeys who had fallen on hard times.

Bentinck's reforming activities, however, did not centre on the Derby and its Epsom home but on Goodwood, from where their influence spread to other racecourses. One improvement, which seems obvious now but which had not occurred to the authorities until Bentinck came along, was to scrap the procedure by which the starter of a race, seeing that the horses were roughly in a line, shouted 'Go!', and devil take the hindmost – a procedure that was particularly confusing at Goodwood, where the starter had a speech impediment and often struggled to enunciate the 'G'. Bentinck's innovation was to employ a man with a flag, lowered at the command 'Go' in full view of the jockeys. It meant that jockeys who may have been bribed to pull their mounts were denied the excuse that they had missed the instruction, and were heavily fined.

Bentinck introduced various enclosures, among them one for gentlemen who wished to smoke cigars. He improved the racegoing experience for spectators in further ways: by requiring that the horses parade in front of the stands; by introducing a consistent numbering system, so that the numbers on racecards corresponded with those on boards at the course; and by fining clerks of the course if races started late.

He was something of a dandy. Here he is in the words of the sporting journalist 'Sylvanus': 'A tall, high-bred man of the true Anglo-Saxon tint and countenance . . . who seemed to still the Ring when the quiet, rather womanish tones of his voice were heard, offering some mighty sum against a horse in the Derby. He had the genuine cut of an English gentleman – so countrified, yet refined – so quiet, yet determined in his air.' Bentinck did not appear to be especially committed to politics, and would be seen in the House of Commons, when he condescended to visit, with hunting gear visible beneath an overcoat. So it was something of a bombshell when, at the Goodwood meeting of 1846, he sold his string of horses for the 'ridiculous' (Roger Longrigg) sum of £10,000, in order to devote himself to the cause of Protectionism. He left the sport with only one unfulfilled ambition: to win the Derby.

It was an unhappily timed move. Among the horses in the dispersal sale was a yearling called Surplice. In 1848, Surplice won the Derby. (We have seen Bentinck's reaction to this blow in the Epsom chapter.) Four months later, Surplice won the St Leger. Two weeks after this further blow, Bentinck died of a heart attack, at the age of forty-six.

Another significant influencer at Goodwood was Edward VII, a regular here as he was at Ascot and at Doncaster during the St Leger meeting. His predecessors George IV and William IV had also patronised the course, and it was no doubt royal glamour that led to Goodwood's status as, in the words of the authorised history, 'very firmly the racecourse of choice for the aristocrat'. A painting by Walter Wilson and Frank Walton of 'The Lawn at Goodwood' – in the same genre as, but more exclusive and less characterful than William Powell Frith's *The Derby Day* – shows four princes, nine dukes, sixteen earls, and eighteen barons. If they did not live nearby, they were entertained during the week at grand house parties by peers who did.

Edward, as Prince of Wales, echoed the behaviour of Charles II at Newmarket in sharing his company at Goodwood both with his mistresses and with his tolerant wife. Society did not demur. Alice Keppel was described by one lady as having 'a wonderful way with her, a pleasant word for everyone and gracious to all', while Lillie Langtry, who was knowledgeable about racing and owned horses under the pseudonym – ownership was unladylike – 'Mr Jersey', became known as 'The Goddess of Goodwood'. Edward viewed the Goodwood meeting as 'a garden party with racing tacked on', and once king, pioneered the pale-linen-and-panama fashion still encouraged today.

Relaxation and tolerance extended only so far, especially after Edward had ascended the throne. Due deference had to be paid. His host the sixth Duke of Richmond was required to meet the royal train at the station, sometimes with a guard of honour, and with a carriage for the royal personages along with further carriages for guests and luggage.

The duke would ensure that the road to Goodwood had been watered, so that the arrivals would not be troubled by dust. At a new grandstand, opened in 1903, the king's lavatory was constructed of monogrammed marble with a marble frieze; the seat was mahogany, and the chain was silver-plated. His queen, Alexandra, instructed that the pavilion housing her own room be turned round so that she could look out over the picnic area, and that her lavatory be fitted with mahogany shelves and an electro-plated towel rail. The bill for these improvements went of course to the duke.

Dim basement canteen notwithstanding, Goodwood mostly aims for the upmarket garden party atmosphere that Edward VII relished. The Earl's Lawn boasts the white loungers I mentioned, somewhere between sofas and beds, and white food huts with crescent roofs. One of the entrances to the lawn is a greenery-festooned trellis, and there are containers of plants dotted about. The paddock-side bars are glass-fronted, under white gazebos; on the Sussex Stand, and on the bar in Lennox, there are Chinese hat roofs.

In Gordon, you get access to only a corner of the pre-parade ring, which is on a slope with most of the saddling boxes on the lower side and hidden behind lime trees. Trainers or their assistants saddle the horses here, the racehorse stables being too far away; but some of them do so, as at Sandown, without allowing the horses to walk round this ring first. It's disappointing.

To repeat: the enclosures here are Richmond (Members), Gordon (Tattersalls) and Lennox (Silver Ring). If I wanted to enjoy a garden party with racing tacked on, I'd choose the happier, more relaxed atmosphere of Lennox. There's a nice bar, Goodwood Organic Food, lots of greenery and places to sit, and a grandstand that gives you a good overview of the races, if not of the last two furlongs. Squinty McGinty's Band are playing: not quite my taste, but Mozartian by comparison with what's belting out of the Earl's Lawn loudspeakers. Today, Lennox hosts a pop-up Covid vaccination centre: a volunteer tells me that on the previous day they were busiest at the end of the afternoon, by which time racegoers with a few drinks inside them had lost all fear of the needle.

The fourth vantage point is free: you could take a picnic to Trundle Hill, directly beyond the winning post. It's the site of an Iron Age hillfort, and home to copious wildflowers, as well as brown hairstreak and grizzled skipper butterflies; hovering overhead are buzzards, red kites and kestrels, so don't leave your food unattended.

No doubt there remains a certain amount of skulduggery in horserac- ing today. But there's a lot less than there was in Bentinck's time, and a lot less than many punters, disgruntled when results do not go their way, conclude. 'How the fuck does he get away with it?' I hear one disappointed Goodwood racegoer complain, presumably referring to the trainer Kevin Ryan, whose mare Last Empire wins the Oak Tree Stakes in a style that witnesses of her previous run – fifth of six when she was favourite in the betting – may not have expected. But Last Empire, forecast 18/1 in the *Racing Post*, comes home at 16/1 – hardly evidence that anyone has profited in bets from this reversal of form.

The big race today is the Sussex Stakes, the flat season's first mile race that pits three-year-olds against older horses. It is heralded as a show- down: between three-year-old Poetic Flare, winner of the 2000 Guineas and Ascot's St James's Palace Stakes, and described by paddock expert Ken Pitterson (see Sandown chapter) as the most impressive horse he has seen this year; and Palace Pier, the highest-rated miler in the world. With a week to go, we learn that Palace Pier has suffered from a blood disorder, is not fully recovered, and is scratched. But he doesn't leave a penalty kick for Poetic Flare, who still faces strong opposition, and, it turns out, soft ground. Inconvenienced by it, he is overtaken in the final furlong by a filly called Alcohol Free. Poetic Flare and Palace Pier meet a few weeks later in the Prix Jacques le Marois, where Palace Pier comes out on top. Alcohol Free heads to York, and I follow her there.

YORK

Flat

18 August 2021

What a legend

Like a bookmaker paying out before the contest is over, I'll say it now: York is the best racecourse in Britain and Ireland. No course I've yet to visit can possibly match its all-round excellence. I don't mean that it's my favourite: I enjoy the smaller courses, the ones punters fondly call the 'gaff tracks': the likes of Fakenham, Plumpton, Brighton. But judged by the quality of the racing, the quality of the facilities and attention to detail, York is a clear winner. Ascot: the grandstand is not hospitable, the food and drink options are more limited, and on crowded days it's a trial. Goodwood: I've mentioned the minus points. Epsom, Newmarket, Cheltenham: thrilling places to be for any racing fan, but with less to offer the casual spectator on a day out.

There are buses to ferry you from York station to the racecourse, but I prefer to take the half-hour walk, past detached, porticoed houses in stucco or dark grey brick. At the County Stand entrance, a smiley woman is giving free racecards to every arrival; these programmes are packed with more information than I've seen any other course provide. Immediately past the entrance is a flower-encircled statue of the great Frankel, as well as an area dedicated to a tribute to his late trainer, Henry Cecil. Frankel put up one of his many scintillating performances here, and now stands as a stallion at Juddmonte Farms, a longtime York sponsor. He has two sons running in today's big race, the Juddmonte International.

Further along on your right are the paddock and pre-parade ring, as well as the weighing room, in front of which is a gallery in wrought iron with a white rose motif. Unlike at some other courses, such as Sandown and Goodwood, you get to see most of the runners in the pre-parade ring before they're saddled up and sent to the main paddock. It's a treat, and informative (even for me, and certainly for those with a keener eye for horseflesh), to see these thoroughbreds without rugs or tack. You notice that they carry quite a bit of 'condition' – their bellies are rounded – while also showing their ribcages and taut muscles.

The horse who makes the biggest impression on me is the gleaming dark bay Mishriff, the Juddmonte International favourite, who strolls past as if sleepwalking. Earlier, outside the weighing room, a couple of lads had accosted his trainer, John Gosden, and asked for a selfie. Gosden, though always forthcoming in media interviews, is not some- one whose patience I'd care to try, but without hesitation he said: 'Fire away.' 'Yess!' one of them responded, perhaps as surprised as I was. 'What a legend!' I decide I want Mishriff to win.

On the left are a low, immaculately trimmed hedge, long beds of flowers, lawns in front of various food and drink outlets, and roof ter- races, where racegoers are enjoying cool drinks; ice buckets housing champagne bottles are plentiful. At other courses on big race days, you must be prepared to enter a competitive scrum to eat, drink and be seated; here, there is plenty of room. As I make my way behind the stands, I recognise outlets that were also at Ripon: the Little Yorkshire Coffee Company and Ice Cream Company vans (from the latter, I buy a delicious vanilla scoop, flecked with vanilla seeds), and Knead'n'Feed Pizza. Also on offer are Cornish pasties, Big Phillie's burgers and steaks, Whitby scampi, Ged Bell of Yorkshire's pies and burgers (salespeople harnessed to trays of pies roam the stands later), and noodles from the Dragon Noodle Bar. All this is available outdoors; in the stands, there are various cafés, buffets, sandwich bars and restaurants – eight of them, according to the racecard, plus the outlets in the Clocktower Enclosure in the centre of the course. Then there are all the bars: the racecard lists twenty-one. I buy a hog roast bap from the Striped Pig Co; I don't have to queue, and I find a seat at which to eat it. There are some 20,000 people here. Amazing.

York claims to have been the first racecourse in the world to have erected a grandstand, in 1750. (Before this, courses assembled make- shift stands, while the grander folk would watch from their carriages or on horseback; some mounted gentlemen would join the runners a few furlongs from home and ride alongside them, yelling encouragement and curses.) Now it has five stands. Melrose, in red brick and with a pitched roof, houses private boxes as well as a club lounge, offering among other treats what is described as a 'Yorkshire platter'. The elegant, listed Gimcrack stand, supported by red, white and blue barber's poles and again with wrought ironwork, has an interior like that of a boutique hotel. Then there are the substantial Ebor and Knavesmire stands, opened in 2003 and 1996 respectively. Last, there is the basic Bustardthorpe stand: steppings, stanchions, tiled roof, that's about it. Here, I find that you have a pretty good vantage point – it's not like being exiled in Goodwood's Lennox enclosure. I get a close-up view of the start of the two-mile handicap, make my way up the steppings, and am close enough to the top of the home straight to appreciate Jamie Spencer's progress from last to first on Arcadian Sunrise. The big screen here is bigger than Goodwood's, too; and Mike Cattermole's commentary is entirely audible. (The only fault I can find with York is that the acoustics are muffled in the Ebor and Knavesmire stands. Oh, and there is even less ethnic diversity among the crowd than there is at Goodwood.)

Whence these names? Bustardthorpe is the local manor. Ebor is from Eboracum, the Roman name for the city. James Melrose was chairman of York racecourse for fifty years, retiring in 1929, shortly before his death at the age of one hundred.

Knavesmire is the name of this site, to which York races moved in 1731. A mire is a low, marshy stretch of ground. The derivation of 'Knaves' is disputed: a common assumption is that it refers to miscreants who were hanged here, but some argue that it is a version of a word indicating a poor person or servant. Another matter of uncertainty is whether the local authorities staged hangings – the gallows were situated near the mile-and-three-quarter pole, where the runners in the Ebor handicap set off – as part of the raceday entertainments. What is certain is that, until the start of the nineteenth century, the hangings took place, bringing to a premature end the life of the highwayman Dick Turpin among many others.

Gimcrack was one of the most popular horses of the eighteenth century. A grey the size of a pony, he took part in thirty-six races and won twenty-six of them, counting among his losses his only two races at

York, which nevertheless commemorates him with the stand and with the Gimcrack Stakes, a prestigious race for two-year-olds. He was, according to Lady Sarah Bunbury (née Lennox, married to Jockey Club supremo Sir Charles Bunbury), 'the sweetest horse . . . that ever was . . . he is delightful'. The great equine artist George Stubbs painted him three times. One especially impressive canvas shows Gimcrack in the background leading a trial race, while in the foreground he is at the rubbing house, following the race, with his trainer, groom and jockey; as in so many of Stubbs's paintings, there is a mythical, timeless atmosphere, as well as an impression of physical power.

Another Stubbs subject was Eclipse, who raced twice here. Or rather, he raced once and walked over once: his first engagement merely required him to walk over the course, no opponent having turned up to challenge him. In his second, he raced against two rivals: Tortoise, reflecting a fashion of the time for ironic nomenclature; and Bellario, owned by Sir Charles Bunbury, whose wife Lady Sarah had by this time eloped with Lord William Gordon. Eclipse set off in front, and extended his lead relentlessly, prompting one layer to offer the price of 100/1 *on* – betting-in-running is not an invention of the internet era. The great horse came home 'with uncommon ease', a result that Bunbury, who objected to the cut of the owner Dennis O'Kelly's jib, did not take well. O'Kelly was in disgrace at the time, having been apprehended at Blewitt's Inn in York after invading the bedroom of Miss Swinburne, daughter of a prominent local figure. He was compelled to take an advertisement in the *York Courant* to acknowledge that he had been '(when in liquor) lately guilty of a very gross affront and rudeness to a young lady of a very respectable family', and to pledge the considerable sum of £500 to charity. You'll find the Eclipse restaurant on the fifth floor of the Ebor stand.

Among the races this afternoon is the Great Voltigeur Stakes, a trial for the St Leger, to be held at Doncaster a month hence. Voltigeur took part in the most famous match race in the history of the sport. Owned by Yorkshireman Lord Zetland, he had won the 1850 Derby and had gone on to defeat 1849 Derby winner The Flying Dutchman, whose jockey had been drinking, in the Doncaster Cup. In the spring of 1851 Voltigeur and The Flying Dutchman met again, at York, attracting 'the biggest crowd on the Knavesmire since Eugene Aram [a murderer] was hanged there the previous century'.* Voltigeur set off in front, but the Flying Dutchman kept him close, and overtook him in the final furlong. Voltigeur carried eight stone, and the Flying Dutchman carried eight stone and a half – weights set by the most imposing turf figure of the day, Admiral Rous.

Horseracing has boasted three men who came to earn the informal title of 'dictator' of the turf: Sir Charles Bunbury; Lord George Bentinck, whom we met in the Goodwood chapter; and Admiral Henry John Rous, 1795–1877. Rous served in the Royal Navy for thirty years before enjoying what the *Biographical Encyclopaedia of British Flat Racing* describes as 'a rather featureless interlude' as Tory MP for Westminster. All the while, he was gaining influence in the Jockey Club. He was, the *Encyclopaedia* states, 'the best type of Englishman of his class and era', a man of 'unsullied integrity'. He had inflexible views on how racing should be run, and on the hierarchies in the sport: he 'firmly believed that jockeys should be kept in their place; and that place a comparatively humble one . . . He himself was courteous and considerate to jockeys, but nothing would have induced him to invite one to his dinner table.'

Rous brought his commanding presence and huge energy to the role of official handicapper at the Jockey Club. He attended every important race meeting, surveying the action through his naval telescope, and was a regular on Newmarket Heath as horses took their exercise. At Newmarket race meetings, he would park himself at the Bushes just over two furlongs from the winning post, roaring at jockeys he deemed to be making insufficient effort.

Owners and trainers rarely believe that the handicapper has treated their horses fairly, but they seem mostly to have respected Rous' authority. He devised the Weight for Age Scale: a system assigning weights based on age, sex, and the time of year when a race is to be run. With a few tweaks, it remains in use all round the world.

In this afternoon's Juddmonte International, for example, the four-year-old colt Mishriff carries 9st 6lb, the four-year-old filly Love carries 9st 3lb, the three-year-old colt Alenquer carries 8st 13lb, and the three-year-old filly Alcohol Free carries 8st 10lb. Three-year-olds are reckoned not to be fully mature; colts have a slight physical advantage

---

* *Biographical Encyclopaedia of British Flat Racing.*

over fillies – though an exceptional filly such as Enable, who won two runnings of the Yorkshire Oaks at York and has a racecourse bar named after her, would at her peak have beaten the colts at level weights. In the Eclipse Stakes at Sandown in early July, Mishriff carried 9st 7lb, while the winner, three-year-old colt St Mark's Basilica, carried 10lb less (8st 11lb) rather than 3lb less: Weight for Age suggests that three-year-olds have matured rapidly – by 7lb, in racing terms – in the past six and a half weeks.

With all respect to Mishriff, a brilliant winner today, and to other winners such as Frankel and Sea the Stars, no running of the Juddmonte International has matched the drama of the first running of the race, then known as the Benson & Hedges Gold Cup, in 1972. The odds-on (1/3) favourite was Brigadier Gerard, winner of all fifteen of his previous starts and later to be rated as the greatest British racehorse of the twentieth century. His rivals included Roberto and Rheingold, who had fought out the finish of the Epsom Derby, with Roberto, given a characteristically uncompromising ride by Lester Piggott, prevailing. Roberto had gone on to flop in the Irish Derby, and for this race was partnered by Panamanian jockey Braulio Baeza, who had never ridden in Britain before; you could back the Derby winner at 12/1. Baeza set him off in front. As the field entered the home straight, Brigadier Gerard loomed up on the outside, travelling easily. But when his jockey, Joe Mercer, asked him to go on and win the race, the colt could not respond, and Roberto extended his lead. With about a furlong to go, 'the Brigadier' clicked into top gear at last, and began to close – but it was too late. Mercer dropped his hands, accepting defeat; he was three lengths in arrears at the line.

It's hard to know how to sum up this race. Take Roberto out of it, and no one would have suggested that Brigadier Gerard was below par: he broke the course record, and finished a long way clear of the others, among them a horse – Rheingold – who was to go on to win the 1973 Prix de l'Arc de Triomphe. In his next race, a month later, the Brigadier broke the mile course record at Ascot, and in October he won the Champion Stakes at Newmarket for a second time, so you can't say that his form had tailed off. His owner, John Hislop, suggested somewhat ungraciously that Roberto, to have been galvanised into beating his supposedly unbeatable horse, 'must have been stung by a bee';

but Roberto's performance in the Coronation Cup the following year showed how formidable he was on his day, while his performances in all his other subsequent races – four defeats – showed that his day was a rare phenomenon. You could say that Brigadier Gerard ran to his best at York and was still beaten. Was therefore Roberto at his best better than Brigadier Gerard at his best? For fans of the Brigadier, the question is sacrilegious – but the case is arguable. What you couldn't argue is that Roberto was a better horse than one whose record reads seventeen firsts and one second.

What the 1972 Benson & Hedges Gold Cup reveals is the confirmation bias to which we are prone when assessing sporting contests. We think that a 1/3 shot is a certainty, whereas what the odds tell us is that the horse has a one in four chance of losing. We think that champions are unbeatable, and are astonished when they lose, whereas any follower of sport should know that upsets are common occurrences.

No upset today: Mishriff, the favourite, is hugely impressive, and bolts clear in the home straight by six lengths. Alcohol Free, whom I saw winning the Sussex Stakes at Goodwood, fails to see out the extra quarter of a mile of this race. Last year, the Juddmonte International was rated – based on the handicap marks of all the runners – the best horse race in the world. So is Mishriff, the *Racing Post* asks, the best horse in the world? Er, his previous two races ended in defeat, is one possible answer. The paper's handicapper later assigns him a rating one pound below that of Derby winner Adayar, who beat him in the King George VI and Queen Elizabeth Stakes at Ascot.

There are further questions, to be discussed, arising from the history, running and aftermath of the Juddmonte International. Brigadier Gerard was not, in bloodstock terms, well bred. How did he become a champion? As a sire, he had an undistinguished record. Why did he not pass on his ability? Third question: how can a horse's ability be measured in numbers?

BANGOR-ON-DEE

Jumps

24 August 2021

Stables and security

The final day's racing of the 2020/21 jumps season took place on 24 April at Sandown Park. The Celebration Chase, the feature race, starred the great two-miler Altior as well as the 2021 Champion Chase winner Put the Kettle On; but the fanfares turned out to be for jockey Briony Frost, who rode a double: first on Frodon, and then, skilfully overtaking Altior on the inside at the final bend, on the 13/2 shot Greaneteen.

The 2021/22 season opened just six days later, at Cheltenham. Not many people noticed.

While the attention of the racing world switches to the flat, a programme of summer jumps fixtures is quietly unfolding in the background, mostly at smaller tracks such as Newton Abbot, Market Rasen and Bangor-on-Dee. The best horses from the leading stables will not show their faces in public until October at the earliest, but there are plenty of other jumps horses in training who are ready to race, and courses that are happy to host them. Today at Bangor (I'll call it that from now on, assuming you won't think I've switched my attention to the city on the North Wales coast), there are sixty-one runners declared for the six races, and the top-rated, a veteran of thirteen called Asockastar, has a handicap mark of 131 (the scale is 0–175). He won't be challenging at Cheltenham next March, but he is, as they say, no mug.

My visit to Bangor could go wrong. First, there's the journey: a train from Euston to Crewe, another from Crewe to Chester, and another from Chester to Wrexham General; then, a twenty-minute taxi ride from Wrexham General to the racecourse. But, would you believe it, everything runs on time. To Londoners who don't consider transport costs of £170 per person to be somewhat hefty for a day trip, and don't mind spending more time on trains and in stations than they'll enjoy at the racecourse, I can report that a day out at Bangor is feasible.

Then there's the weather. I'm told that it rains quite a lot in North Wales. Rain is especially unwelcome at Bangor races, because the course is the only one in Britain to lack a grandstand – and, in this time of Covid, I don't fancy squeezing for shelter into a crowded bar or restaurant. But again I am lucky. The day is overcast, but warm and dry.

Though short of a grandstand, Bangor has all the other facilities you'd expect. On your left as you enter from the car park side is a bar, a lawn mown into stripes, and a series of four single-storey red-brick buildings, with pitched roofs: the Paddock Restaurant, from £88 (plus VAT) per person at the time of writing; the weighing room; the smartly appointed owners' and trainers' bar and restaurant, in a building that also finds room for the miniature Stable Door café (stools at the window for four); and the Wynnstay bar and restaurant (carvery, from £51 plus VAT). There's a food court, where I unwisely select a Cajun burger, which is rubbery – the much larger queue for the fish and chips van should have told me something. There's another bar at the end of the path.

On the right of the path is the paddock, and beyond it a bank dropping down to the course. This is why Bangor has no grandstand: the bank offers a natural vantage point. The course is flat, bordered on the far side by the River Dee, and then by a row of trees. A bright blue object at the end of the treeline is a pump, used to extract up to 15 million gallons of Dee water with which Bangor is licensed to irrigate the course during the summer months. In the distance are the Welsh Hills.

Beyond the Paddock Enclosure is what Bangor calls the Open Course, with its own car park. For £10 on the day, you can set yourself up with a picnic on the bank. There are families here who have brought along the complete kit: tables, chairs, rugs, food, drink, ice buckets. The view is fine, though you have to go close to the enclosure railings to get a proper sight of the big screen.

There's another unusual thing about Bangor racecourse: the finishing straight is not alongside the spectators' area, but head-on. If you stand near the top of the bank, you get a reasonable perspective on the race for the line; but the experience, certainly for the first-time visitor, is less involving than a conventional layout offers. Perhaps I'm simply noticing that the crowd makes less noise than at most other courses.

There are about 2000 people here today: to my untrained ear, the predominant accent is more evocative of Cheshire or Shropshire than of Wales. The Bangor racegoers know about horses and racing, and radiate a more casual vibe than do their counterparts at country courses such as Fakenham or Taunton. It's their loyalty to the course that has helped Bangor to get through some tough times.

There has been the Covid-19 pandemic: shutdown, followed by racing behind closed doors, and only now a return to something like normality. At the time of the shutdown Bangor had been out of action anyway, because of flooding caused by storms Clara and Dennis; storm Christoph flooded the course earlier this year. All this followed an out-break of equine flu in early 2019 at the local yard of Donald McCain. Like some variants of Covid-19, equine flu has a low mortality rate but is highly contagious. The discovery of the virus provoked an immediate suspension of UK horseracing – in this case, the lockdown strategy was entirely effective.

Bangor – since 2002 part of the Chester Race Company, which runs Musselburgh as well as Chester – has five hundred annual members. In 2020, it offered to give them their money back or to carry their member-ships forward; racecourse manager Jeannie Chantler tells me that only about twenty of them asked for refunds. This year, the members were unable to come racing until late May, but they have continued to leave their money in Bangor's bank account.

Chantler, articulate and businesslike, has associations with Bangor dating back to 1976, the year a photo on the racecourse history board in the Wynnstay building shows her leading a horse round the parade ring. She has been manager here since 2004. Her colleagues include head groundsman Andrew Malam, who has been in the role since 1997, when he took over from his father; John Malam had done the job for twenty-seven years. 'Andrew knows every blade of grass here,' Chantler says. 'That's a huge benefit for us.'

As we chat, in the secretary's office to the side of the weighing room building, the last of today's runners are arriving in the racecourse stables, immediately to the other side of the adjoining B5069. There are eighty-five boxes here, more than enough to accommodate today's entries, a few of whom – who may, for example, have 'scoped dirty' (a scope shoved up their noses emerged showing mucous); or have picked up a late injury; or be unlikely to relish the ground conditions – have been declared non-runners on the day. The BHA through Weatherbys 'ballots out' horses if more are declared than Bangor can accommodate, thus taking the flak that might have been directed at the racecourse management by disappointed owners and trainers.

The stable manager has a list of all the horses and the stable numbers assigned to them. The man in charge today lays shavings or paper on the floors of the boxes, according to what each horse prefers to have underfoot, and he gives vouchers to the trainers' staff for their free meals and (soft) drinks in the canteen. (At the time of writing, stable staff get free food at forty-four of the fifty-nine British racecourses.) He makes sure that a vet and a farrier are on hand if required.

Every racehorse has an identifying microchip and a passport, and on arrival gets scanned by the BHA representative, who also conducts random passport checks. Well in advance of each race, the manager ensures that the runners head across the road to the pre-parade ring, which hooray! (see previous chapters) they all circulate before entering the main paddock. After each race, the stewards may decide to drug test a runner or runners, perhaps because a horse has performed above or below expectations. A member of staff based at the paddock will ensure that the horse goes straight from the track to the sampling unit, without interference.

The misdemeanours that these procedures are designed to stop may be unwitting. Drugs in a horse's system are not necessarily there to boost or impair performance. In 2009, the leading trainer Nicky Henderson was fined £40,000 and banned from making entries for three months after running at Huntingdon the Queen's mare Moonlit Path, who tested positive for tranexamic acid. It's supposed to help horses who have a tendency to burst blood vessels when they exercise. The disciplinary panel accepted the argument that Henderson and his vet had administered the medication without knowing that it was banned. Tranexamic acid had not seemed to boost Moonlit Path's performance: she finished down the field, convincing Henderson that a racing career was not her destiny.

However, more sinister actions remain a threat. In Ireland, at a race at Tramore in autumn 2018, a horse called Viking Hoard, who had been friendless in the betting market, ran sluggishly and was pulled up before completing. He was an obvious candidate for a drugs test. He failed it, with 'a dangerous level' of sedative discovered in his system. It seems that his trainer, Charles Byrnes, had left him unattended at the stable, which in common with every other racecourse in Ireland apart from Leopardstown had no security cameras.* Byrnes got a six-month ban.

I've mentioned the case of Sheikh Mohammed's trainer Mahmood al-Zarooni (Newmarket chapter). In the US, the superstar trainer Bob Baffert blamed contaminated feed after his horse Medina Spirit, who had been first past the post in the 2021 Kentucky Derby, had tested positive for a steroid and was disqualified. It was the fifth medication breach in which Baffert had been involved in thirteen months; in each case he denied any wrongdoing.

On confused identities: one of the most celebrated cases – 'celebrated', oddly, is the appropriate word – took place 125 miles north of here, at Cartmel, on August bank holiday Monday in 1974. At the instigation of Cork business magnate Tony Murphy, a chestnut horse of moderate ability had been sent from Ireland to the yard of Tony Collins, based in Troon. Apparently, the horse was called Gay Future, and he was entered in Cartmel's Ulverston Novice Hurdle, for which he could be backed at generous odds. But the real Gay Future, who was a good deal more talented, was still in Ireland; he did not cross the Irish sea until shortly before the race, and in a layby on the M6 he and the impostor swapped places.

Meanwhile, Murphy's associates were on a tour of betting shops, where they backed Gay Future, along with horses that Collins had entered for races at Southwell and Plumpton, in doubles and trebles. It seemed a bit out of character for the trainer to send one of his charges from Scotland to East Sussex, but it did not arouse suspicion until the Southwell and Plumpton entrants were declared non-runners. All the double and treble bets became singles, on Gay Future.

You couldn't attempt this scam now. First, the identification checks are more rigorous. Second, the conspirators relied on the primitive nature of communications at the Lake District track. Third, the SP

---

* Installations are taking place at the time of writing.

(starting price) system is no longer based on odds available in the betting ring, but on odds generally available.

On learning of the non-runners, bookmakers went into panic mode. They needed urgently to cut Gay Future's SP, and the only way they could do this was by backing him at Cartmel. But they couldn't get through to their representatives at the course: Cartmel's only line to the outside world was via a phone box, mysteriously occupied for the best part of the afternoon. A motorbike rider set off for the course from Manchester with a satchel of cash, but was hampered by bank holiday traffic. Gay Future's price at the course was an attractive 10/1, thanks also to Collins's wife, who went round the ring placing £20 bets on the stable's other runner in the race.

Gay Future, who had been given a soaping before his entry into the paddock to make him look sweaty, won by fifteen lengths. What a coup! But then: whoops! When a *Sporting Life* reporter phoned up Collins's yard to ask about the well-being of the Southwell and Plumpton entrants, an innocent employee told him that they were fine, and that he could see them out of the window – they had never left home. It was a crucial piece of evidence in a trial that saw Murphy and Collins fined, as well as 'warned off' – they could have nothing to do with horseracing – for ten years.

We are inclined to admire the wit involved in scams such as this, and to consider them to be victimless crimes: bookmakers are fair game. Oh, and perhaps there was disappointment for the connections of the other Ulverton Novice Hurdle runners, who may have thought they were in with a chance of winning the race. Cartmel racecourse seems to have thought it was all a bit of a laugh, commemorating the scam on its fortieth anniversary in 2014, with Tony Collins as special guest. He expressed only one regret: Troon golf club had blackballed him.

More recently, there have been innocent mix-ups. For one involving top Irish trainer Aidan O'Brien, Covid-19 restrictions were partly responsible. In autumn 2020, O'Brien sent to Newmarket two contenders, Mother Earth and Snowfall, for the Fillies' Mile, a leading autumn contest for two-year-olds. The Ballydoyle stable's England-based staff, less familiar with the fillies, gave the better-fancied Mother Earth the saddle cloth that should have gone to 50/1 shot Snowfall, and vice versa. 'Snowfall' (Mother Earth) finished third, while 'Mother Earth'

(Snowfall) finished roughly where the betting suggested that Snowfall would, down the field in eighth. It was O'Brien, having scrutinised the race on television, who pointed out the mix-up to the British Horseracing Authority (BHA), which by way of a thank-you handed him a £4000 fine. The coda to this story is that Snowfall, undistinguished at two, emerged as a superstar at three, winning the English Oaks by an amazing sixteen lengths, and the Irish Oaks by eight and a half lengths. Mother Earth, whom we shall see running at the Curragh, won the 1000 Guineas.

No such mix-ups at Bangor today, although I do spot in the parade ring a distinctly grey horse who is advertised in the racecard and in the *Racing Post* as a bay. There are probably, as I've said, no Cheltenham contenders either. But you never know: as Snowfall has demonstrated, racehorses can improve remarkably. There are portraits on the walls here of a good number of great horses who have run at humble Bangor since racing began at the course in 1859: among the more recent ones Grand National winners Amberleigh House (trained locally, by Ginger McCain, Donald's father and of course also the trainer of three-times National winner Red Rum), Ballabriggs (trained by Donald) and Comply or Die, and Gold Cup winners Norton's Coin (who won at Cheltenham at 100/1) and Mr Mulligan. Further back, Bangor hosted the subsequent National winners Gamecock (who won at Aintree in 1887) and Cloister (1893). The course was also the venue for the first winning ride by Fred Archer, who was to become the greatest flat jockey of his era; at twelve years old and weighing 4st 11lb, Archer steered the mare Made of Trent to victory in the 1869 Galloway Steeplechase. (This is the version according to racecourse histories and Archer biographies. The Bangor website says that the race was for ponies, run in 1868, and that Archer was ten at the time.) Dick Francis also rode his first winner here, in 1947; he was to go on to suffer heartbreak on board the Queen Mother's Devon Loch in the 1956 Grand National, and on retirement to become one of the bestselling thriller writers in Britain.

Probably the best horse ever seen at Bangor was Denman, winner of the Gold Cup in 2008. 'The Tank' raced here in 2006, on a day of awful weather when it was mid-morning before the fixture got the go-ahead; his trainer Paul Nicholls, deciding that he really did want to see Denman in action, hired a helicopter to get him to the course from Somerset on time.

By terrestrial routes, I leave Bangor at 4.30 p.m., and arrive home four hours later.

SALISBURY

Flat

2 September 2021

With Racing TV

Travel advice: if you're going by public transport to Salisbury or any other course that is some distance from the nearest train station, book a taxi in advance. On my way to Ripon, I would have got stuck at Thirsk had I not spotted a notice on the train advising that there was no taxi rank there. Wrexham General station (for Bangor-on-Dee) has a taxi office, with helpful staff, who nevertheless cannot guarantee that a car will be readily available. Arriving at Salisbury at 11.45 a.m., three-quarters of an hour before she was due to go on air, my host for the day Lydia Hislop of Racing TV found a deserted taxi rank – apparently some festival was also taking place in the area, she discovered, incredulous that a city hosting an excellent day's racing would also schedule a rival attraction. Only a chance encounter with a friendly racehorse owner, who did have transport, got her to the course on time. I *had* booked a taxi, with a service that for reasons not entirely clear to me would not allow a return journey reservation; had I joined the massive queue at the taxi rank outside the course after the last race, I would have waited until nightfall. Hislop, who did have a 4 p.m. taxi reserved, kindly took pity on me when I cadged a lift.

There's further evidence that she's a nice person. First, she tolerates my getting in her way all afternoon. Second, a young man approaches her during a pause between races, says he's about to start studying for a degree in broadcast journalism, and asks for advice in gaining experience in the field. I know from my day job in the book world how one can weary of such inquiries ('Could you advise my daughter how to get a job in publishing?'; 'Could you recommend a literary agent?'; 'Could you

144

read my manuscript and give me an honest opinion?' – this last really means, 'Could you recommend my book to an agent/publisher?'); but Hislop has a friendly and helpful chat with him, and takes his email address.

Salisbury racecourse, in common with Epsom and Brighton and Goodwood, is on high downland. It can be a calm day when you arrive in the city, and windy up here. As it was for most of August, the weather today is overcast, and barely warm enough for an afternoon outdoors in shirt and jacket; the small gazebo accommodating Racing TV is threatened by, but just about withstands, the sudden gusts.

As you approach the ticket office from the taxi drop-off point, you can see on your right a venerable stone building. This is the rubbing house, where horses would be attended to after their races, and is thought to have been built in the late seventeenth century. It was given Grade II status in 2020. Racing at Salisbury dates back further, to at least 1584, when a horse owned by the Earl of Cumberland won him a golden bell, worth £50 and donated by him as the prize for the following year. According to legend, Elizabeth I stopped here for an afternoon's recreation before meeting Drake as he prepared to do battle with the Spanish Armada. Queen Elizabeth II has been a visitor, too, and today has a horse called Intelligentsia running in her colours in the feature race; I spot her bloodstock adviser, John Warren, in the stands, and conclude that Intelligentsia carries high hopes. But what seems to be a clue is a red herring: Intelligentsia flops, coming home last, with her trainer's representative explaining that she didn't care for the undulating track.

Eclipse had two engagements at Salisbury, walking over the course on 28 June 1769 – he didn't have to run, because no opponents turned up to challenge him – for the King's Plate, and a day later defeating two rivals for the City Plate. Two of the greatest horses of the twentieth century raced here in the same year. Mill Reef was trained by Ian Balding (broadcaster Clare's father), a past director of the Bibury Club, which has run Salisbury since 1899; the horse won the Salisbury Stakes before going on the following year to win the Derby, Eclipse, King George, and Prix de l'Arc de Triomphe. Brigadier Gerard, owned and bred by John Hislop (no relation of Lydia's – and neither is *Private Eye* editor Ian), won the Champagne Stakes, and went on to beat Mill Reef in the 2000

Guineas during a career of seventeen victories and only one defeat (see the York chapter).

Bar names pay tribute to a couple of further significant figures from Salisbury's history. A rooftop terrace bar commemorates the great jockey Lester Piggott, who in 1948, as a twelve-year-old apprentice weighing five stone, rode his first race here. He finished unplaced on a horse called The Chase, trained by his father Keith; six years later, Lester would ride the first of his record nine Derby winners. His son-in-law, William Haggas (Lingfield chapter), is the trainer of two runners on today's card: Persist, backed into favouritism for the two o'clock, finishes third, and in the big race of the day, the two thirty-five, Perfect News (10/1) is unplaced.

The Persian Punch bar is named after a popular stayer (specialising in distances further than a mile and a half) who won here twice and was owned by Jeff Smith, current Bibury Club chairman. We've seen Smith's filly Alcohol Free win the Sussex Stakes at Goodwood and fail to stay in the Juddmonte International at York. Today, his filly Quickstep Lady is favourite for the fifth race, named after another of his celebrated runners, Lochsong; Quickstep Lady seems to have it all set up for her, but alas comes home fifth of seven.

You don't quite get the broad vistas here that other downland courses offer from their stands, but the surroundings are very attractive. Like those courses, Salisbury has a weird layout. The mile-long straight rises from the start, dips, then rises again until the finishing post. As at Goodwood, there's a loop, and horses racing at longer distances gallop the wrong way up the straight before turning left, negotiating a short circuit, and coming back. Runners in the loop are invisible to the spectators. There are big screens, of course: one for occupiers of the stands, and the other opposite the paddock, which is alongside the track beyond the winning post. I like this arrangement: you can view the horses as they circulate before the race, and simply turn round to watch them cantering down to the start.

At the other side of the paddock, on the weighing room terrace, I meet the Racing TV team of three. Strictly speaking, it's two: cameraman Geoff Lyle works for RaceTech, owned by the Racecourse Association and provider of pictures from all fifty-nine British courses. Also at the course is a RaceTech staffer in charge of liaison between the channel and the camera crew. Lydia Hislop, presenter, is joined today by James Millman, form expert. Millman is son of trainer Rod Millman, and was a jockey for eight years before retiring at twenty-five and going to law school. After a brief legal career, he worked for William Hill Radio before joining Racing TV's roster, combining punditry on five or six days a month with work as assistant trainer at his father's yard.

As I arrive, Hislop and Millman are profiling for Racing TV viewers the runners in the feature race, the IRE Incentive Scheme Dick Poole Fillies' Stakes at 2.35. I'm standing only a few feet away, but I cannot hear them above the voice of today's racecourse commentator Richard Hoiles, whose assessment of the card is blaring out of the racecourse tannoys; Hislop and Millman are unfazed. Then it's off with Lyle and his camera to the paddock, to give their assessments of the form and appearances of the runners in race one. Lyle may be quite relieved that Hislop does not do that thing of Francesca Cumani's on ITV, walking alongside the horses as the camera operator backpedals in front of her.

This segment may be broadcast on delay, so there is no dead air as the trio return to their weighing room spot. Lyle's work is done for the time being; Hislop and Millman now take their places in front of the monitor, commentating on the pictures that the viewers see as the horses make their way to the start and race back. The monitor picture isn't bad, and today it's uncompromised by sunlight, but the screen is a good deal smaller than the ones you and I have at home; from this, the presenters have to offer their detailed appraisal of how the race is run.

Hislop and Millman tell me that their preparations for the broadcast include about half an hour's studying of the form for every race. I'm amazed it doesn't take longer. They each have large printouts of the *Racing Post* cards, on which they've written notes about every runner: form, going preferences and other idiosyncrasies, pedigree, running style, and a good deal more. Then there's what they observe, and what data their observations remind them of. Going down for the first, the favourite Rectory Road (whom we saw winning at Yarmouth) comes to a halt at the furlong marker and needs considerable urging before he condescends to canter the remaining seven furlongs to the start. 'He did this at Lingfield,' Millman notes – I mean, it's impressive enough to retain all the horses' form, let alone their pre-race behaviour, their breeding, and relevant details about their jockeys and trainers. Will it be a problem for Rectory Road's apprentice jockey, Alice Bond, that this is a 'hands and heels' race, and she's not allowed to use her whip? (The racing calendar includes a number of races such as this, designed as part of apprentices' training.) Yes: Rectory Road is last to leave the stalls, loses further ground when Bond switches him to the outside, and despite finishing strongly never has a chance of winning. Millman wonders also if Piselli Molli might need a bit of encouragement to get going, while also noting that his trainer Sir Mark Prescott, who likes to run up sequences of wins, may be able to take advantage of the conditions of this race and enter the horse again within eight days without incurring a weight penalty. Piselli Molli jumps sharply from the stalls, travels sweetly for jockey Morgan Cole, and is never headed. (At Chester eight days later, I see his name on the racecard; but he is a late withdrawal.)

Among further observations during the afternoon: what going and distance this horse's granddam liked; trainer Ralph Beckett's record this season with his juveniles (two-year-olds); how quickly this jockey is riding out her claim (as she rides winners, the amount of weight that is reduced from her horses' allocations diminishes); is Intelligentsia mimicking the record of her older sister, who won on her first start and was beaten on her next two?

With all this knowledge, do Hislop and Millman bet? She does, though not as seriously as she once did; he doesn't. 'You have to devote yourself to it 24/7,' they both say.

Hislop grew up in Wolverhampton. She caught the racing bug from her grandfather, 'a punter – but not a very good one'. She would go racing with her family to the local course, where she once tipped her mother a 66/1 winner, and from the age of ten was allowed to accompany her grandfather to Cheltenham for Champion Chase day. For her, 'racing was a safe place'. After studying at Oxford, where she read English at University College, she wrote to the *Sporting Life* and the *Racing Post*, heard from the *Life* by return, and began work experience at the paper before landing a job at the Racenews agency. She was at Racenews, she says, for 'ten months and four days' – one infers that she didn't find the work entirely fulfilling, but on the plus side one of her colleagues was Steve Curry, her partner ever since. Next, she wrote to Max Hastings, editor at the time of the *London Evening Standard*, and he offered her, then twenty-two, a role as feature writer. Later, when the racing correspondent retired, she took over. 'I was outlandishly young and also, in the press box, conspicuously female,' she recalls. But she has never allowed herself to be daunted. When a prominent trainer patted her on the bum, she would not let him leave the room before she had told him plainly why such behaviour was unacceptable. It's certain that he found being spoken to like that an entirely novel experience.

It's not only sex pests in racing who don't reckon on being called out: the sport, like other communities, expects insiders to be uncritical. Asking a question, in some people's view, is no different from making an accusation, and jockeys including Ryan Moore and AP McCoy – who, as a pundit himself now, may well see matters differently – have in the past bristled at Hislop's perfectly fair comments about their riding tactics. For example, at Ascot in 2010, McCoy gave a horse called Get Me Out of Here what is euphemistically known as an 'educational' ride, not pushing too hard – in contrast to his usual uncompromising style – when it was clear that victory was impossible. 'I just don't think he was persisted with in a way you would expect [of] any horse,' Hislop said on air. McCoy responded: 'On my three-year-old daughter's life, I did not stop that horse.' You see the problem? She said, 'He gave him a lenient ride'; he heard, 'He cheated' – which she hadn't suggested or believed. It's very difficult to do a reporter's job in circumstances where powerful people – McCoy was a multiple champion jockey and has since been knighted – call you out on possible interpretations, rather than on what you actually say or write. You'd be tempted to avoid making such comments in future. But Hislop hasn't flinched, has continued to talk straight, and has won the respect of viewers: online, where slagging off TV presenters is a favourite sport, she comes in mostly for praise. She was Racing Broadcaster of the Year in 2019 (and this December is to win the award again).

She worked for the pay TV channel At the Races, for Channel 4, and spent just over a year at the BBC, where she was not happy: there appeared to be a loss of faith that the sport could be presented to viewers without popularising gimmicks. Racing TV suits her much better. 'We're talking to people who often know at least as much as we do,' she says. 'If you're confident in the product, you should be able to deliver it in an accessible way.'

For many of us as we grew up, racing meant Peter O'Sullevan, the voice of the sport, on the BBC. Technically, contemporary commentators such as Richard Hoiles and Simon Holt are more proficient than O'Sullevan was, but none can enhance the pictures as he could. It's sad that the channel for which he called Arkle's three Gold Cups and Red Rum's three Grand Nationals no longer covers racing at all, and that the BBC does not have a racing correspondent after dropping Cornelius Lysaght in 2020. Terrestrial racing coverage is exclusively on ITV, which at the time of writing has a three-year deal reportedly worth £8–9 million. (To put that into perspective, Sky is paying £1193 million *a year* for its Premier League package.)

There are two pay TV racing channels: Sky Sports Racing, which has evolved out of At the Races; and Racing TV, owned by umbrella organisation the Racecourse Media Group. Racing TV has rights to broadcast from Ireland's courses and most of the top British courses, though it lost Ascot to Sky in 2019, and will lose Newbury in 2024. None of these channels has outside broadcast units, and they contract RaceTech to provide the pictures. ITV, Sky and Racing TV distribute the pictures to TV viewers; firms including SIS (Sports Information Services) distribute them to betting shops and streaming services, in this country and overseas; another company, the Racecourse Data Company, licenses the use of data – runners and riders, colours, form and so on.

The critical view of these arrangements is that they encourage too much low-grade racing, staged merely as 'betting shop fodder'. The supportive view is that they give opportunities for people with modest budgets to venture into racehorse ownership, because their modest horses will get opportunities to run. The critics respond that there are too many horses in training, and that rewards are spread too thinly; owners may get to see their horses run, but they're highly unlikely to win much of their money back. Salisbury is one of five meetings today, with Haydock, Sedgefield, Newcastle and Chelmsford City. Racing TV is also showing the Irish meetings at Clonmel and Dundalk.

As the last runners enter the stalls, Hislop hands over to Richard Hoiles. The pay channels, along with betting shops and streaming services, use the racecourse commentaries – which is why during lockdown the words of Hoiles and his fellow commentators boomed out of tannoys in empty enclosures. Hislop and Millman watch the race, sharing only the odd observation. Hislop cuts in to the broadcast after the horses pass the post. 'It was a long final furlong,' is her opening remark following the first, in which the runners – apart from Rectory Road – charged out of the gate and finished tired. She and Millman comment on the runners as the race replays, first as we saw it originally, and second from a head-on camera, which reveals how the horses veer from a true line and can cause interference. Next, it's back to Angus McNae in the studio; meanwhile, Hislop has her eye on the jockeys as they return, and books a slot after the weighing-in with the victorious Morgan Cole.

At meetings that ITV is covering as well, the usual arrangement is that ITV gets the first interview with the winning jockey and/or trainer, Racing TV the second, and the press the third. (You sometimes see members of the press crowding round with their notebooks and recorders as the TV interviews take place.) The scheduling was often tricky during lockdown, when some press interviews had to be arranged via Zoom, and is always tricky during the Cheltenham Festival, when the atmosphere in the paddock is manic. 'Sometimes you have to have sharp elbows,' Hislop says. I tell her that the jockeys seem to be more informative in conversations with her than they are when talking on terrestrial TV. 'I've media-trained them,' she says.

There's disappointment for Millman in the fifth, as the family-trained fillies Crazy Luck and Silent Flame finish second and third, collared on the line by Ryan Moore on Chocoya. But Millman is philosophical: the winner has been running in higher-grade races, while Crazy Luck has earned a good deal more in prize money than the £9000 she cost. Last year, she won a race here worth only £3777, but picked up an extra £20,000 thanks to an incentive called the Great British Bonus Scheme. Crazy Luck's owner, the Crown Connoisseurs syndicate, may not agree that the racing calendar is overloaded.

Back in Salisbury after the racing, there's time for a quick pub visit and gossip with Hislop before I catch the train home. What an excellent day out.

CHESTER

Flat

10 September 2021

Good breeding

Chester is the second-best racecourse in Britain. (The top Irish courses match it.) I felt confident last month in declaring York to be the best, and I feel the same way, despite the number of courses I have never visited, about placing Chester in the runner-up spot.

It's atmospheric. Beyond the stands you can see the Roman walls that provided a harbour when this area was entirely flooded, and in the centre of the course there is a mound and stone cross where a statue of the Virgin, having fallen from a height and brained the wife of a local dignitary, fetched up after being thrown into the water upstream. Or it may have been a wooden cross that did her in. The name of the site, the Roodee, derives from 'Roodeye', the 'rood' part meaning cross and the 'eye' part meaning island. Or perhaps the cross was known as the Rood Dee (Dee Cross), because it was near the River Dee. We're talking legend rather than verifiable history.

A more modern historical nudge is the name of Chester racecourse's premium restaurant, 1539. Horseracing had taken place in Britain before this date: no doubt the Romans raced horses as well as horses attached to chariots, and there are reports of races in the seventh century, in the twelfth century at Smithfield in London, and on other occasions during the medieval period, as well as numerous records of imports of barbs and other admired breeds to improve the racing stock. But it was in 1539 that Mayor of Chester Henry Gee, immortalised in expressions such as racegoers' 'We're off to the gee-gees', instituted a race over five circuits of the Roodee, with a silver bell for the owner of 'the horse that [runs] before all others'. As Smithfield is otherwise occupied these days,

Chester can boast that it has been staging horse races for longer than any other venue in Britain. York comes second. Chester also staged one of the first races for which we know some of the rules, when during the reign of Charles II the high sheriff won the prize with a horse that he had borrowed for the occasion, having taken the precaution of disqualifying a couple of rivals on the grounds that they had arrived in the city after the prescribed time. It was not a popular ruse, inciting, a report stated, 'all the gentry to relinquish these races ever since'.

The paddock bars and notices at the course recall more recent history. Buffalo Bill brought his travelling show here in 1903, we learn. In 1946, as people flocked to sporting events following the war, a crowd of more than 100,000 came through the gates on Chester Cup day. There are bars named after Chester Vase winners Old Vic, who went on to win the 1989 French and Irish Derbies, and Henbit, who won the 1980 Epsom Derby despite running the last furlong with a broken cannon bone. You might also stop for a drink in Enable, named after the 2017 Cheshire Oaks winner whose brilliant CV was to include the Epsom, Irish and Yorkshire Oaks, the King George VI and Queen Elizabeth Stakes, and the Prix de l'Arc de Triomphe (that year and next).

A board on the paddock railings commemorates the most famous Chester winner of all. Shergar arrived here after a ten-length victory in the 1981 classic trial at Sandown, a performance that inspired the *Observer* racing correspondent Richard Baerlein to write, 'At 8/1 Shergar for the Derby, now is the time to bet like men' – not a choice of wording that you'd find in the *Observer*, or in many other places for that matter, these days. Shergar won the Chester Vase by twelve lengths and went on to win the Derby by ten lengths – 'You need a telescope to see the rest!' shouted BBC Radio commentator Peter Bromley. Baerlein's winnings from his manly bets went towards the purchase of a house, which he named after the great horse.

The sad coda is well known. After one season as a stallion at Ballymany stud in Ireland, Shergar was kidnapped by masked gunmen, probably in a misguided attempt to raise funds for the IRA. When it became clear that no ransom would be forthcoming, the gang murdered him. The body has not been found.

The present-day Chester is immaculate. Trim lawns, neatly pruned trees, lovingly tended beds of bushes and flowers. Even the cheap Dee enclosure has loos with stalls and panelling in dark wood. (The gents' does, I mean; I assume the ladies' does too.) The bars and restaurants are modern, while the older facilities, such as the Tattersalls stand with its half-timbered gables, are in fine condition. My lunch is a 'handmade, all-butter pie', featuring '14-hour braised Swaledale grass fed beef'. Fourteen hours may have been more than enough, I conclude; but the flavour is splendid, and the pie crust is both crisp and melting.

Why then does Chester get a slightly lower mark than York? An obvious, though not by itself decisive, criterion is the quality of racing: York's is higher. At York's May meeting, the Derby and Oaks trials (Dante and Musidora Stakes respectively) slightly outrank Chester's Chester Vase and Cheshire Oaks – though the examples of Shergar and Enable among others show that the Chester winners may prove themselves superior to their York counterparts. Chester has no Group 1 races; York has the Juddmonte International and the Nunthorpe. The Chester Cup handicap is valuable, and venerable; but the Ebor handicap at York is the richest flat handicap in Europe.

Of course, if quality of racing were the only criterion, Ascot and Cheltenham would be joint number one in perpetuity.

Perhaps it's unfair to downgrade Chester for operating the most officious entry system I've come across since racing returned. I arrive at the course through the Watergate in the Roman wall, after a walk down Eastgate Street with its shops in half-timbered houses (Victorian restorations rather than Tudor originals), and regretting that I didn't have time to take the short detour to see the largest Roman amphitheatre in Britain. There are lot of people milling about, many of them stewards; the racegoers ask the stewards where to go, and the stewards direct them to other stewards. Eventually, I'm pointed to a corridor of barriers. I walk down it, turn, and come back up the adjacent corridor: it's a dead end. I push aside the barrier, and gain access to the entrance proper.

The paddock with its surroundings of horticultural displays, bars, food outlets and corporate entertainment marquees is in the centre of the course. The Roodee is the shortest flat racing circuit in Britain, at only a mile round; but the constructions in the paddock area block most positions in the stands from a view of the back straight. The best vantage points, I discovered, are the two galleries accessible from the Dee enclosure – and, as I've mentioned, there's a well-appointed loo there, so it's win-win. The locals who watch the racing from over the Roman walls enjoy a good view for free.

You get to the paddock through a tunnel, accessible from the County stand and Tattersalls. If you're in Tattersalls you'll find that the stewards won't let you into the paddock bars, and if you have a County badge only you'll be denied entry to the Winning Post and Champagne Bar areas. The Winning Post pumps out loud music, but not as relentlessly as the disco on the Earl's Lawn at Goodwood.

Everywhere there are windows and mobile pitches advertising Chester Bet, with which the Chester Race Company replaced the Tote some ten years ago. The service is unpopular in some quarters. It is not a pool betting operation, in which the total bet is shared among holders of winning tickets – the Tote has a monopoly on pool horseracing bets; and the Chester Bet odds are often less generous than those you'd find in the betting ring. Then again, the prices may be more generous than the Tote would have returned (except at courses where the Tote matches starting prices); and you may find the betting ring somewhat scary. It's complicated. Chester now offers accumulator bets with the Tote, which is the sponsor of the Chester Cup, and you can place any kind of bet with the Tote at sister course Bangor-on-Dee.

It's a young crowd, with a shortage of racing nerds. The pre-parade ring, well frequented at every other course I've visited and always favoured by the sorts of spectators who make notes on their racecards, is almost deserted – I spot only one note-taker all afternoon. The young men have tight suits; the circles in which they congregate are arenas for body language competitions. The women are dressed in styles that will prove to be impractical when, in mid-afternoon, there is a tremendous, forty-minute downpour. One of the young men on the Crewe–Chester train has a theory about women's attire. 'Women are weird,' he avers. 'They don't feel the cold. I've seen women wearing short skirts and no tights in winter, and not shivering at all. And,' he adds, 'they don't feel pain.'

I wonder whether Hayley Turner, who during her riding career has suffered a serious head injury as well as breakages of ankle and collarbone and vertebrae, would agree. Today, she's riding the favourite, Bookmark, in the 2.50. The horse leaves the stalls slowly, and Turner allows her to settle before making a move. Then she gets blocked.

Again, Turner stays cool, switches to the outside, applies the burners, and wins, as commentator Stuart Machin puts it, 'cosily'. It seems that the trainer and owners, Middleham Park Racing, think that Bookmark may be talented. 'There's quite a bit of class in her pedigree and you would probably want to side with her next time,' the Middleham boss tells reporters.

Bookmark was bred by the Queen. So will the Queen be kicking herself for selling the filly? Probably not: if you're a breeder, you accept that you may sell horses who will be successful for others.

To get an insight into the world of the owner/breeder, I pay a visit to the grand Chelsea mansion of Sir Anthony Oppenheimer, proprietor of Hascombe & Valiant stud.* Sir Anthony, a former president of diamond firm De Beers, is said by one source to be the seventh richest owner of racehorses in the world, but he, like the Queen, does not believe that his racing operation should be a route to becoming poorer, as it would be if he kept all the offspring of his mares for the track. (The Queen was Champion Owner twice in the 1950s. Such an achievement by the monarch would be frowned upon nowadays – 'Why should the taxpayer fund her hobby?', etc.)

Sir Anthony's father, Philip, became involved in racing through a friend, and barely knew what he was doing. Sir Anthony, who was to join him after starting out in the army, was similarly ignorant: 'The last time I'd ridden I was sixteen and hated it, because I had to do dressage all the time.' Nevertheless, the Oppenheimers found themselves owners of a stud farm that was home to a collection of broodmares and foals. Fortunately, there were people around to advise, and Anthony's then wife Penny had 'a tremendous talent for horses and riding – I mean, she was absolutely brilliant'. The Oppenheimers travelled round France, Ireland and the US, eyeing up potential impregnators of their charges. In 1981, they bought a share in Shergar, giving them the right to send a mare to the great horse each year. Their first nomination, as the sending of a mare to a stallion is called, did not result in a foal – it happens occasionally. Then Shergar was kidnapped. The Oppenheimers were insured against the loss, as was Shergar's owner, the Aga Khan. It's not a happy ending, of course, but it shows why the kidnappers' plot was so misguided.

---

* See also the Doncaster chapter.

Sir Anthony, divorced from Penny in 1983 and married since 1989 to Antoinette, is the proprietor of about 300 acres at Hascombe and Valiant, home to about twenty-eight mares and, for a period of each year, their foals. Why no stallions? (Actually, he has half shares in two stallions, Golden Horn and Cracksman.) The answer is that to stand stallions he'd need a lot more acres. As I've mentioned, top stallions 'cover' more than a hundred mares, and sometimes more than two hundred, in a season lasting from mid-February to June; you need a big farm to accommodate the waves of mares as they arrive. A few operations, such as Coolmore in Ireland and Darley (Sheikh Mohammed) in Newmarket, are dominant players in this market.

Each spring, the mares leave for their meetings with the stallions that Sir Anthony reckons to be suitable. There is no artificial insemination in horseracing: physical coverings, the industry believes, guarantee the integrity of the system. One can imagine dodgy tradespeople selling sperm that they claim to have been produced by Frankel or some other champion; and the potential to milk stallions for even more sperm than they produce now would cause a collapse in prices.

How does Sir Anthony choose? Expense is one consideration. A covering by a top stallion may cost £75,000 to £100,000, and in the superstar league, headed for a long time by Coolmore's record-breaking Galileo, breeders were reported to be charged up to €600,000 a pop. Will your mare and the stallion be suited? It's not a question of whether they'll fancy each other, but whether they possess genes that will combine in a way that will generate talent. The judgement is not very scientific, and Sir Anthony is uninterested in DNA analysis and other tests that purport to bring science to the breeder's art. Instead, he has a thorough knowledge of the stud and form books; now in his mid-eighties, he occasionally struggles for a name, but no more frequently than I do.

He mentions a Galileo mare who won a nine-furlong race in France. (When racing people use this formulation – a 'Galileo mare' or a 'Sea the Stars colt' – they mean that Galileo and Sea the Stars are the fathers.) 'But it looks to me as if she's a bit more of a stayer [preferring to race at longer distances] – a slowish Galileo. I suspect it wasn't a very good race in France.' He doesn't want to send her to a staying sire – he'd probably end up with a slow horse. Sea the Stars was 'by' a miler, Cape Cross (sire), and 'out of' a Prix de l'Arc de Triomphe (one mile four furlongs) winner, Urban Sea (dam). He won top-class races at a mile, one mile two furlongs, and one mile four furlongs. He had the dream combination, speed and stamina. Breeders tend to set store by – despite scepticism about the theory in some quarters – 'nicks': the magic alliance in pedigrees of certain sires and mares with particular forebears. The cross of Galileo with mares sired by Danehill was one such venerated nick, producing among others the great Frankel.

The question of nicks and of Sir Anthony's wariness of French form leads him to look with a good deal of interest at Coolmore's expensive purchase of the stallion Wootton Bassett, who had been standing in France and siring an extraordinary number of successful racers. Now that Galileo has died, Coolmore needs another superstar, and hopes rest on Wootton Bassett to fill the role. Fortunately, he's not feeling the pressure. During his first season at the stud, he made what the *Racing Post* described as a 'blistering' start, covering 244 mares. That's in roughly four and a half months.

On the day I went to York, the prestigious two-year-olds' race the Acombe Stakes went to a 25/1 outsider, Royal Patronage, owned by Highclere Thoroughbreds. His sire is Wootton Bassett. Two days later, Coolmore sponsored the Group 1 sprint the Nunthorpe Stakes, renamed for the occasion the Coolmore Wootton Bassett Nunthorpe Stakes. It's all good publicity. At the end of September, Royal Patronage wins the Royal Lodge Stakes at Newmarket, raising talk of the 2022 Derby. If he were to line up there, the reflected glory for Wootton Bassett would probably be more valuable to Coolmore than victory by one of its own, Ballydoyle-trained colts.*

'Wootton Bassett has a slightly plebeian breeding,' Sir Anthony observes. 'He has been successful in France, but the question on everyone's minds is, would he have been as successful here, where the competition is so much hotter?' The owners of 244 mares appear to have decided that it's worth finding out.

One attraction for them is that Wootton Bassett offers an 'outcross'. Sometimes, a certain amount of close inbreeding can work very well: Frankel, for example, has Northern Dancer as his paternal great-grandfather and as his maternal great-great-grandfather (the breeders'

---

* He does make the 2022 Derby line-up but finishes sixteenth of seventeen.

formula is that he's inbred to Northern Dancer 3 x 4). But such has been the influence of Coolmore's stallions, many of them Northern Dancer descendants, that the inbreeding may be overdone. Northern Dancer, from whose influence no modern thoroughbreds are free entirely, is in Wootton Bassett's family tree 4 x 5 x 5 (once in the fourth generation and twice in the fifth). These days, this counts as an outcross.

Coverings are usually successful. In the event that one doesn't take, the stallion's stud will throw in a second go. Of Sir Anthony's twenty-eight mares, twenty-six got in foal this year. When the mares were covered, the stud farm informed the racing administrator Weatherbys, and guaranteed that the coverings were natural. The mares will give birth next spring; the foals will be registered, a sample of their blood will be taken, they will be microchipped, and issued with passports.

It used to be Sir Anthony's unwavering practice to sell the colts at the yearling sales, retain one or two fillies whom he believed would enhance the stud, and sell or race the remainder of the fillies. More recently, he has raced a few of the colts, with, in the cases of Golden Horn and Cracksman, spectacular results.

After two straight victories, Bookmark faces the starter as favourite for her next race at Chester, but finishes only fourth of eight; a month later, she is fifth of thirteen on the all-weather track at Kempton. Impeccable breeding, and even a few racecourse performances, may flatter to deceive.

PERTH

Jumps

22 September 2021

Name that horse

Invited to summarise his ideal day at the races, the late author Simon Raven offered: 'A weekday afternoon at Perth, with not too many people about.' Raven was living at the time on charity in the London Charterhouse, bereft of savings thanks to a history of reckless betting, and with the income from his scabrous novels of misbehaviour among the upper classes and from TV scriptwriting (*The Pallisers, Edward and Mrs Simpson*) having slowed to a trickle. His memory was of mid-century jaunts. Perth may have livened up since then: it seems to me to be quite buzzy when I visit, for the first day of its two-day 'Glorious Finale' meeting. There aren't too many people, though: you can find a vantage point in the stands without having to jostle for position, and you can get up close to the winner's enclosure, to eavesdrop as the jockey debriefs the trainer and owner. Buzzy plus uncrowded: the ideal combination.

Where have these people come from, and how have they managed to create so much traffic that, at the end of the afternoon, booked taxis arrive at the course half an hour late? I ask because my first impression of Perth, on arriving shortly after 5 p.m. on the afternoon before race-day, brings to mind the old (pre-Covid lockdowns) joke about visiting New Zealand: 'It was closed.' Scarcely a pedestrian is visible on the main thoroughfares, and the traffic is about as light as you'd find during off-peak hours in a southern market town. Most of the shops are shut. Tesco Metro, Sainsbury's Local, and Marks & Spencer entertain a few late customers. At intervals, a bar door opens, and snatches of conversation and music erupt into the lonely streets.

I'm not complaining. It's pleasant to stroll through this compact city, admiring the sandstone buildings. My base is an impeccably maintained, friendly B&B, where the following morning I enjoy a fortifying breakfast – no rubbery eggs or flabby pink bacon here – before setting out on the hour-plus walk to the racecourse. (I prefer to walk to racecourses if the journey is feasible: it gets me in the mood, I find.) I pass detached houses with lush gardens – the climate here is damp and, for Scotland, mild – before entering open country. On my left is the entrance to Scone Palace, occupying the site where Scottish kings – Duncan, Macbeth, Robert the Bruce *et al* – were crowned. Further along is a left turn, and then I arrive at the racecourse sign, pointing to a path through rolling lawns and banks of trees. Perth racecourse is part of the Scone estate, home to successive Earls of Mansfield; the Countess is at the races today, to present a prize. Among the Mansfields' contributions to Perth races are two trophies, one of them a miniature replica of the Stone of Destiny, a sanctified slab of sandstone that was integral to the Scottish coronation ceremony until purloined by Edward I of England. This trophy goes each August to the winner of what was the Summer Champion Hurdle, now more romantically named the Stone of Destiny Handicap Hurdle. The original stone – though some say that it isn't, and that the original was hidden away before Edward could get his hands on it – is back in Scotland at Edinburgh Castle, and is due to move to Perth City Hall in 2024. The Mansfields' second donated trophy is a replica of a saddle quern, an implement for grounding grain discovered at a Roman fort nearby.

We move forward in time to the early seventeenth century for the first records of racing in Perth. They date from 1613, when a sporting fixture at South Inch offered a silver bell to the winner – this being a standard prize at the time, as we know from the history of Chester races. The city changed its racing venue to North Inch – an inch is an area of low-lying land near a river – in the late eighteenth century, holding a series of what seem, to judge by the anecdotes in James Gill's racecourses book, a series of ill-starred fixtures. In 1807, according to a *Sporting Magazine* report that Gill quotes: 'The scaffold erected on the racecourse for the accommodation of the stewards gave way soon after the horses had started and all the spectators upon it, among whom were His Grace the Duke of Athol and some other persons of distinction, were precipitated to the ground. There was a scene of great confusion for some minutes, but we are happy to state that only two persons were seriously hurt' – neither of them the duke, one infers, so that was fine.

The first meeting here at Scone Palace Park took place on 23 and 24 September 1908. This is the northernmost racecourse in Britain, and the only jumps course to confine its meetings to the summer months: the soil is too heavy to provide raceable conditions in the winter. Behind the stands are rows of poplars; as you look across the course, the view is dominated by oaks. Only from certain parts of the stands is there evidence of habitations at Old Scone, a twenty-minute walk away and not, to judge by this evidence, as entirely picturesque as it sounds. The circuit is about one mile two furlongs round, offering good visibility; if you rely on the big screen rather than binoculars, you're best off in the members' stand, which the screen faces.

The facilities appear to have been rudimentary here when James Gill was writing his racecourse profiles in the 1970s. Now, they are pretty smart. The Dewhurst Stand, beyond the winning post, houses private boxes and, on the ground floor, the One for Arthur bar, named after local trainer Lucinda Russell's Grand National winner. The members' stand is an attractive, largely wooden construction, with a clock on its front-facing gable. Next along is the Nelson Stand, with the Galileo restaurant, Perth's 'flagship eatery', on the first floor. I think you get the best all-round view from the steppings here, even though you're half a furlong from the winning post and don't have an ideal angle on the big screen.

I go for 'Paddock and Chips', an outlet near the racecourse entrance. My haddock, if that's what it is, looks somewhat drab on its perspex-covered counter, but turns out to be fresh and delicious, with light and crisp batter. Good chips, too. After this lunch on top of a B&B breakfast, I tell myself to stick to salad this evening.

Behind the paddock is a row of low wooden buildings: the owners' and trainers' bar and restaurant, the racecourse offices, the weighing room, and a dinky press room ('max capacity: two') next door to the loos. The loos – a significant barometer of racecourse management, I'm coming to find – are smart.

The principal sponsor today is Weatherbys, a firm that has long been at the heart of racing. James Weatherby set up the business, of which his seventh-generation descendants Sir Johnny Weatherby and Roger Weatherby are now chairman and non-executive director respectively, in 1770. That was the year James was appointed secretary of the Jockey Club, and when he set about outmanoeuvring a few rivals to become the sole publisher of the *Racing Calendar* – like 'racecard', an initially confusing term. The *Calendar* is not a chart of dates that you hang above your desk, but a record of racing results and fixtures. Weatherbys' publication also included bits and pieces of information about pedigrees; but he soon realised that a far more thorough repository of such information was required if a market in racehorses were to flourish. In 1791, Weatherbys published *An Introduction to a General Stud Book*, following it with the *General Stud Book* (*GSB*) in 1808: as later research has confirmed, these books were, with a few exceptions, remarkably accurate – though in places incomplete – accounts of the pedigrees of racehorses dating back to the somewhat misty origins of the thoroughbred in the late seventeenth and early eighteenth centuries. If someone is trying to sell you a horse, or if you're wondering whether to send your mare to breed to a stallion, or if you're a punter trying to determine whether your fancy will have enough staying power for the mile and a half of the Derby, the *GSB* record will be a key factor in your decision. Today, Weatherbys is the administrator as well as the record keeper of British horseracing, conferring official thoroughbred status on horses it deems qualified for *GSB* entry. It also offers banking, insurance and equine research services, and publishes racecards.

The racecard is the programme of the day's events. Weatherbys is responsible for the racecards at most British courses, and is the administrator of the information it contains except the form comments and summaries, which at most courses come from the Timeform ratings organisation.

The first details you'll take in from the listings for each race are the horses' names. The owners will have registered them with Weatherbys, adhering to certain rules: eighteen characters (spaces included) maximum; no living or recently deceased (past fifty years) person may be referred to without permission; no name associated with a racing great – you cannot call your horse 'Arkle' or 'Nijinsky'; no names that are 'vulgar, obscene or insulting' – a rule that did not exist in the early days of the sport, when King William I – not a monarch usually associated with frivolity – raced a horse named Stiff Dick. Mike Butts of Weatherbys told the *Racing Post* that the firm had set up a rigorous screening system against such undesirable nomenclature: for example, he said that the team's antennae would immediately be alerted by 'anything . . . that starts with the name Norfolk'. But even Weatherbys' most suspicious minds, the *Post* reported, let through Wear the Fox Hat.

The names on the card today seem innocent enough. A number of them refer to pedigrees: Silver Star Mix by Fair Mix; Placedela Concorde by Champs Elysees; Dalileo by Galileo; Jaunty Soria, who wins the seventh (it's a packed, eight-race fixture), is out of the mare Jaunty Spirit; Fernhill Lad is by Dylan Thomas. Teescomponents Lad is the latest in a line of horses owned by and advertising the North East-based manufacturer. Clondaw Caitlin is in a line of Irish-born – the 'IRE' after his name tells you this – Clondaws. Drumlee Watar, who wins the third, was also foaled in Ireland; the second part of his name, that of his sire, is obscure, with the commentator pronouncing it to rhyme with 'cat' and 'far', while the racecourse announcer goes with 'water'. There's a place in India called Watar, Google tells me.

Next to each listing on the card is an illustration of the colours – 'silks' – registered to the horse's owner through the British Horseracing Authority. You design your own, with a tool on the BHA website.

Most of the racecard data administered by Weatherbys is the BHA's property. It is known as 'pre-race data', and licensed to organisations such as broadcasters, newspapers, and bookmakers. As I've noted elsewhere, racecourses get income from these licensing deals, from media rights sales (rights to broadcast from courses), and from the Levy, a fund drawing on bookmakers' profits.

Not many people read the small print on the racecard's inside back cover. It outlines the conditions of each race: owners' stakes (entry fees); horses' eligibility; weights to be carried; and prize money.

Trainers usually make entries, but the owners pay – whether the horse eventually runs or not, although unforeseen factors such as abandonments will enable waivers. You must have an account with Weatherbys, which, on the day following the race and in the absence of unforeseen factors, subtracts your money and, if you're lucky, pays your winnings. Sometimes, Mike Butt of Weatherbys tells me, an owner will phone to ask why the firm has charged the stakes for several races. It's because the trainer has made several entries. 'Some trainers take a scattergun approach,' he says, while pointing out in mitigation that if you have a horse of moderate ability, you may want to maximise your chances of getting a run – if there are too many runners entered in a race, or more runners entered for a meeting than the racecourse can accommodate, Weatherbys and the BHA will 'ballot out' the surplus. It's usually the less talented horses that get the chop.

Within an hour of the entries deadline, Weatherbys sends the lists of runners to the press. The team's next job is to check whether each entered horse really is eligible for that race. Then they assign the weights. In race two today, Not the Chablis has the highest BHA handicap mark or rating (102), and therefore gets the top weight, which for this race is 12st. The forlorn hope Instingtive is rated 66, and so in theory should carry 9st 6lb (the 36lb difference between 102 and 66). But the lowest weight allowed in this race is 10st. So as well as being right out of form, with a string of noughts next to his name, Instingtive must carry more than half a stone on top of the weight that should give him a fair chance. He is 'out of the handicap', or as the racecard puts it, 'eight pounds wrong at the weights'. He starts at 66/1, and finishes last.

For the top races, the entry stages begin early. Entering the Derby is a bit like putting down your child for a top public school: you must be quick off the mark – in this case, making a provisional commitment in the December of a horse's yearling year. Powerful stables such as Ballydoyle and Godolphin may make dozens of entries, costing more than £500 each, before their charges have started training, let alone raced. There are further entry stages, all requiring further stakes; and after entries have closed there is a supplementary stage. Sir Anthony Oppenheimer (Chester and Doncaster chapters) entered Golden Horn for the 2015 Derby at this point, gambling a fee of £75,000; the horse more than repaid him by winning.

Further prestigious races are 'early closing'. But for most, including every race on the Perth card today, entries take place six days ahead.

Declarations – final confirmations that horses will run – come in by 10 a.m., forty-eight hours before the relevant race meetings. Confirmations of the jockeys booked to ride arrive by 1 p.m. Now Weatherbys starts work on the racecards, or sends the relevant information to the few other racecard publishers.

The Perth racecard includes a preview of the meeting by Weatherbys' Paul Ferguson, who is here today accompanying copies of his colourful and information-packed *Jumpers to Follow*, on sale for a very reasonable £10. He gets off to a flyer, albeit with some caution: 'Of [the] three Scottish-trained runners [in the Weatherbys'-sponsored first race], arguably the most interesting is . . . Clearly Crazy,' he writes. 'It could be significant that [Lucinda] Russell relies on Clearly Crazy, who could keep the prize close to home.' Clearly Crazy looks like a horse about whom to be cautious for most of the race, being pushed along urgently and making little progress while most of her rivals are galloping within themselves, but she keeps going as the others get tired, hits the front before the final hurdle, and extends her lead to win by seven lengths. Interviewed in the winners' enclosure, Russell reveals that she was in a Sainsbury's car park when she bought the mare, adding, in a line that may not have been spontaneous: 'I didn't even get any Nectar points!'

Weatherbys may be disappointed that only four horses face the starter in what is supposed to be the feature race on the card, the Weatherbys nhstallions.co.uk David Whitaker Handicap Steeplechase; but the runners put on a good show anyway, arriving at the final fence in a line, and justifying Ferguson's unwillingness to commit to a firm prediction in print. Go Another One, ridden by Sean Bowen, prevails, reminding me that earlier I had heard a cameraman advise a racegoer: 'I don't bet – but the Bowen family only come up here [from Haverfordwest in Pembrokeshire] if they think they've got a chance.' Brother James Bowen rides Island Mahee, placed second in race one; their trainer father, Peter, saddles two runners on the card, without reward. That racegoer should instead have followed another southern family, the Twiston-Davies. Nigel Twiston-Davies, who has travelled up from Gloucestershire, trains Goa Lil, ridden by his son Sam and winner of race five. Sam also rides Jaunty Soria to an all-the-way victory in the seventh.

The atmosphere resembles that at Fakenham, with the county set well represented; as at Fakenham, you're allowed to bring your dog. It is a knowledgeable crowd. But one racegoer gets it wrong. 'How's The New One, Nigel?' he shouts across the parade ring, in reference to a favourite horse at the yard. Several people wince. Nigel Twiston-Davies looks up, startled. 'He's dead,' is all he says. Having retired from racing, The New One contracted colic, often a cause of equine fatalities. Even I knew that. But I feel sorry for the questioner: Twiston-Davies, who for a period during his career declined all media appearances, is not the kind of person to ease your social embarrassment. Perhaps he enjoys it: when Sam is interviewed following Jaunty Soria's victory, Nigel stands behind the interviewer, making faces.

Punters refer to the last race of the day as 'The getting-out stakes': you're in debt following previous results, and here's your last chance to get out of it. The name is ironic – certainly so in the case of race eight today at Perth, The Scottish Game Fair in Scone Parklands Handicap Hurdle Race. Scots Sonnet has a career record of twenty-four races, twenty-four defeats. The racecard gives his recent form figures as 04406F (the 'F' indicates a fall), and comments: 'Modest on the flat and over hurdles. Beaten a long way all three completed starts in handicap hurdles this summer.' He wins. Perhaps his starting price, at 17/2 much less generous than his form would seem to have warranted, was a clue.

If we were sensible, we'd use the racecard to tell us the names of the horse, jockey and trainer, and for identifying the horse's colours, and leave it at that.

DONCASTER

Flat (also stages jumps racing)

23 October 2021

The Derby dream

The roar begins while the runners are still a quarter of a mile from home, as the favourite Luxembourg makes progress on the outside, travelling easily. Can all these fevered people have backed him, to win only £4 for every £6 wagered? I like to think that the excitement is more disinterested: it comes from seeing a splendid horse justify the claim that he's one of the best of his generation – one who, as soon as he passes the post with more than a length to spare over his nearest rival, causes bookmakers to halve his price at the top of the betting for next year's Derby. Luxembourg sparks something fundamental in our love of sport: our longing to dream.

The race is the Vertem Futurity Trophy Stakes, which has also been known as the Timeform Gold Cup, the Observer Gold Cup, the William Hill Futurity, and the Racing Post Trophy. It is for two-year-olds and is run over Doncaster's straight mile. Among two-year-old races in Britain, it ranks in prize money behind only the Dewhurst Stakes, run earlier in the month over seven furlongs at Newmarket. The extra furlong of the Vertem implies that it attracts horses who will, as more robust three-year-olds, race over longer distances next season; but this does not stop them from going on to win the mile classic, the 2000 Guineas, as Saxon Warrior and Magna Grecia demonstrated in 2018 and 2019, and as Luxembourg's sire Camelot demonstrated in 2012. These horses were trained, as is Luxembourg, by Aidan O'Brien, today scoring his tenth victory in the race.

Camelot's involvement is poignant. In 2012, he won the first two legs – the 2000 Guineas and the Derby – of the Triple Crown. Would he go on to race in the St Leger at Doncaster, bidding to become the first Triple Crown winner since Nijinsky in 1970? There were strong reasons to avoid the challenge. Even in Nijinsky's day the St Leger was going out of fashion, as breeders, keen to get speedy horses, increasingly avoided the kind of stallion whose racing career had included victory over the St Leger distance of a mile and three-quarters. Why speedy? In part because speedy horses are more likely to be precocious, giving you a chance of earning your money back faster. And in part there has been a feedback loop: as breeders have gone for speed, race programmes have reflected the bias, which has reinforced the trend, and so it has gone on.

However, fair play to Coolmore – the 'Coolmore Mafia' as some call them, or 'The Lads' to O'Brien, who trains for them at Ballydoyle. Their championing of middle-distance stallions such as Sadler's Wells, his son Galileo and grandson Camelot has made a significant contribution to the promotion of traits that might otherwise have become devalued. Not usually known for placing romantic above commercial considerations, they sent Camelot to Doncaster.

He lost. Held up at the back of the field by jockey Joseph O'Brien (Aidan's son), he made steady progress in the home straight, had to check his stride when another horse got in his way, and couldn't engage top gear in time to catch Encke, trained for Sheikh Mohammed's Godolphin operation by Mahmood al-Zarooni. In April the following year, twenty-two horses in al-Zarooni's care tested positive for banned steroids. Among them was Encke. (He had passed a drug test after his St Leger win.)

No St Leger winner has sired a Group 1 winner in Europe in the past twenty-five years. The owners of some of them have not even tried to establish them as flat racing sires, employing them instead to service stamina-laden mares to get National Hunt offspring who will race over two miles-plus. But of course Camelot, had it not been for Encke, would have broken this trend. Luxembourg is his ninth Group 1 winner, and he has a good many other talented horses on his record.

What makes a top stallion? It is not necessarily ability on the track. Sea Bird II, Secretariat and Brigadier Gerard – ranked 1, 2 and 4 in John Randall and Tony Morris' authoritative survey of the greatest flat racing horses of the twentieth century – did not go on to become superstars at stud. One who did was Sadler's Wells, the champion European stallion of the late twentieth and early twenty-first centuries: he was a very good racehorse but not a great one. Sadler's Wells' son Galileo (who died in July 2021) was an example of a great horse who became a great stallion; and Galileo's even greater son Frankel looks as though he will fulfil at stud all that was hoped of him. There are no rules.

All you can say is that some stallions are especially proficient at passing on their talents, and sometimes talents beyond those they themselves exhibited. The same is of course true of mares: the remarkable Urban Sea, for example, was the mother of Galileo, Sea the Stars, and several other top performers. Some sires also become influential as damsires, with their female offspring going on to be prominent in pedigrees: this has been Secretariat's principal contribution to the breed.

Just as there is no guarantee that an outstanding racehorse will be an outstanding sire, there is no guarantee that your talented mare, having been covered by Galileo or Frankel, will produce an outstanding racehorse. Only a few of the hundred-plus matings that a top stallion will enjoy each season will produce top-class offspring. Entered in the first race at Doncaster today is Frankelio, a son of Frankel with a British Horseracing Authority handicap rating of 66. Frankel's rating was 140. Frankelio finishes seventh of the twelve runners.

Such questions are never far from the mind of Sir Anthony Oppenheimer, whom we met in the Chester chapter. Coolmore's heavily hyped stallion Wootton Bassett, about whom Sir Anthony is reserving judgement, has a son running in the Vertem Futurity: Royal Patronage, whom we saw winning the Acomb Stakes at York and who went on to win the Royal Lodge Stakes at Newmarket, but who here finishes last – later, we learn that he was struck into by another horse and came home injured. A couple of weeks later, Coolmore announces that it is raising Wootton Bassett's covering fee from €100,000 to €150,000.

Of more immediate concern to Sir Anthony is the performances at stud of stallions Golden Horn and Cracksman, in whom, unusually for an operation centred on female horses, Sir Anthony has half shares. They both stand at Dalham Hall, part of Sheikh Mohammed's Darley bloodstock operation, which owns the other halves.

Sir Anthony bred Golden Horn, born in 2012. His sire was Cape Cross, who despite having sired the outstanding racehorse of 2009, Sea the Stars, was suffering a dip in popularity. 'I was probably looking for a stallion who wasn't too expensive,' Sir Anthony tells me. 'I had a mare, Fleche d'Or, who was useless – no, it's unfair to say useless: she had got injured. So we sold her, but only after we had got two foals by her: Golden Horn, and Eastern Belle [by Champs Elysees], who's in our stud now.' Some years later, Fleche d'Or's new owner sent her to Frankel, getting a colt who fetched £3.1 million at the yearling sales. 'I like buying mares from such successful breeders as Anthony Oppenheimer,' was the owner's unsurprising comment.

Following his usual policy with colts, Sir Anthony planned to sell Golden Horn. As a yearling, the horse came up for auction at Tattersalls' book two sale in autumn 2013, with a reserve price of £190,000. The highest bid was £160,000. So Sir Anthony kept him, and immediately felt justified in doing so when two leading trainers, John Gosden and William Haggas (of whom more later), told him that they would love to welcome the horse to their yards. They knew something. Gosden got the gig, and trained Golden Horn to win the Derby, Eclipse Stakes, Irish Champion Stakes and Prix de l'Arc de Triomphe – despite evidence in the horse's pedigree that he would be suited to races at shorter distances.

Understandably reluctant to part company with a champion, Sir Anthony struck his deal with Sheikh Mohammed and Darley. But so far, he and Darley are experiencing the rough side of the 'no guarantee' rule. 'Golden Horn is not doing as well as he should be,' he admits. He does not mean that Golden Horn's performances in the breeding shed are sub-par; he is referring to the disappointing results recorded by the stallion's offspring on the track. 'Even [Golden Horn's] staunchest supporters would have to admit that one Group 3 winner and four listed scorers are not really a good enough return from three sizeable crops of racing age bred off a fee of £60,000,' the *Racing Post* commented in 2021. By the following year, this fee has come down to £10,000, and in summer 2022 Sir Anthony and Darley sell Golden Horn to Overbury Stud, where he will mostly cover jumps mares.

On the track, Golden Horn was for an owner and breeder the horse of a lifetime. But two years after sending Fleche d'Or to Cape Cross, Sir Anthony had the extraordinary fortune of breeding a colt who was almost as good. Cracksman, a son of Frankel, was beaten as favourite in the 2017 Derby, but won the Champion Stakes twice as well as the

Coronation Cup. He too stands at Dalham Hall; at the time of writing it's too early to say whether he'll become a leading sire.

As in the football transfer market, there is not a great deal of scrutiny of how bloodstock transactions are conducted. A racing insider once said to me: 'In the breeding business, everyone is very charming, and everyone lies to you all the time.' Disguising a horse's true ability – high or low – is one ruse, and Sir Anthony mentions that an agent in the sale of one of his horses was accused of it – 'but I'm not sure that's what happened'. In 2019, a British Horseracing Authority report identified 'a culture of unethical, and in some cases unlawful, business practices by a small number of unscrupulous individuals': it mentioned conspiracies to inflate horses' prices during auctions, and – as has been known to happen in football – payments to agents from both vendors and buyers. Sir Anthony says: 'There are one or two people who never buy my horses – but I suspect they're slightly crooked and want some sort of a return. I'd never do that.'

His bigger worry is the state of British breeding following the recent deaths of three prominent figures: David Thompson, managing director of Cheveley Park; Khalid Abdullah (Juddmonte); and Sheikh Mohammed's brother Hamdan Al Makhtoum (Shadwell). Cheveley Park appears to be carrying on as normal, but Juddmonte has cut back, with the emphasis now on its leading sires Frankel and Kingman rather than on racers; and Shadwell has been selling. 'Hamdan used to spend £10 million at the Goffs sale, and £10 million at the Tattersalls book two sale,' Sir Anthony says. 'That £20 million has gone, and will never come back.'* But, in the weeks following our interview, and no doubt to his and many others' happy surprise, the market defies gloomy predictions, with buyers at the leading sales splashing their cash. At Tattersalls book two, for example, there were plenty of gung-ho bidders to step into Sheikh Hamdan's shoes, inflating revenues to a record-breaking 54 million guineas (a denomination still used in the bloodstock market).

This is good news for breeders, the only downside being that the cost of nominations – matings with stallions – will also reflect the going rates for the offspring that these matings produce. If you charge £10,000 for

---

* But, at the autumn 2022 sales, Shadwell starts buying again.

a nomination to a stallion whose offspring regularly fetch £50,000 at the sales, you're going to raise the fee.

What also influences covering fees is performances on the track. This is why Luxembourg's trainer Aidan O'Brien is at Doncaster today, for this single race. The Vertem Futurity is important for three reasons, of which Luxembourg's advertisement of his status as a potential future champion may be, financially, the least important. It advertises him as a future stallion – even if he were to retire now, he would, as a Group 1 winner, command a decent nomination fee, with potential earnings far in excess of what any horse could earn on the track; and it advertises Camelot, his sire. At the same time as raising Wootton Bassett's covering fee, Coolmore announced that Camelot's would also go up, from €60,000 to €75,000.

O'Brien was not here in September for the St Leger, staying in Ireland for the Irish Champion Stakes, held on the same day at Leopardstown. The St Leger was won by Ballydoyle's great rivals Godolphin, with Hurricane Lane, while the Champion Stakes went to the Ballydoyle-trained St Mark's Basilica. But missing a classic race he has won six times was not a choice influenced by prescience or patriotism; O'Brien knows that, sad as it may be for traditionalists to acknowledge, a Group 1 race over a mile and a quarter is of greater consequence than one – no matter how venerable – over a mile and three-quarters.

The St Leger is the world's oldest classic, first run in 1776, when the winner was a filly called Alabaculia. Two years later, the race took the name of one of its first subscribers, Lieutenant General Anthony St Leger, and moved from Cantley Common to the current racecourse site, Town Moor. Epsom first staged the Oaks in 1779, and the Derby in 1780; at Newmarket, the 2000 Guineas followed in 1809, and the 1000 Guineas in 1814. As these races acquired the status of classics, the notion of a special accolade for winning them in sequence took hold. For colts, the Triple Crown is the 2000 Guineas, Derby and St Leger; for fillies, the 1000 Guineas, Oaks and St Leger – though fillies are eligible to race in all five of them. In 1902, the filly Sceptre won four classics, and might have enjoyed a clean sweep had her jockey not given her an ill-judged ride in the Derby.

The St Leger meeting has never enjoyed greater popularity and status than when Edward, Prince of Wales ('Bertie'), later Edward VII, patronised it as the third essential racing festival, after Ascot and Good-wood, in his annual schedule. The wealthy and the socially ambitious competed to entertain the royal party, but sometimes regretted their hospitality. Bertie graced with his presence houses such as the Duke of Devonshire's Chatsworth and Lord Savile's Rufford Abbey, leaving behind bills totalling thousands of pounds, or hundreds of thousands in today's money. 'If a house was not grand enough [for Bertie],' writes George Plumptre in *The Fast Set*, 'a suite of rooms set aside for his use would . . . have to be redecorated and refurnished for each visit.'

There might be fifty guests at these parties, and therefore several times that number of servants, a good many of them required to accompany the guests, by carriage or motor car or private train, to the racecourse, bearing enormous hampers of food and drink as well as tables, chairs, linen, silver, china and glassware. Plumptre writes: 'Lord Dupplin and Lord Hardwicke both ruined themselves entertaining the prince, as did poor old Christopher Sykes.' Sykes, variously depicted as 'an incurable snob' and Bertie's 'court fool', lived beyond his means in the grand country house Brantingham Thorpe, and was saved from bankruptcy only after Bertie, berated by Jessica Sykes as the cause of her brother-in-law's misery, bailed him out.

With Sykes no longer in a position to entertain him, Bertie took his 1890 St Leger holiday at Tranby Croft, owned by a shipping magnate, Arthur Wilson. A scandal ensued. At Bertie's instigation, guests settled down each evening after dinner to games of baccarat, at which members of the Wilson family thought they saw Sir William Gordon Cumming, a lieutenant-colonel in the Scots Guards with a reputation for arrogance and womanising (some of his conquests, such as Lillie Langtry, overlapped with the prince's), cheating. The story got out, allegedly circulated by another of Bertie's mistresses, Lady Brooke, thereafter nicknamed 'Babblebrooke'. Sir William sued for slander, and lost. Bertie was a loser too: disreputable behaviour in his presence was held to be his responsibility. There were vicious cartoons, damning leader articles, outraged sermons. Having been compelled to give evidence when the case came to court, he grew tired of the proceedings, and chose to spend the last day of the trial at Ascot, where he was booed. Under pressure, he wrote an open letter to *The Times*, claiming to believe that gambling was 'one of the greatest curses that a country can be affected with'. But, strange to say, it was racing that a few years later was to confirm the prince's return to popularity, when to public jubilation his horse Persimmon won the 1896 Derby.

Doncaster racecourse, like the St Leger, is no longer so fashionable. York outshines it. If Bertie were alive today, he'd still be frequenting Ascot and Goodwood, but probably would have dropped Town Moor from his schedule, unless the local aristocracy were laying on some spectacular hospitality. What is there to say about it? It's a half-hour walk from the railway station. The track is just under two miles round, mostly flat, but with a slight incline known as Rose Hill near the far end of the back straight. If I were a trainer, I'd send my horses here knowing that they'd get a fair chance. The facilities are decent. The food in the grandstand is acceptable. A solid 7.5/10.

In the Doncaster parade ring, Aidan O'Brien submits to a series of media interviews. Eventually, the course announcer gets his turn; it's unfortunate that only one word in three of his words is audible over the muffled PA system, and none of the softly spoken O'Brien's. One would be even more keen to hear what O'Brien and Luxembourg's jockey Ryan Moore have to say to each other in their earnest, protracted private chat following the trophy presentation. Another race is run, another trophy is handed over, and O'Brien is still in the ring, talking on his mobile.

On my journey home, running fifty minutes late because of a signal failure outside York, I catch up with O'Brien's thoughts as quoted on the *Racing Post* app: Luxembourg has 'always been very exciting . . . Today he had to get down and stretch in the last furlong, which was good for him really.' Ryan Moore tells the *Post* reporter: 'He feels like he's going to be a better horse next year.' No great insights there. Exciting, nonetheless.*

---

* Luxembourg finishes third in the 2000 Guineas of 2022. He sustains an injury, and doesn't run in the Derby.

LINGFIELD

All-weather (also stages turf flat and jumps racing)

28 October 2021

She wanted to go

William Haggas is not at Lingfield to watch his filly Sea La Rosa win the feature race of the day, the Coral EBF River Eden Fillies' Stakes. Many of his fellow trainers are absent too. The heads of the bigger yards send horses to the races most days of the week, and usually have other priorities than to go with them, even if they wanted to – and Haggas does not.

'I don't go racing very often,' he tells me. 'I have a wife [Maureen] who likes going, but I don't really like it – it's too time-consuming.' Nevertheless, his previous experience at the races, two weeks ago, was a grand one: on Champions Day at Ascot, his colt Baaeed won the Queen Elizabeth II Stakes (£623,810 first prize), defeating the highly rated Palace Pier, trained by Newmarket rivals John and Thady Gosden; the Haggas stable's Dubai Honour claimed second prize of £270,900 in the Champion Stakes; and Aldaary won the concluding Balmoral Handicap, earning a less bounteous but still useful £103,080. But the day, though triumphant, was not a jaunt. You wouldn't have found Haggas enjoying a leisurely lunch while buttering up his owners. 'For me, lunch is not a culinary experience. I'll go to lunch if an owner wants lunch, but very few of our owners do. We aim to go to the course, get the job done, and come home.' If you want a trainer who'll give you a good time, he suggests, try George Baker. 'George sets out to entertain the owners and make it all great fun. That's what they get out of him – the craic.'

Haggas goes racing at Yarmouth from time to time, because he likes to send two-year-olds there for their first outings, and he finds it valuable to see how they take to the experience. Otherwise, an assistant trainer will be there, along with a groom for each runner. Grooms look after the horses in the racecourse stables, send the right horses to the right races, lead them round the paddock, and make sure they're refreshed afterwards. The trainers or assistants declare the runners, sort out as many complimentary badges for their owners as the racecourse is inclined to spare, chat to the owners, saddle up the horses, and give instructions to the jockeys. Talking to me the day before the Lingfield race, Haggas says that he is not sure that Sea La Rosa will 'get' (have the stamina for) the one-mile-five-furlong trip; but either his assistant Andy McIntyre tells jockey Tom Marquand something different or Marquand takes matters into his own hands, because he sends his mount charging up the outside of the field on the home turn as if stamina is not an issue, powers clear, and wins by four and a half lengths.

Ninety-eight miles away at Somerville Lodge stables in Newmarket, back to which McIntyre and colleagues will drive their horses once their last runner of the day, Alvediston, has run unplaced in the 3.58, William Haggas will have been woken by his alarm clock at 4.25 a.m. He and a select group of horses walk to the nearby Warren Hill gallops at 5.45 a.m. Newmarket is a town of some eighty training establishments and, during the flat racing season, some 3000 racehorses; the gallops are busy. The trainers learn to accommodate each other. Haggas is often there at the same time as Roger Varian. 'I rarely clash with John Gosden, but I do clash with Roger,' Haggas says, 'and we've learned to go five minutes earlier or five minutes later. We get used to it.' At the yard, other horses will exercise on the horse walker, or trot round the trotting ring for about three furlongs. The staff watch them closely, reporting if any horses seem below par or unsound. After the first lot of gallopers comes home, another lot goes out. There may be three lots in a morning.

In the early days of the sport, training regimes were brutal. The horses galloped hard every day, sometimes clothed in thick rugs to ensure maximum sweating, and were kept on tight water rations. Modern trainers are more sympathetic. They build fitness gradually. They may ask their charges to undertake a stiff uphill gallop only once, and not more than twice, a week, and for the rest of the time restrict outdoor exercise mostly to cantering. Haggas likes to get sprinters to run at three-quarters pace over longer distances: 'If we do constant speed work, they think they've got to get from A to B as fast as possible – which they do, but in a controlled manner, not in a frightened-rabbit manner.' Trainers recognise that understanding their horses, and preparing them for the mental challenge of competing on the track, is as important as getting them fit.

'I always liken my job to headmaster of a public school,' the Harrow-educated Haggas says. 'Every year we get rid of the sixth-formers and bring in the new boys. Horses are my pupils, and the owners are the parents. When the new pupils arrive we try to work out what makes them tick and how to get the best out of them. Some are idle, some are very talented but difficult, some are not very talented but try like hell, some are rude, some are polite. What we're trying to do is find the ones that are gifted to start with. They can't tell us, and we have to find out. Often it's nourishment not punishment that gets the best out of them.'

By about midday, the stables shut down. The stable staff, part of an eighty-strong employee roster at Somerville Lodge, return later in the afternoon to muck out and to give the horses their evening meals. At a yard such as this, grooms all have four or five horses in their care. The horses often have regular work riders too, though sometimes leading jockeys will step in to assess the well-being of the most talented racers.

The pay for stable staff is low. In April 2021, their rates ranged from £4.50 an hour to £9.50 an hour. Some of them get free accommodation and meals.

Trainers, meanwhile, charge hefty fees. When the *Racing Post* analysed trainers' income, the highest publicly quoted fee it found – not many trainers advertise such details – was Mark Johnston's, at £78 a day including vets' bills. Johnston has more than two hundred horses in his yard. He also gets roughly 10 per cent of the prize money the horses earn.

No doubt Johnston, Haggas and John Gosden (now listed as joint trainer with his son Thady) are comfortably off. But their expenses, itemised by the *Post*, are scary. There are staff wages – not extravagant as we have seen, but 40 per cent of the total; bedding (for the horses, I mean); hay; feed; regular removal of the muck heap; medications and supplements; vets' bills; transport costs; utilities; rent or mortgage payments; fees for access to the gallops; equipment; and equipment breakdowns. A jumps trainer with one hundred horses told the *Post* that monthly costs at his yard were £100,000. Gosden, in a season when he won the trainers' championship with more than £8.5m amassed, earned from his cut of the prize money only enough to cover his expenses for three or four months, the *Post* estimated; and most trainers are competing in races offering much lower rewards. For saddling the winner of race one on the Lingfield card today, Roger Teal took home about £250. Haggas says that the contribution of racecourses to prize money is inadequate. 'They seem more interested in building hotels,' he observes.

Racecourse hotels are indeed fashionable – there were hotels at the last three courses I visited, and there's another one here. The parkland walk from Lingfield station takes you not to Lingfield racecourse but to 'Lingfield Park Resort', housing in addition to the racecourse the Lingfield Park Marriott 'Hotel and Country Club' and a golf course. The Marriott is situated where you might expect to find the silver ring grandstand, and may be the only hotel in the country with a terrace for spectators outside its ground-floor rooms. At the far end there is a small, fenced area where guests sip drinks and watch the races on this mild autumn day.

The subject of racecourse developments has acquired an awful topicality following the suicide of Rose Paterson, chairman of Aintree racecourse and a Jockey Club steward. After Surrey councillors had turned down the Jockey Club-owned Sandown Park's application to build a hotel and more than three hundred houses, it was reported that housing minister Robert Jenrick had intervened in the appeal process – by implication, because of connections between Jockey Club members and the Conservative party. (Another Jockey Club steward, Dido Harding, was put in charge of the much-derided Test and Trace initiative against Covid-19.) A year later, Rose's widower Owen Paterson resigned as an MP when it became clear that the government would not back him in fighting claims that he had broken lobbying rules on behalf of two firms, one of which was Randox – sponsor of Aintree's Grand National. He alleged that the investigation of his affairs had contributed to his wife's depression and death. (There has never been any suggestion that there was impropriety in Aintree's Randox deal, but the connection may have heightened Rose's fears about being dragged into the controversy.) Sandown Park's appeal was eventually dismissed.

I couldn't say whether a company that runs resorts such as Lingfield's, as well as fifteen other racecourses, while also receiving Levy and media rights income, is offering fair prize money. Arena, Lingfield's owner, seems to come under fire over the issue more than most. But in racing there are so many interest groups, all with their own agendas, that it's hard to untangle these arguments. Ten days before the Lingfield meeting, Arena announced a £4 million increase in its contribution to prize money in 2022, but added that the racing industry would miss out on a further £5 million owing to trainers' and jockeys' opposition to the introduction of nine-race cards on all-weather courses during the winter months. Owners – who you might have thought would have been in agreement with the people they employed – reacted with dismay to the rejection of the nine-race proposal. 'It cannot be ignored that the inability to reach a progressive outcome that worked in the interests of racing and a majority of its participants derives from the sport's structure and governance,' the Racehorse Owners Association commented. 'We have to find a way forward for our sport that supports progress and professionalism.' Yes, people keep saying this.

Arena gets quite a bit of stick, too, from racegoers, or at least from those who post at the Racing Forum. A couple of days after this meeting a contributor starts a thread entitled 'Lingfield jumps. Do Arena know what they're doing?', complaining about being charged £23 plus a £2.50 'facility fee' for a low-grade, Sunday card, with half the facilities shut. I look back at the prices at the courses I've visited for this book, and I see that most of the independents are cheaper. I paid less than £20 at Plumpton, Fakenham, Chelmsford, Ripon, Bangor-on-Dee and Ayr.

Admission prices are too high, the forumites agree, 'and the food on offer is usually rubbish'. It's true that the canteen fare at the Lingfield brasserie, though half the seating area is a bright conservatory, is not tempting. I head for the burger van. The burger is so-so, and rivals Goodwood's overpricing at £12, but I like the skinny chips, and I am relieved to find a squeezable bottle of mayonnaise rather than those infuriating sachets. I eat my lunch at a table on what Lingfield describes as the 'Paddock Lawn' but that I'd call a field, and nonetheless attractive for it. At the top of this sloping green space, with its horse chestnut, lime and cypress trees, is the pre-parade ring, better patronised than at some other courses, perhaps because horses and grooms have to pass through it on the way from the stables to the paddock.

Lingfield – 'Leafy Lingfield' or 'Lovely Lingfield' to some – is the only British racecourse to stage jumps, turf flat and all-weather racing.

The turf course is vulnerable to waterlogging. A wet spring is a shame, because Lingfield stages trial races for the Derby and the Oaks, on a circuit that offers decent evidence about whether a horse will be suited to those races: like Epsom, it drops sharply from the far end of the back straight until the field comes round the corner for home. Classic dreams have been fuelled here, or have shattered as horses have hurtled down the incline and carried on hurtling when they should have been turning left.

Today, as on some eighty occasions during the year, the racing is on the all-weather track. All-weather racing is no longer the poor relation of the sport that it was for many years, and racing pundits are less inclined to label all-weather enthusiasts 'the bucket and spade brigade'. As we have seen, top trainers Haggas and the Gosdens are represented here, along with Godolphin's Charlie Appleby, whose Modern News wins the race following Sea La Rosa's. A November card includes two further listed races, and in the spring Lingfield stages what it bills as the all-weather championships vase fixture, with £395,000 in prize money.

This, my travels have taught me, is my kind of raceday. Midweek spectators, who tend largely to be racing followers; not too many of them, but enough to generate an atmosphere; a few decent horses on show. And – what's this? – more ethnic diversity than usual. The charity Racing to School – a very worthwhile initiative – is in action, giving educational days out to groups of young people.

Back at Somerville Lodge: to exhausting hours and scary expenses, add painstaking administration. With up to 170 horses in his care, William Haggas must spend many hours with the programme book identifying suitable races for them, as well as keep on top of the day-to-day paperwork and management tasks necessary in running a business involving dozens of employees, wealthy and demanding clients, and highly strung, expensive animals. 'I do most of the admin,' he says. 'I enjoy it.' The Queen is one of his owners. Does that bring extra pressure? 'No,' Haggas says, 'though of course we want her to have as much success as possible. It's fantastic for racing that she is so involved.' He's not a great one for holidays, though he takes a few days off at the end of the flat season and might get away for a bit in January. 'It's our choice to have this life,' he says.

He was not born to it. After leaving Harrow in the seventies, he joined his father's textile business, but soon gave it up to make his way to Newmarket. He has been training at Somerville Lodge since the mid-eighties and has on his CV victories in both the Derby (Shaamit, 1996) and Oaks (Dancing Rain, 2011). His filly Sea of Class – like Sea La Rosa, a daughter of Sea the Stars – won the Irish Oaks in 2018, and in the Prix de l'Arc de Triomphe that year was unlucky, accelerating from the back of the field but not in time to catch Enable. This season, Baaeed has been undefeated in six races, earning nearly £1 million in total. With these achievements and others, Haggas is certainly a racing insider now – a status enhanced by marriage to Maureen, daughter of the great jockey Lester Piggott. Running Somerville Lodge is a joint operation, Haggas's account makes clear.

Another aspect of the job is buying horses. Some trainers, such as Richard Hannon, are busier in the sales rings than others, ferrying dozens of purchases back to their yards, and selling them on to their regular owners, perhaps after a nice lunch. William and Maureen do less of this. 'Maureen and I like to buy horses that we want to look at. If I really like a yearling at a sale, I go and find him in his box. I walk in, look at him, and say to myself: "Do I want to look at you every day for two years?" If the answer is yes, I buy him.'

He adds: 'The bit that's most important when we're buying young horses is the bit we don't see: the heart, the way it beats, the strength of it.' He uses an expression I'm not familiar with, to point out a truth that owners, breeders, jockeys and punters as well as trainers know well: 'If they're duck-hearted, it doesn't matter how beautiful and well bred they are. If they don't wanna go, they won't go.'

AYR

Jumps (also stages flat racing)

16 November 2021

Winning is everything

I approach Ryan Mania for an interview at the right time. The Grand National-winning jockey is on a high after one of his biggest successes since his return to the saddle in 2019, having justified a twelve-hour round trip from his home near Kelso to steer Midnight Shadow to victory in the Paddy Power Gold Cup at Cheltenham. (The race used to be sponsored by Mackeson milk stout – 'By golly, it does you good', the TV ads assured us.) He spent the next day, Sunday, with his wife, daughter and son. He has since had to work to lose the weight he put on then: today's slimming exercise is a run over four circuits of Ayr's one-and-a-half-mile course. It works, and after he gets the leg-up on Well Planted, his mount in race one, he and his saddle weigh no more than the 10st 12lb that the horse has been allotted to carry. In a brief chat outside the weighing room, Mania – pronounced 'man-e-ah', with the stress on the first syllable – tells me he is a bit tired. Tiredness, with hunger and pain, are familiar accompaniments to jockeys' working lives; today, rain and a chill wind join the mix.

Unhindered, Mania rides Well Planted, priced at 22/1, into second place, which is certainly the best result he could have hoped for against the 1/2 winner. In the next race, he comes second again, this time on a 50/1 shot, and once more losing to a hot favourite. Then he does it again, on 12/1 shot Salvino, also beaten by a 1/2 favourite. Normally, you'd be exasperated to be runner-up three times in a row; but to do it when the market says you have outperformed the odds (the combined place return on these horses is 247/1), and against very well-fancied rivals, at least allows you to feel that you've ridden well. Later, as Mania has predicted to me, he finishes unplaced on his two further mounts; but, following him through my binoculars, I can see how sympathetically he handles the horses, giving them every chance. He is very good, as he shows again the following day at Hexham, where he has winners at 13/8 and 22/1 (a 59/1 double). One of the winning trainers says: 'Ryan is a huge talent and we're very lucky to have him.' Mania is friendly too: I think he would have given me his time even if he hadn't just ridden the winner of the Paddy Power, one of the showpiece handicaps of the season.

Today, it's back to low-key racing. Ayr may be the leading racecourse in Scotland, but on this grey, soggy Tuesday it lacks the vibe of a premier venue. The rain comes down all afternoon, in line with what the weather forecast – which may account for the low turnout of spectators – warned. Bookmakers seem to have predicted the weather too. There are only seven of them, and none in the betting ring: five are next to the paddock, and two have set up their boards in the grandstand bar, for punters who don't fancy moving from indoors. There are two bars, and an owners' and trainers' restaurant; no other facilities are open.

Ayr scores ten out of ten for its loos, with their cream tiles, sparkling porcelain, posh soaps, and wooden stalls. But I'm sorry to report that the food, on the same one to ten scale, gets a rating of minus one thousand.* There are no food vans or sandwich outlets; you have to make do with the grandstand bar canteen, with its beige curry, grey hamburger patties, off-white chicken pieces, and pale yellow macaroni cheese – all served with chips, unless you fancy a couple of limp pieces of lettuce and an under-ripe tomato claiming to be 'salad'. A woman behind the counter has an expression that says: 'This is what there is. It's nothing to do with me, and I don't give a stuff whether you like it or not.' Can the curry, I wonder, be as horrid as it looks? By golly, it's worse.

The dismal experience of trying to swallow and keep down a few mouthfuls of this meal seems to be a symptom of the more depressing aspects of Ayr. Parts of the town look left behind: there are empty and crumbling picture palaces, boarded-up shops, and vacant business premises; the town in November has the poignant atmosphere of all

---

* I have stolen this joke from the satirist Craig Brown.

out-of-season resorts. But my blue-fronted B&B is spotless, warm and comfortable; the nearby seafront has an impressive expanse of sandy beach, with a view of the Isle of Arran; Wellington Square, also nearby, features an imposing sandstone courthouse and a statue, also imposing, of Lord Eglinton, a key figure in Ayr racing history.

We know that there was racing at Ayr in the late sixteenth century, thanks to a report of a meeting in 1576, when a racecourse quarrel got out of control and two men were shot in the leg. But it wasn't until 1771 that the *Racing Calendar* first took notice of the town. The Royal Caledonian Hunt Club, of which Lord Eglinton was to become a key member, began to patronise Ayr races, as well as supporting local causes such as the publication of a volume of verse by local poet Robert Burns – a charitable act that prompted the course secretary to observe in retro-spect: 'While we are gratified by the spirit of the resolution, it is to be lamented that at that time the funds of the Hunt did not permit a larger premium to Burns, the Ayrshire poet, than was given in 1803 to Blaze, the black stallion from Biggar.'

The Western Meeting Club took control of the course in the 1820s. (Ayr is now in private ownership.) The Western Meeting, in September, tends now to be known by the name of its feature race, the Ayr Gold Cup, the richest sprint handicap in Europe. A paddock bar, closed today, bears in faded lettering the name Be Friendly, in honour of the 1967 winner, owned by the great racing commentator Peter O'Sullevan.

Racing in Ayr moved to the current site in 1907. The course first staged jumps racing in 1950, and in 1966 took over as the venue for the Scottish Grand National. Outside the adjacent Western House hotel there's a statue of Red Rum, who won the Scottish National in 1974, a few weeks after the second of his three Grand National victories; he's the only horse to have achieved the double in the same year. Two years later, Ayr was the venue for another singular achievement: 28-year-old mother-of-one Muriel Naughton drove her horse Ballycasey to the racecourse, saddled him, and rode him to finish sixth of eight – a plucky adventure, yes, but it made history too, because it was the first ride by a woman under National Hunt rules.

From the stands, you would look out over attractive Ayrshire coun-tryside were not the view over the back straight interrupted by a cluster of nondescript houses. I cannot blame Ayr's management for this, but I am a bit cross with them for not giving number bands to the stable staff accompanying the horses in the pre-parade and parade rings. Unsaddled horses in the pre-parade are therefore anonymous, and if in the main ring they wear blankets that cover their number cloths, only the sponsor's name on the blanket can give you a clue about their identities.

Let's not be unrelievedly downbeat. I cannot go along with James Gill, who in the 1970s wrote: 'By common consent pretty well the perfect racecourse, Ayr has a style and elegance to match the quality of the racing it stages'; but I must acknowledge that judging the course on a dreary Tuesday is not entirely fair. The grandstands are smart and their interiors well appointed; no doubt with the sun shining, a festival crowd, and all the restaurants and bars in operation, Ayr would present a more stylish and elegant face. And perhaps, were they open, the Eglinton Food Court or the food court on the Champagne Lawn would offer a cornucopia of gourmet treats.

Ryan Mania arrives at the course, after a two-hour drive from his home in the Borders, at about 10 a.m. One of the first things he must do is check his weight. Uh-oh: he needs to lose a few pounds. He sets off on his run. When he gets back, he has a shave ('We're all clean-shaven – you've got to look the part') and a shower. All being well, he has burned off enough energy to make room for a cup of coffee and, if his metabolism has been particularly kind, a light snack – though the food that racecourses provide for jockeys and stable staff is notoriously grim. 'Ayr is one of the better ones,' he tells me when we chat again, a couple of weeks later. 'The PJA [Professional Jockeys Association] has been working on upping the standard. We had a trial day at Doncaster a few weeks ago showing what could be done, and it was unbelievably good, so let's hope that catches on.'

Mania is 5' 11" tall. Maintaining his weight at about the 10st 7lb mark requires constant vigilance – a discipline that, in the first part of his career, became too much for him. He should have been on a high, having achieved at his first attempt every jump jockey's dream of riding a Grand National winner. But struggles with weight were making him miserable. In November 2014, just over eighteen months after victory at

186

Aintree on board 66/1 shot Aurora's Encore, he hit a crisis point when he got on the scales one night and found he needed to lose half a stone before the races the following afternoon. 'I went to bed and told myself that I'd be lighter when I woke up, but there was no change and that's when I snapped, it's when I realised I couldn't do it any more,' he told the BBC recently. 'All the love of racing had been drained out of me. I needed to stop.' He did.

Looking back, a more chilled Mania says: 'I don't think I really had a weight problem. My personal life wasn't great at the time, and I allowed everything to get on top of me. I was complaining about waking up in the morning eleven stone. Well, that can happen to me now, but I don't stress about it.' He got married, to Annie, stepdaughter of trainer Sandy Thomson; they have a daughter (called Aurora) and a son. A happy home life as well as progress in sports nutrition have made the difference. Now, he is confident that his weight is within his control. He made his comeback in October 2019. The Paddy Power and the Ultima Handicap Chase at the Cheltenham Festival in March 2021 have been his biggest victories since then.

At Ayr, a valet, who looks after Mania as well as several other jockeys, prepares his saddle and silks. Mania's next task is to weigh out: to get on the scales carrying the saddle. If the combined weight (with a 3lb allowance for the body protector he wears) is 10st 10lb: ideal. If it's 10st 9lb, no worry: the clerk of the scales will instruct him to use a weight cloth under the saddle bearing a 1lb lead weight. If it's 10st 11lb, Well Planted will have to carry one pound overweight; an announcement to that effect will be broadcast over the racecourse tannoys, and the trainer and owner(s) will not be pleased. Jockeys can lose work for such an offence.

The saddle passes to the horse's trainer or groom. Once saddled, the horse enters the parade ring, and trainers or assistants, with owners and sometimes friends and families, congregate in the centre. A bell rings, summoning the jockeys, whose task is to be charming to the owners and to listen to any instructions the trainer might have. Mania does not study the form as intensively as do some of his colleagues, but he will have done enough preparation to know what his tactics will be. If, however, he has planned to start the race quietly towards the rear of the field but the trainer wants him to take up a prominent position, he'll take up a prominent position. Otherwise, here is another way of losing work. 'The first rule is, if the trainer tells you to do something, you do it. Because if you don't do it and you get beaten, you're probably never going to get a ride from that trainer again. But if it all goes wrong and you've been following instructions, then it's not your fault.'

Mania rides mostly for Sue Smith (trainer of Aurora's Encore), Mike Smith, and for his father-in-law Sandy Thomson. These trainers trust him to make the right decisions during races. They also understand that in jumps racing, random things can happen that are no one's fault. Mania will debrief them afterwards: he may report, for example, that the horse needs to race over shorter or longer distances, or did not like the ground (too soft, too firm), or might benefit from wearing blinkers (which can encourage concentration in horses who tend to get distracted). The discussions are brief, because Mania must hurry to weigh in: get back on the scales, which should give the same reading as when he weighed out. 'Weighed in' comes the announcement over the tannoys once the clerk of the scales is satisfied that there are no discrepancies (in Ireland, the announcement is 'Winner all right'); in theory, this is the signal for bookmakers to settle bets, though if the provisional result appears un- likely to be altered, they'll have started paying out already.

The person most likely to be critical of his rides is Mania himself, reviewing the videos of every race when he gets home in the evenings: what did he do wrong, what could he have done better, and what dif- ference might he have made? 'To be honest, I could count on one hand the times where I thought that if I'd done something different, I would have won. And if you think, "If I'd done this, I'd have been second", it doesn't matter.' It's not that he is dissatisfied with his three seconds at Ayr; but Mania has the sportsperson's mentality, that winning is everything.

Every time he goes to work, he is at risk. Jumps jockeys fall or are un- seated in about 10 per cent of their races. Sometimes they escape injury when sent crashing to the turf; other times, they are not so lucky. Ruby Walsh, generally recognised as the most gifted jumps jockey of recent years, suffered breakages of a good dozen bones during his career, as well as concussion, crushed vertebrae and a ruptured spleen. Just a day after his Grand National victory, Mania was riding in a low-key race at Hexham when he fell, got kicked in the back by half a ton of racehorse, and had to be airlifted to hospital, fearing that he was paralysed. He turned out to have what a jockey would describe as minor injuries – a cracked vertebra, with some soft tissue and ligament damage. Since his comeback he has got off relatively lightly.

'There was a point last season when I did a count and realised that I hadn't had a fall in over two hundred rides,' he says. 'That made me think, "Shit, I'm definitely due one", and sure enough I did fall soon after, and it really hurt.' This season he has had a broken arm, and miraculously escaped without a fracture when a horse kicked him in the leg at Wetherby.

There are dark days. The worst are when a horse you ride dies on the course. 'It completely deflates you,' he says. 'But you're just the person riding the horse for the day. The people you feel for are the owners and the girl or the lad who looks after the horse at the yard. It leaves a big hole.' It's especially poignant, he says, because the horses who die are often the ones that enjoy racing the most, and who fall as a result of over-enthusiasm, or of pushing themselves to the limit. Later in the season, his Paddy Power Gold Cup-winning mount Midnight Shadow, with Mania on board again, has to be put down after crashing into a fence in a race at Doncaster.

For this gruelling and emotion-sapping job, the basic salary is not generous. Jumps jockeys get £194.63 for each ride. (This rate was set in April 2022; flat jockeys' rate was set at £142.90.) If they win, they get 9 per cent of the prize money; if they finish in one of the other places that carries prize money, they get lower percentages. A few jockeys may attract sponsorship – Mania carries on his breeches the name Envelicus, a company specialising in PPE. Some may get appointments as 'ambassadors' for gambling firms. Sam Twiston-Davies has a column in the *Racing Post*. Mania writes blog pieces for £150 each. When he and I talk for a second time, he is staying at Sue Smith's yard, where in the morning he will 'ride out' – ride the horses at exercise; but mostly he does this for no payment, as part of their long-standing association.

There are a good many expenses. Fuel is a big one, reckoned by the *Racing Post* in 2020 to cost a jockey more than £6000 a year. There are saddles and other equipment. You pay for the valet service, per ride. There are fees to Weatherbys for administering your payments, to your agent, to the Professional Jockeys Association (PJA), and to the Professional Riders Insurance Scheme, from which Mania drew this summer when sidelined with his broken arm. There is a fee to pay for on-course physiotherapists.

The *Racing Post*'s 2020 survey reckoned that some leading jockeys on the flat, where prize money is higher, were earning seven-figure sums each year, while the 'average' jockey was taking home about £30,000 after tax and expenses. This is while risking serious injury, and with uncertain career prospects once your sporting days are over.

Why would you do it? For what Mania and his colleagues describe as the 'unbelievable thrill' of riding winners, is one reason; and now, in this second stage of his career, he loves the day-to-day business of horseracing too. It's addictive. But, as we talk, an unflattering spotlight is illuminating the weighing room camaraderie he so enjoys. In London, a panel is considering accusations of bullying and harassment made by Briony Frost against fellow jockey Robbie Dunne, and a few days later finds Dunne guilty, banning him from the sport for eighteen months (later reduced to ten months on appeal). During her testimony, Frost says that she has been ostracised by other jockeys – male and female – after reporting her treatment. The PJA, which Frost says gave her no support, responds to the verdict with a statement acknowledging only that she had 'felt' bullied – a wording that causes outrage, and from which the association hastily backtracks.

The chair of the panel expresses 'real concern' about a 'deep-rooted, coercive' culture in the jockeys' weighing room. The PJA is particularly upset about these words, describing them as 'grossly inaccurate and wholly unfair'. It is a response with which Mania – who mostly rides in the north, while Frost mostly rides in the south – would agree. In his view, the weighing room is 'one big family – which is a strange thing because we are all competing against each other. I think we all respect each other, because we're going out there risking our lives, our bodies.'

He describes the weighing room atmosphere as safe and happy. 'We do have our fallouts – it's like any family. And some people are more aggressive than others. I try not to be. I'll just say my piece and hope that the person will learn from it.'

My guess is that the weighing room fits Mania's description most of the time. But enclosed, self-regulating worlds, as other exposés have revealed, can allow unacceptable behaviour to which insiders are either wilfully or unconsciously blind. The values and practices of horseracing have come under increasing scrutiny in recent years, not always to the credit of the sport.

NEWBURY

Jumps (also stages flat racing)

27 November 2021

Weighty matters

If you're wrapped up in a world, you may have lost your ability to tell whether your language and customs make sense to outsiders. Here, for example, is a form comment in today's Newbury racecard, which is supposed to be a helpful guide for all racegoers, whether they be racing fans or newcomers to the sport: 'Mark looked a stumbling block thereafter last term.'

What on earth does this mean? Is 'mark' a verb, in the vocative? No: 'mark looked' doesn't make sense. It's probably not a person called Mark. Is it a noun with a missing 'his' implied, meaning blemish? The horse in question is called Grand Sancy. What kind of blemish is Grand Sancy suffering from that could be a stumbling block? And when was last term?

The form expert is in fact referring to Grand Sancy's handicap mark, or rating, which the racecard tells us is 139 at present. ('Last term' was the last jumps season, ending in April.) But what does this mean? As today is one of the big jumps racing Saturdays of the year, with a handicap carrying a quarter of a million pounds in prize money as the centrepiece, now seems a good time to ask.

Newbury racecourse is worthy of the occasion. It's smart and well tended (in the club bar: wooden floors, dark pillars, cream and sand-coloured walls and ceiling, recessed lighting); the staff are good-humoured and friendly; it scores high on my loo-o-meter; the bars gleam – though whether you enjoy relaxing in the grandstand hall, which has the echoey atmosphere of a railway terminus, is a matter of taste. There are food and drink vans everywhere you look: pizza,

Loaded Fries and Dirty Dogs, Chinatown oriental noodle bar, Car-
bonis ('natural food – naturally cooked'), roast pork, fish and chips,
and of course burgers. I enjoy an excellent pork bap, with crackling that
really crackles. On the day that Storm Arwen hits the UK, the mulled
wine stall and the Winter Warmer bar are busier than the Pimm's and
Prosecco vans.

The weather forecast led me to fear that I'd arrive at the racecourse,
get cold and wet, learn at midday that racing had been called off ('We'll
be monitoring wind speeds closely,' the racecourse had advised on Twit-
ter), and cross the road back to the station to find that all services to
London had been cancelled. Yes, the wind is brutal, and I'm too cold
to hold steady my binoculars – the image judders like that on a mal-
functioning computer monitor; but I reflect, as I catch up with the big
races from Newcastle on the course TVs and see only dim shapes in a
blizzard, that people elsewhere have got it worse.

The other thing about today is that we have a new, possibly more
easily transmissible and vaccine-resistant Covid strain, Omicron, to
worry about – one that causes Prime Minister Boris Johnson, moving
with a decisiveness for which he has not always been noted, to announce
the return of travel restrictions and compulsory mask-wearing. But
you wouldn't guess that Omicron was a matter of concern from observing the thousands of racegoers at Newbury. In the packed bars and
marquees, there's hardly a mask to be seen. The pumped-up clientele
of the Crafty Filly bar, where there is musical entertainment, belts
out an accompaniment to the band's rendition of 'Sweet Caroline', in
superspreader style. The Carnival Marquee, with a disco as well as live
music, is also chock-a-block, but nevertheless attracts a long queue of
people eager to add to the crush at the racing after-party, due to run
from the end of race seven (3.35 p.m.) to 7 p.m. Young people having it
large are much in evidence. They pile into the loos *en masse*, whooping.
One of them enters a cubicle. 'Miller's having a shit!' his friends, rat-
tling the door behind which Miller had no doubt been hoping to enjoy
a few moments of privacy, chorus. Come 7 p.m., one fears, the racecard
plea for 'a special effort . . . to respect our neighbours with particular
regard to noise in the surrounding residential streets' will have been
in vain.

The occasion for these larks is, principally, the sixth race on the card, at 3 p.m.: The Ladbrokes Trophy Steeplechase (Handicap) (Class 1) (Grade 3), with a prize fund of £250,000. This is one of the great races of the jumps season, with a roll call of past winners including such legendary steeplechasers as Mandarin, Mill House, Arkle, Burrough Hill Lad and Denman. For many years, it was sponsored by Hennessy, a brand that became associated in racing fans' minds with the great achievements of these horses, and to which – oddly, given the commercial rather than sentimental reasons for the nomenclature – they became attached; the Ladbrokes Trophy, they feel, is somehow a diminished event, as is the Betfair Hurdle (previously the Schweppes Gold Trophy) and the Bet 365 Gold Cup (previously the Whitbread). There are a few top-class horses among winners of the big handicaps on the flat, but they all became stars later; eligibility for these races meant that at the time they were below top class by definition. Whereas you can't be too good to take part in the Ladbrokes Trophy, or in the Grand National, and you'll really set fans' pulses racing if you defy the handicapper's attempts to slow you down. Arkle won what was then the Hennessy twice, carrying 12st 7lb on each occasion. Burrough Hill Lad and Denman both won while also carrying top weight. I, along with many others who were at Newbury for the 2009 running, recall as one of the highlights of our racegoing experiences Denman's second victory, when supposedly past his best and with 11st 12lb on his back.

The racecard tells us that the top weight in the Ladbrokes Trophy today, Brahma Bull, is – as was Denman – assigned 11st 12lb. (Race conditions are more lenient than in Arkle's day.) Next to this information is a box bearing the legend 'BHA [British Horseracing Authority] 158'. This number, the racecard glossary advises, is Brahma Bull's rating. Next on the card is Eklat De Rire, carrying 11st 8lb and with a rating, or mark, of 154. Ah: Eklat De Rire is rated four points behind Brahma Bull; a point seems to equal a pound in weight; and the weight discrepancy must be designed to even up the horses' chances. The betting market feels that the concession is more than enough: Eklat De Rire is 3/1 favourite, while you can back Brahma Bull at 40/1. From this, we can infer that a rating is not necessarily a predictor of a horse's performance on any given day: it is based on past performances.

Further down the racecard is Kitty's Light, trained by Christian Williams and ridden by Jack Tudor – we saw this trainer/jockey pair enjoying success at Fakenham. Kitty's Light's assigned weight is 11st 3lb (rating: 149); but next to Tudor's name is a (3), indicating that he is a conditional jockey, one serving a kind of apprenticeship, and, owing to inexperience, entitled to ride the horse at 11st.

Racehorses usually qualify for BHA ratings after three racecourse runs. (The exceptions include flat racers whose first two runs are victorious.) A handicapper who suspects that a horse hasn't been trying, in order to earn a low mark, may decline to give a mark until the horse has run again – making an effort, this time.

There are various reasons for this system. The most obvious is that more than 60 per cent of races run in Britain are handicaps: owners, trainers, bookmakers and punters need to know that a scrupulously designed methodology lies behind the assigning of weights in these races. In non-handicaps, assessments of the horses' past performances are also valuable, giving owners and trainers guides to the classes of races they might enter, and adding to punters' information about horses' abilities. The marks are essential for the breeding industry too: breeders who send their mares to Frankel know that they are buying the sperm of a stratospherically rated animal.

The BHA employs eleven handicappers, all of whom have had to miss out on live racing for the past twenty-one months. Some BHA staff, such as stewards, have essential roles at the races; during the pandemic is not a good time for others to be seen to be enjoying their privileged status. Dominic Gardiner-Hill, head of handicapping, tells me that he misses the buzz of racecourses, but concedes that most of his team's essential work is done in front of TV screens. In the winter months, six specialise in jumps racing, while five follow the all-weather flat programme. In the summer, eight will handicap flat racers, while three will keep track of the low-key summer jumps fixtures.

A handicapper may have up to ten races a day to assess, with every runner to be given a performance rating. It means watching a race numerous times, because you cannot simply decide on the winner's mark and score all the rest on where they finished and the distances they were beaten. Or rather, such a method will reveal how the horse performed on the day, but may be a misleading guide to the horse's fair handicap mark. All sorts of factors in addition to raw ability may influence the result of a horse race: the pace of the race, the state of the ground, whether the race distance suits, the draw (if for example, you're drawn on the outside for a sprint race at Chester, you're at a serious disadvantage), bumping and barging, an error by the jockey, a burst blood vessel, lack of fitness, ill health, not trying; fillies and mares may run badly if in season. Gardiner-Hill and his colleagues must be alert to these considerations.

'We dig into the profile of every horse to find out why it may have run poorly or below its perceived best,' he says. 'Conversely, we're always looking to see why a horse may have run its best ever race. Is it because it's been stepped up in trip? Is it because they put blinkers on it? Is it because they've changed tactics? If anybody asks me why I've done what I've done with a horse – whether it be put it up [raise the horse's mark], drop it, or leave it where it is, I've got a number of reasons that I can give to explain and justify what I've done.' Justification is a necessary though no doubt tiresome aspect of the job. Certain trainers are on the phone regularly, complaining about high ratings for their horses, who therefore, the trainers complain, will have to carry too much weight in handicaps to be competitive.

The handicappers have various tools with which to determine performance figures. Particularly valuable when assessing inexperienced, unrated horses are comparisons with previous runnings of the same race; the stopwatch may be an indicator of ability too; even more valuable, though not available for every course, are sectional times, enabling you to assess how finishing positions were affected by the pace of a race – did the runners go off too fast or too slow, or was the pace steady?

If the form of the runners is well established, the handicappers aim to find those who have run as their ratings suggest they should have done, and build the ratings for the whole race around them. But a performance rating does not equal a handicap mark. Disappointing the many fans of jockey Rachael Blackmore, the Irish-trained Eklat De Rire has an off day in the Ladbrokes Trophy; she pulls him up on the second circuit. The handicapper cannot drop him a stone to 140 and see if he runs better off that mark. 'It's quite a difficult one, because clearly that wasn't his [Eklat De Rire's] running – whatever happened to him, it had nothing to do with his handicap mark,' Gardiner-Hill says. 'I thought the horse never looked comfortable. Right from the start, he seemed to be lugging left.' The BHA's Irish counterpart, Horse Racing Ireland, leaves Eklat De Rire on the 154 mark.

Trainers sometimes claim that the handicapper is quick to raise their horses' marks, and slow to lower them. Gardiner-Hill's response is: 'What we don't want to do is set a precedent where every time a horse gets beaten it gets dropped three pounds, because all that's going to do is create a cheat's charter.' Punters already suspect that the practice of disguising a horse's ability until it reaches a handicap mark that will almost guarantee a win, with the aim of landing a gamble, is rife. But such skulduggery is extraordinarily hard to prove, as cases that have come before courts or tribunals have demonstrated. When Top Cees, trained by Lynda Ramsden and ridden by Kieren Fallon, won the 1995 Chester Cup soon after getting beaten as favourite in a race at Newmarket, many eyebrows rose. Everyone knew that Ramsden's husband, Jack, liked a gamble. But the Ramsdens and Fallon sued the *Sporting Life* over a piece implying that they had cheated; they won the case, receiving £195,000 in damages. On the other hand, what does the trainer Mark Johnston mean to imply about his contemporaries by operating under the motto 'Always trying'?

There are grey areas. The week after the Ladbrokes Trophy, Briony Frost rides 12/1 shot Greaneteen to victory in the Tingle Creek Chase at Sandown, one of the big two-mile races of the season. When asked why Greaneteen could finish only fourth on his previous outing, his trainer Paul Nicholls says: 'He had his first run at Exeter to take the freshness off him and he was never going to win that day carrying top weight. That was a prep run and his improvement since then has been tremendous.' To be fair, Nicholls described the earlier race as a prep run at the time – though if you missed that detail and backed Greaneteen at Exeter, you would be a bit miffed on reading later that you never had much chance of a payout. But what's a trainer to do? Some horses need races to get fit. There may be a conflict between this demand and the one to be trying all the time.

The Ladbrokes Trophy winner, Cloudy Glen, gets a reward for his efforts of a rise in the weights of 10lb. It means that if he had competed in the race off his new mark of 150, he would have carried 11st 4lb rather than 10st 8lb. He beats by half a length the horse that does carry 11st 4lb, Fiddlerontheroof, whose mark as a result goes up to 159. If Cloudy

Glen and Fiddlerontheroof meet in a handicap again, off 150 and 159 respectively, the handicapper reckons that they should finish side by side.

Such a contest is unlikely in the near future. Cloudy Glen will remain a handicapper (a horse is a handicapper if he or she tends to compete in handicap races), while Fiddlerontheroof looks likely to compete in graded races, off level weights. (But he also takes part in the 2022 Grand National, finishing fifth.) Cloudy Glen's Ladbrokes Trophy victory is an unlikely one on recent form, and his odds are 33/1, although plenty of people around me at Newbury are yelling 'Come on, Charlie', as jockey Charlie Deutsch and his mount jump the final fence in the lead and gallop to the line. Perhaps sympathy rather than financial interest prompts their encouragement. A few years ago, Deutsch spent time in jail after being stopped when driving over the limit, panicking, accelerating away, and leading the police on a high-speed chase. One's sympathy is limited; but Deutsch's supporters, including Cloudy Glen's trainer Venetia Williams, felt that he was a fundamentally decent though troubled young man, and stood by him. This is his biggest victory since his return to race riding. It's an emotional outcome in other respects: Deutsch is wearing the colours of the late Trevor Hemmings, who had seen his horses win the race three times and who is remembered today in a double-page spread in the racecard. (Not the only fitting victory: the Sir Peter O'Sullevan Memorial Handicap Chase is won by Kapcorse, running in the great commentator's colours.)

Gardiner-Hill is delighted with the result too – and not because he backed the winner: handicappers and jockeys, the humans in the best positions to influence racing results, are barred from betting. 'It was a great result for us, because we'd achieved what we set out to do which was a nice, open handicap,' he says. 'We thought we were putting Cloudy Glen on a competitive mark of 140, and so it proved.' Gardiner-Hill once compiled ratings for the *Racing Post*, where his task was different: the *Post*'s ratings, or those of Timeform, are designed to help punters pick winners; the BHA's aim is to give every horse a theoretical chance. Cloudy Glen does not feature in any tipster's predictions for the race, even as an each way shot. 'Private handicappers would much rather have a 6/4 winner than a 33/1 second,' Gardiner-Hill says. (To be fair, Cloudy Glen's *Racing Post* rating for the Ladbrokes Trophy is only three pounds lower than the paper's top-rated runner, Cloth Cap, and is the same as that of Eklat De Rire.)

The handicapper's task has an extra layer of difficulty when some of the runners come from overseas. Irish dominance at the 2021 Cheltenham Festival, where the Ireland-Britain score was twenty-three to five, was a subject of much debate: higher prize money and more attractive taxation were two widely advanced reasons why the best horses were coming from Irish stables. But these factors should not affect handicaps, in which imbalances are ironed out by weight allocations. At the previous three festivals, the British and Irish scores in the handicaps were level, but in 2021, the victory tally was 7-2 in Ireland's favour, and in the Grand National a few weeks later, Irish-trained horses filled ten of the first eleven places. Dominic-Hill's team and their counterparts in Ireland have made changes to their systems that they believe will restore parity.

Other recent adjustments have addressed 'ratings creep', a phenomenon known in the education system as 'grade inflation': the tendency for overall ratings gradually to rise. What I find a little hard to grasp, but which Gardiner-Hill assures me is perfectly in keeping with the integrity of the system, is how some horses can break through ratings barriers. Over the jumps, the ratings scale is 0 to 175. But, to take two recent examples, Sprinter Sacre achieved a top rating of 188, and Kauto Star of 193. (Arkle raced before there was a centralised handicapping system, but Timeform put him at 212.) On the flat, Frankel achieved the notional maximum mark, 140.

Sprinter Sacre and Kauto Star did not compete in handicaps (though Arkle did). Nevertheless, their marks matter, and these days the marks at the higher end of the scale are determined by international agreement. On the day I speak to Gardiner-Hill, he was up at 4.30 a.m. for a conference call with counterparts in time zones ranging from the west coast of the US to the east coast of Australia, to determine the rankings that will be released at the end of the year.

I ask Gardiner-Hill if, were he a betting man, he would follow the BHA ratings or those of his former employer the *Racing Post*. 'I'd use my own ratings,' he replies, without hesitation. 'I know why I've done what I've done; I don't want to be trusting anyone else's judgement.'

As he and his colleagues illustrate, and as James Millman told me at

Salisbury, form study is a full-time job. Since my brief training from Ken Pitterson (Sandown), however, I have taken a closer look at the horses in the paddock, and as Cloudy Glen walks past I utter an inward 'Wow!': his dark coat is trace clipped (hair removed from only part of his body). This is what punters contemptuously refer to as 'after-timing', or what anglers know as 'the one that got away'. Did I back Cloudy Glen? No.

AINTREE

Jumps

4 December 2021

Twenty-one started . . .

Storm Arwen was last week, and the wind and rain rampaging through Aintree today have not qualified for a name. I could call them a few things. At times, I barely make headway as I attempt to walk behind the stands, or through the passages in between. But on the racecourse side, the stands offer protection, and it's not as cold as it was seven days ago at Newbury; some relief for the spectators, but not for horses and jockeys on the track, where the wind-breakers are too far away to be effective, and where even half-ton racehorses seem to be disconcerted by the force of the gusts. There are more fallers today than I've seen on any other day at the jumps courses I've visited – always an issue of concern at the home of the Grand National. There is also, I'm sorry to say, a fatality: Bombs Away, the favourite for race one, does not fall, but having come home second is later discovered to have suffered an irreparable injury.

I learn about Bombs Away's death from a website called Race Horse Race Death Watch, run by Animal Aid, an organisation that would like to see horseracing banned. I can find no mention of the fatality anywhere else – not in race reports or the results section of the *Racing Post*, nor in the weekly video blog of Olly Murphy, Bombs Away's trainer. Racing is leaving the dissemination of such news to the harshest critics of the sport, it seems.

The local train service to the Liverpool suburb of Aintree drops you next to the Ormskirk Road, a dual carriageway with the racecourse on the other side. You cross the road at the lights and walk down the Grand National Way. Inside the course on the right is the Red Rum Garden, at the centre of which is a statue of the great horse, winner of the Grand National in 1973, 1974 and 1977. Red Rum's grave is close to the Aintree winning post. A bust of his trainer, Ginger McCain, surveys the parade ring. Today, those passing by McCain's gaze include Rachael Blackmore, who earlier this year defied his prediction that a woman would never ride a Grand National winner.

To be more precise about Red Rum: he was a great Grand National horse, running in the race five times and finishing second on the two occasions when he didn't win; he won a Scottish Grand National too. Away from these races, he was merely good. At the start of his career, he looked as though he would achieve no level of distinction at all, competing in low-grade races on the flat, though twice having the honour of carrying on his back another racing great, Lester Piggott. Red Rum joined McCain after passing through various training yards, and took up residence in the stables behind McCain's used-car salesroom in Southport; he got fit for his races by galloping on Southport Sands.

'Rummy' was no national treasure in 1973, when he broke many spectators' hearts by pipping at the Aintree post an Australian-bred horse called Crisp. Carrying 12st to Red Rum's 10st 5lb, Crisp had put on an exhilarating display of front running, and was at one point thirty lengths clear of the field; he was still fifteen lengths ahead of Red Rum at the final fence, but slowed almost to a halt on the long run-in as his relentless pursuer chased him down. We all, apart no doubt from McCain, Red Rum's jockey Brian Fletcher and the horse's owner, and perhaps also from the punters who had backed him, felt that Crisp was the moral victor. But we had all forgiven Red Rum for being a spoilsport by 1977. 'They're willing him home!' Peter O'Sullevan yelled at BBC viewers as Rummy jumped the final fence, clearly having got the better of Churchtown Boy, who had seemed threatening a short while earlier. The twelve-year-old was as perky as a fresh horse as he galloped to the line, O'Sullevan reported. 'It's hats off and a tremendous reception – you've never heard one like it at Liverpool!' For racing fans of my generation, O'Sullevan's commentaries are as inextricably linked to great races as musical scores are to movies.

A hotelier called William Lynn set up the Grand Liverpool Steeplechase in 1836. It was won by The Duke, ridden by the most celebrated rider of the day, Captain Becher. Whether this race and the follow-ups in 1837 and 1838 took place at Aintree or at a nearby course is a subject of unresolved debate. In any case, most agree that these races were only precursors to the Grand National proper, which, though still called the Grand Liverpool, was first run in 1839. This time, Captain Becher had a less happy experience, falling when in the lead on Conrad and taking shelter in the brook at the fence as the other runners leapt over him, while reportedly observing to spectators, 'Water is no damned use without brandy!' ('whisky' in some accounts); he remounted, but another fall put him and Conrad out of the race for good. The winner, ridden by Jem Mason, was Lottery, soon to become so dominant in the sport that he hastened the development of handicap steeplechases. The Grand Liverpool became a handicap in 1843, and got the name Grand National in 1847.

Becher's Brook, as it came to be known, is not the largest of the sixteen fences on the course, but it is the scariest (the brick wall obstacle that was a feature of the early races must have been pretty alarming too, but was soon removed), because after you've cleared the four feet ten inches on the take-off side, you find yourself, like a ski jumper shooting off the ramp, with a terrifying drop to the landing side. 'Falling off the edge of the world,' is one jockey's description. But all the fences, uniquely covered in spruce, are challenging. There is Valentine's Brook, named after a horse who supposedly came down on the far side of it hind legs first. The turn at the Canal Turn is ninety degrees, and horses and jockeys must negotiate it immediately on landing. The Chair – so named because a judges' chair used to be sited alongside it – is the largest fence on the course at five feet, two inches, with a ditch in front; a pile-up here in 1979 resulted in the falls or refusals of nine runners. But the smallest Aintree fence has also been responsible for havoc. It is called Foinavon.

Many of the most memorable episodes in Grand National history involve calamities. The fences have not always been guilty of causing them. In 1956, the Queen Mother's Devon Loch, ridden by Dick Francis, was within yards of the winning post when he suddenly splayed his legs like a horse in an eighteenth-century painting and belly-flopped onto the turf, allowing ESB to snatch the prize. Francis, who was to go on to write bestselling racing thrillers, patiently answered questions about the bizarre collapse for the rest of his life: Devon Loch had suffered a sudden cramp, was his theory. The Queen Mother took the blow with a fine display of regal composure: 'That's racing,' was her reported summing-up.

The calamity of the 1993 Grand National took place before a fence had been jumped. First came an invasion of the course by animal rights protestors, and there was a nerve-wracking delay while officials rounded them up. When eventually the starter Keith Brown – officiating at his last Grand National before retirement – tried to send the overwrought runners on their way, several riders got tangled up in the tape, and Brown called a false start. At the second attempt, jockey Richard Dunwoody got entangled, and this time Brown's recall flag failed to unfurl. Only nine of the thirty-nine riders pulled up their mounts, while the rest charged off towards the first fence. Gradually, as they made their way round the circuit, a number of them realised that something was wrong, and left the race; but seven completed, led by 50/1 shot Esha Ness, ridden by John White and trained by Jenny Pitman. The jockey and horse's efforts, and Pitman's preparation, counted for nothing: the race was declared void. It was 'the National that never was'.

In 1929, a pile-up at the Canal Turn accounted for most of the field, and by the final fence only Billy Barton and 100/1 shot Tipperary Tim were left. Billy Barton fell, leaving Tipperary Tim to canter to victory, with his remounted rival a distant second. In bog-like conditions in 2001, the winner Red Marauder was one of only two horses to complete the race without mishap, though two others crossed the line after being remounted. At least the many fallers had soft landings, and there were no injuries to horses or riders.

Racing fans of my generation can remember where they were when they watched the 1967 Grand National. They probably think they can remember Michael O'Hehir's commentary from the far end of the course too (the BBC fielded four commentators, situated at various points on the two-and-a-quarter-mile circuit; Peter O'Sullevan occupied the grandstand box), though O'Hehir's superbly alert account of the dramatic events may have become imprinted on memories through repeated viewings.

The runners were on their second circuit. There were twenty-eight left, all of whom had just negotiated Becher's Brook and were approaching fence 23, apparently a nice, easy one as respite before the next two, the Canal Turn and Valentine's. All would have been fine, had not a horse called Popham Down, who had fallen at the first fence but who had carried on without his jockey, suddenly veered to the right. He crashed into Rutherfords, bringing about a pile-up of horses who either fell, refused, or could find no way through. In O'Hehir's words: 'Rutherfords has been hampered, and so has Castle Falls – Rondetto has fallen – Princeful has fallen – Norther has fallen – Kirkle Lad has fallen – The Fossa has fallen – there's a right pile-up – Leedsy has climbed over the fence and left his jockey there – and now with all this mayhem, Foinavon has gone off on his own.' Foinavon, a 100/1 shot, had been plodding along some way behind the leaders, and his jockey, John Buckingham, had time to steer him to a gap through which he could jump the fence. Other jockeys either remounted or, their horses having refused the first time, persuaded them to have another go, but by then Foinavon was thirty lengths clear. The gap narrowed, but never looked like being closed.

Red Rum is sometimes credited with saving the Grand National, reviving interest at a time when the race was losing its lustre, and when the Aintree finances were precarious. The race and racecourse eventually found a more secure footing in 1983, when the Jockey Club took over. Now, the Grand National faces different threats. For years, incidents such as the pile-up that led to Foinavon's victory seemed to me to be all part of the fun of 'The world's greatest steeplechase', but by the 2011 and 2012 Nationals, in each of which two horses died, the fun had begun to pall. Viewers saw runners bypassing fences while ground staff held up screens concealing stricken horses; after these images, I felt enjoyment of the sport was impossible. Others felt the same. The Aintree management made changes, which had some effect. The number of Grand National deaths from 2012 to 2021 was two, by far the best record since the race began. (But the 2022 running, after which two horses died, was to be a sobering reminder that no matter what adjustments are made to the fences, the race will always be dangerous.) Some racing fans regret the modifications: it's just another steeplechase now, they complain. They may underestimate the vulnerability of racing to charges that it regards horses as expendable. Four deaths in ten years are four too many – and they have not been the only ones at the three-day Grand National meeting, where total fatalities since 2012 are twenty.

Objections to the Grand National are not solely a phenomenon of the era of animal rights. In 1829, the equestrian writer John Lawrence noted: 'I do regret the cruelty of driving brave, and generous, and useful animals into useless and unprofitable dangers and hardships, from which they can scarcely escape with impunity and soundness, and through which so many have been rendered miserable cripples ever after.' Reporting that year on the first Grand National, the *Liverpool Mercury* said: 'It was no doubt a very exciting spectacle, but we can no more be reconciled to it on that account than we are to cockfighting, bull-baiting, or any other popular pastime which is attended with the infliction of wanton torture on any living being.'

The risks of jumps racing are not the only matter on which the sport faces charges of cruelty. Whipping horses – a sight confronting the viewer of every horse race – does not look good, and the British Horseracing Authority (BHA) has rules about whip use, among them that a jockey cannot strike a horse more than seven times during a flat race, or more than eight times during a jumps race. But this is all about perception rather than welfare. A jockey's whip, devised with input from the RSPCA, is foam-padded: he or she could whack you quite hard with one and you wouldn't be hurt. Decriers of whip use point out that some horses nevertheless return to the stables with marks on their skin. One might reply that some humans bruise or suffer welts easily too: the marks are not evidence of pain. The argument, however, is lost. At the time of writing, the BHA is pondering the results of a consultation into whip use, and is odds-on to tighten the rules further.* In some jurisdictions, jockeys may wield their whips for safety reasons only: to stop their mounts from drifting into others' paths, for example. Making judgements on this rule must be tricky.

The third matter is racing's dirty secret, not fully acknowledged for far too long. There are more than 20,000 horses in training in Great Britain and Ireland: what happens to them at the end of their racing days? A BBC *Panorama* programme broadcast in summer 2021 revealed, with footage recorded on cameras concealed by Animal Aid, what had been happening to some of them: transportation to an abattoir in Wiltshire and, in appalling conditions and at the hands of amateurish executioners, death by bullet. *Panorama* asserted that 4000 racehorses,

---

* It does. Among new rules introduced in autumn 2022 is that jockeys hold their whips in the backhand position – pointing back, towards their elbows.

most of them from Ireland, had suffered this fate since 2019. The programme brought further bad publicity for Irish trainer Gordon Elliott, who at the time was serving a ban following the release of a photograph showing him sitting on a dead horse: the previous recorded whereabouts of three horses appearing on the abattoir footage was Elliott's stable in County Meath. Contacted by *Panorama*, he said that he had sent two of the horses to a dealer 'to be rehomed if possible, and if not, to be humanely euthanised', and the third horse – Vyta Du Roc, once trained in England by Nicky Henderson to win three races at Grade 2 level – to another 'rider'. He added that he had ensured the appropriate and proper treatment and welfare of animals who had been in his possession, and had rehomed a substantial number of them.

Races in Ireland tend to attract large fields of runners – evidence, I used to think, of a thriving industry. Now I look at them in a different light.

Horse Racing Ireland and the BHA have guidelines for owners and trainers about making provisions for their retired horses. In Britain, the BHA with the Horse Welfare Board and Retraining of Racehorses is improving its traceability protocols, and introducing more rigour to its funding policies. Amid the fallout from the *Panorama* broadcast, the BHA reported that more than 9000 horses were registered on the Retraining of Racehorses website – an encouraging figure, but one put into context by a comparison with the larger one for horses in training. The authority said that it was aiming for 100 per cent traceability, but admitted that there were 'gaps in the industry's knowledge of the whereabouts of thoroughbreds bred for racing'.

For injured or unwell horses, as for injured or unwell cats and dogs, euthanasia may be the kindest option – though not in the way it was carried out in Wiltshire. Other victims, one suspects, were not injured at all, but just weren't wanted any longer. The BHA told the *Racing Post*: 'British racing has in place euthanasia guidance to ensure euthanasia is used only in the correct circumstances . . . [It] states that elective euthanasia of a horse should be carried out only when those who have responsibility for its welfare, usually the owner or designated keeper, often in consultation with a veterinary surgeon, have considered all available options and decided it is in the best interests of the horse.'

'I just want him to come back in one piece,' I hear a racegoer say of Tiger Roll (trained by Gordon Elliott), twice winner of the Grand National but today running on the Mildmay course, a mile and a quarter circuit inside and in part alongside the National circuit. Races on the National circuit are spectator-unfriendly: from the National start, the runners head away from you for some three-quarters of a mile before, at the end of a line of six fences, they meet Becher's Brook, after which they disappear from the view of most grandstand positions until they get close to the home turn. You rely on the big screen and the commentary, emitted from a much clearer sound system than some other courses provide. Granted better light than today's murk, you would be able to follow every stage of a race on the Mildmay course through binoculars. I find that I like to watch from the terrace in the Earl of Sefton stand beyond the winning post, although the front-on perspective on National and hurdle course finishers is uninformative. Roof terraces in the Princess Royal and Lord Daresbury stands would give a commentator's-eye view of the action, but in this weather are not for the faint-hearted.

One of my fellow spectators on the Earl of Sefton terrace is John Hales, met in the Cheltenham chapter as the owner of Azertyuiop, and here to see his horse Protektorat – co-owned with ex-Manchester United manager Sir Alex Ferguson and two others – score an impressive, 25-length victory, ridden by Bridget Andrews. Now in his eighties, walking with a stick and apparently on his own, Hales makes unsteady progress down the steps on his way to greet Protektorat in the winner's enclosure. It's time to forgive him for owning the rival to one of my favourite horses, and I offer him a hand, which he declines. 'My horse has just won that race!' he tells me. I congratulate him.

What of Tiger Roll? He does come home in one piece, having been let off jumping half the fences by jockey James Bowen, who pulls him up, trailing the field, after the first of the two circuits. Respectful and affectionate applause breaks out.

There follows the Becher Chase, run on the National course but over a distance of three miles two furlongs – one mile short of the Grand National distance. In these conditions, it's gruelling enough. Twenty-one horses start; ten finish. When at last Tout Est Permis (ninth) and Hogan's Height (tenth) pass the line, more than seventy lengths behind the winner, it's almost time for the next race. Snow Falcon, Top Ville Ben, and Mac Tottie fall; Vieux Lion Rouge, Via Dolorosa, Chris's Dream, and El Paso Wood unseat their riders; the other four contenders are pulled up. All the horses and jockeys emerge unscathed. They are lucky. But with more than one horse falling or unseating in every jumps race, some will not be lucky. In 2020, there were 86 fatal injuries from 25,188 runs in jumps races in Britain; in percentage terms, 0.34 per cent of runs ended in the deaths of horses.

Is this acceptable? Here's what racing people say: horses enjoy racing, they lead pampered lives at racehorse stables, and no one is more distressed than racing professionals and owners when horses die. Racing makes a substantial contribution to our economy; it engenders love and respect for horses; for the vast majority of people, it offers a safe, challenging and enjoyable way of indulging the human urge to gamble; it's a thrilling sport to watch or take part in.

If current trends continue, there may come a time in which society regards the risks of jumps racing, or perhaps of all racing, as invidious, and grants horses the right not to be employed by humans for sport. That time won't arrive for a while – but it may come sooner than racing people expect. After the 2022 Grand National, a friend texts to tell me he won't be watching or betting on the race again. I can see his point.

TAUNTON

Jumps

8 February 2022

The view from the stewards' room

At most courses, there's a loud, synthesised klaxon, and the announce-ment: 'Stewards' inquiry; stewards' inquiry.' At Taunton, the klaxon may be on the blink, or they never bother with one; anyway, at this unpretentious venue we get the verbal announcement only. The run-ners in race three have returned, either to the parade ring as winners or runners-up, or to the unsaddling enclosure as also-rans, and they've had their showers and drinks; the bookmakers – though not the Tote, which waits for 'weighed in' to be called – have started paying out. But weighing-in has been the problem: Harry Bannister, rider of Taylors Three Rock, weighs out at eleven stone before the race; when he gets on the scales after the race, he is two pounds lighter. A meeting with the stewards is inevitable.

Taylors Three Rock had gone haring off at the start, as if energised to find two pounds less on her back than she had expected, and at one point was twenty lengths clear of her rivals. The loss of two pounds, though, does not give a twenty-length advantage, and by the time the runners came into the home straight Bannister's rising agitation in the saddle was in inverse ratio to Taylor Three Rock's speed. Rivals reeled her in, and coasted past. She didn't stop trying. Having stumbled over the last hurdle, she arrived wearily at the post in fourth and last place, while the three others from the seven-strong field had been pulled up or had fallen (unharmed). It was all in vain: the stewards disqualify her. Bannister and a representative for Tony Carroll, Taylors Three Rock's trainer, cannot explain why the jockey and his saddle and his saddle cloth are lighter than they were before the race, and indeed no one would try to cheat in this way: you'd have a 100 per cent chance of being found out. Nevertheless, the stewards are there to enforce the rules, whether broken unwittingly or not. Bannister gets a day's suspension, and Carroll gets a £250 fine.

There is a lot of activity behind the scenes at a race meeting, and one notices it only when something goes wrong, as it has done here. The Taunton racecard lists as officials for today five stewards, a judge (who calls the results), a clerk of the scales (who weighs Harry Bannister), one vet and four veterinary surgeons, six medics, three equine welfare and integrity officers, and a betting ring manager. There are two starters: you certainly notice them if there are false starts or delays. Among these roles, that of the stewards seems the most obscure: they pass judgements, and sometimes they can decide that the horse we backed and thought was a winner must be demoted, but who are they? What is their authority? I have had a very pleasant chat with former chief steward Paul Barton, and may be able to give at least partially informative answers to these questions.

First, Taunton. You'd think it was the kind of place always to have had a racecourse. It certainly has a horsey, rural atmosphere. Green jackets are much in evidence: either waxed, or in checked tweed, with matching caps. If you fear you don't look the part, 'The Farmer's Friend' clothing stall will set you right. Racing has been taking place in the area since at least the start of the nineteenth century, and has always attracted an up-market crowd: 'At Taunton races the company was more numerous and brilliant than ever before assembled in that part of the country: some of the equipages were very superb, and the number of vehicles, filled with fashionable company, conferred on the scene peculiar animation,' the *Sporting Magazine* reported in 1826. As at Epsom in William Powell Frith's famous painting, *bon ton* rubbed shoulders with skulduggery, or was intertwined with it: a local historian quoted on the racecourse website (itself quoting John Tyrrel's *Chasing Around Britain*) recalled:

Whilst the horses were running the thieves were busy in easing the spectators of their purses and the carriage people of their silver tankards. I saw a fellow steal a silver tankard from a carriage belonging to the Misses Patton; he must have passed it to an accomplice, as it was not found upon him. The thief was captured and taken to the 'Crown and Mitre', where he frightened me out of my senses by telling me I was about to swear to what might hang him, make his wife a widow and his children fatherless. I thought it all so dreadful that I said I was not quite sure that he was the thief.

Fashion is fickle, and to the consternation of local card sharps and pick-pockets no race meeting took place in the area for more than seventy years, until in 1927 the Taunton Racecourse Company, established for the purpose, opened the present course on the Portman Estate, in the parish of Orchard Portman. It was the youngest racecourse in the country until this century, when Great Leighs/Chelmsford City and then Ffos Las came along.

The site, three miles outside the town and with a very attractive view across the course to the Blackdown Hills, is now part of the Crown Estates. The track is one mile and a quarter round, mostly flat, but with a dip that occludes sight of the second-last fence except from the highest vantage points. At ground level, your perspective on the back straight is also unsatisfactory, but you can see it from the top of the steppings, or make do with the big screen. The M5 is nearby; its construction benefited the course, providing 50,000 tons of excavated earth for widening the bends and for other track improvements.

Taunton, in common with many towns of a similar size, has economic problems, particularly on the high street. My taxi driver, who previously lived in South London and Brighton, complains that there's nothing to do in the evenings. The racecourse spectators are 'county' rather than, as they were in 1826, glamorous. Taunton's facilities, while improved from the days when all the course provided was 'a small wooden stand, often surrounded by a sea of mud' (Tyrell), are basic by comparison with those at fellow country venues such as Fakenham, Perth and Plumpton.

The signage and cream concrete on the Portman Stand, opened by His Worship the Mayor J.R.G. Meikle in 1968, are showing their age, as is the adjacent building that houses private boxes. However, the brick and glass stand for owners, trainers and annual members, and the Orchard Stand beyond the winning post, are recent, smarter additions. On the first floor of the Orchard Stand is a bar, where a security guard, intimidating in size though friendly in manner, instructs me to delete the photo I take, on the grounds that it shows a member of staff. I don't argue. On the ground floor is the Saddle Room, with a buffet of 'home-cooked' dishes. I take a look at them and, wiser after my grisly experience at Ayr, move on. There's a small café on the first floor of the Portman stand, glass-fronted and with tables overlooking the paddock and winning post; it offers pasties and sausage rolls, but I choose an egg and cress sandwich and a bar of Cadbury's Dairy Milk. Playing it safe.

The bars display photos and prints, some of them classic but most featuring horses who have raced here. You won't recognise many names. But there is one Taunton winner with a significant place in racing history: Hit Parade, triumphant in division two of the Motorway Selling Hurdle in May 1975. Hit Parade's victory was the first on the CV of trainer Martin Pipe, who after a slow start went on to amass fifteen Champion Trainer titles. Typical Pipe horses would race off in front and, unlike poor Taylors Three Rock, stay there. They were fitter than everyone else's. This physical edge aroused suspicion and jealousy, which Pipe's social awkwardness and non-racing heritage (his father was a bookmaker, who, in common with other fathers of high achievers, rarely expressed approval of his son) did not alleviate. His closely fought battles for the trainers' title with Paul Nicholls were compelling: both driven characters, they clearly didn't like each other much.

Pipe, suffering from a muscle-wasting condition, retired in 2006. (He seems still to be going strong.) His son David Pipe, who has a more sociable manner, runs a stable – at Nicholashayne, fifteen miles away – that is not as supercharged as it was in Martin's day. A 2005 picture in Roy Gill's *From Epsom to Traleee* shows Martin Pipe at Taunton briefing ten jockeys, all booked by him to ride his ten entries in a single handicap hurdle race. David has two runners on the Taunton card today: Kalzari finishes second in the Free Racing 14th March Handicap Hurdle (Class 5), and Seventeen O Four is fifth in the catchily titled Mike Morgan Electrical Services Supporting Love Musgrove Handicap Hurdle (Class 4) (the afternoon's racing is in support of the Love Musgrove medical charity).

A couple of horses on show today could defy my implication that Taunton is a course for plodders: Doctor Parnassus, who puts on an impressive display of acceleration in the opening race, and Dr T J Eckleburg, who is similarly authoritative in the fifth, are both reported to be heading for the Triumph Hurdle at the Cheltenham Festival.* And my comment about top trainers giving low-key meetings a miss (Lingfield chapter) also fails to apply. Dan Skelton and Olly Murphy, trainers respectively of Doctor Parnassus and Dr T J Eckleburg, are both here, as are Emma Lavelle, Philip Hobbs, Harry Fry and Alan King.

It is not a lucrative afternoon for bookmakers. Half an hour before the first race, they look out at a no-man's-land, beyond which racegoers hover like shy members of the opposite sex at a school dance in the 1950s. Eventually, one or two come forward, everyone relaxes, and business picks up. But the results don't help: four favourites win, two further winners are well fancied, and only Marettimo, who takes the novices' handicap chase at 22/1, provides the kind of result that bookies favour. Taylors Three Rock was quoted at 16/1 before her race, but started at 12/1, so a few punters must have lost their money on her.

It would have been a pain had Taylors Three Rock won, because the owners would have been expecting a purse of £7079, and punters who had backed her would have been imagining how to spend a twelvefold return or more on their wagers, only for the tannoy announcement to squelch their dreams (unless the punters were with a bookmaker whose policy was to pay out on the first past the post, whatever the official result). As it was, all that was lost was fourth place prize money of £816. The stewards' job was easy. There had been a breach of the rules; the weight discrepancy was not great and did not affect the result; it was highly unlikely to have been a deliberate ruse: entry-level punishments.

There are five stewards on duty today. John Pearn, the stewards' panel chair, is a volunteer, one of about sixty volunteer stewards in Britain. He sits at various courses in the West Country. Then there are the British Horseracing Authority-employed stipendiary stewards – though Paul Barton tells me that he avoids the 'stipendiary' bit, lest it imply a 'them and us', amateurs and professionals, distinction. There are Richard Westropp and Chris Rutter; Chris Hill, who has the Covid-era title of social distancing officer as well as raceday assistant; and Stephanie Swanney, working remotely to provide admin support.

---

* It turns out that Dr T J Eckleburg doesn't run in the Triumph Hurdle; Doctor Parnassus finishes seventh.

Westropp and Rutter arrive a good couple of hours before the first race. Pearn will have walked the course with the clerk of the course, and will confirm the going description (good to soft today), any movements of the running rails, and any – please none – unsafe patches of ground. Equine welfare and integrity officers, also part of the BHA contingent, will have checked that the horses have arrived at the stables with microchips, certificates of vaccination against equine flu, and passports in order. Hill and the clerk of the course will make sure that horses arrive at and leave the parade ring on time; he'll also check to see that the horses' accoutrements, such as headgear, are correct, and he'll note post-race comments from jockeys. The stewards must give their permission for various privileges: a trainer may want a horse to wear a hood, or earplugs, before a race, or to go down to the start early.

With the first race due in just over an hour, all the officials meet. The clerk of the scales notes non-runners, jockey changes, or alterations to the colours the jockeys will wear. Are there any veterinary issues – dodgy vaccination paperwork, for example? Have there been any unusual betting patterns? If so, the stewards will pay close attention to the performances of the horses concerned – especially if the BHA's integrity team in London have alerted them to suspicious factors, such as a poor performance last time by a horse who is attracting punters' money today.

Next stop is the paddock, where the stewards will try to familiarise themselves with the runners: who has a noseband or cheekpieces, who has blinkers, who is grey, who has a white blaze, who is large/small: it all helps them to 'read' a race. Barton liked to watch every pre-race parade, but quite often, once the afternoon's action was under way, was too busy to get out of the stewards' room.

The BHA employs seventeen stewards, on contracts that require them to go racing on more than half the days of the year. Nice work, one imagines; Barton certainly enjoyed it, and took pride in it. But racedays for stewards are not like racedays, or like any other sporting occasions, for you and me. Stewards are not concerned with the contests; they're not invested in who wins and who loses. Barton tells me of his paddock watching and race reading: 'I'm not interested – it sounds awful – in the horse itself. The horse is just part of the event for me, and I just want the event to go without incident. If there is an incident, I need to be able to identify it and the stewards can deal with it in the quickest and most efficient way.

'Which horse wins the race is of no interest, other than that I'll want to know if a horse that won shouldn't have, or if a horse that didn't win should have. I'm not looking at the race as an exciting event. I'm looking at it in cold blood to deal with whatever happens.' Hmm. Perhaps stewarding wouldn't be for me.

The next task is to keep an eye on the horses as they canter down and mill about before the start. Courses offer stewards at least three viewing rooms: a head-on box, not used much as a vantage point these days, when head-on cameras are standard; a side-on box, which should command a view of the entire course; and the stewards' room, where screens broadcast the action from various angles, and where a further screen shows the betting market.

What happens if a horse rears, throws the jockey, and runs loose – not an uncommon occurrence? 'We need to find out whether the horse has been caught or has headed off to the town centre,' Barton says. If the latter, or if the horse gallops too far to be still fit to race, a 'Rule 4' comes into play, cutting payouts on winning bets, because there has been no time to form a new market without the errant, and now withdrawn, competitor. If a horse lines up for the start but refuses to race, the stewards must determine whether the horse has come under starter's orders, in which case Rule 4 does not apply. (The standard commentary is: 'They're under starter's orders – and they're off!')

Race one at Taunton, the Injured Jockeys Fund Novices' Hurdle, passes without obvious incident. In the winner's enclosure, trainer Dan Skelton seems to be concerned about Doctor Parnassus's near back leg, but doesn't report any problems later. Skelton – currently under investigation by the BHA after falling out with a group of owners over a horse he was involved in selling to them – has placed Doctor Parnassus well, finding for him a race in which he turns out to be the only four-year-old, allowed to carry less weight than given to his older rivals. The stewards asked, or were vouchsafed information, about two beaten horses: 'James Best reported that Pol Ma Cree, unplaced, hung badly right, and Tom Bellamy reported that Rebel Intentions, unplaced, ran too free,' the report notes. Sometimes, a vet's observations may be relevant: 'The veterinary officer reported that Zulu, which was pulled up, had twisted its right fore shoe . . . the veterinary officer reported that a post-race examination of Clondaw Dancer [also pulled up] failed to reveal any abnormalities,' the report notes after race two. Horses who arouse the stewards' interest, either through unexpectedly good or unexpectedly bad performances, may be drugs-tested. Other tests are carried out at random.

Michael Nolan, rider of Iberio in the second race, jumps the last fence three lengths behind the leader. He gives Iberio a crack of the whip. Iberio responds, Nolan keeps up the treatment, and the pair come home more than a length in front. But whipping the horse all the way to the line takes Nolan over the eight-stroke limit, earning him a two-day suspension – a more expensive punishment than his share of the winner's purse will cover.

The decisions that the stewards take today are all straightforward. They don't, for example, have to rule that a jockey and trainer are responsible for a 'non-trier'. The consensus on the racing message boards is that jockeys and trainers cheat regularly; but there is never consensus about the incidents when cheating has been alleged. Some years ago, a jockey in a steeplechase appeared not to fall or be unseated but to jump off his mount, in an incompetent bid to throw the race; even then, some argued that the mishap was accidental. Yet stewards must come to judgements, invariably to the outrage of those condemned. Two days after the Taunton meeting, the Doncaster stewards dish out a £4000 fine to trainer Gary Hanmer, and suspend jockey William Shanahan for eighteen days; Shanahan, they rule, has failed 'to ride his mount in such a way that he could be seen to ask for timely, real and substantial effort to obtain the best possible placing'. Hanmer tells the *Racing Post*: 'I'll speak to the owners, but they were amazed and, like us all, disappointed by what's happened.'

Also contentious are matters of interference: has a horse crossed the path of another, is it the jockey's fault, has it affected the result? The stewards will summon the jockeys concerned, and invite each to give an account of the incident. The conclusion may be that someone is guilty of careless riding, prompting a suspension of a day or longer, or of improper riding, which may mean that the jockey will spend the best part of a month watching the racing on television; but even the most egregious errors may not cause the result to be changed, if the finishing order would have been the same had they not been committed.

Barton was on duty at the 2015 St Leger, when he and his fellow stewards ruled that Bondi Beach would have won had not Simple Verse, first past the post, barged into him a couple of times. They gave Bondi Beach the race; eleven days later, following a BHA disciplinary panel verdict, Simple Verse got it back. Barton is phlegmatic about the controversy now.

He doesn't quite put it like this, but I think it's fair to say that his position is that such cases are not matters of right or wrong – how can they be, when there are differences of opinion among participants, spectators, and stewards themselves? What the stewards must do is come to a conclusion that they are satisfied is based on the evidence and is acceptable to everyone in the room. 'Our job is to explain our decision, not to justify it,' Barton says. 'If a hundred journalists can't agree, that's just how it is. As long as you follow the guidelines, you've done what you're expected to do. So when they cross the line and there's been interference between the winner and second, you have to call it. It shouldn't make any difference to your decision if it's the St Leger or the Derby [or a selling hurdle at Taunton, he might add] – and if it does affect your decision-making, you're probably in the wrong job.'

The last question to someone who has been a steward for more than thirty years (Barton is now a consultant), who has attended thousands of race meetings, and who has watched, again and again and from every angle, tens of thousands of races: is racing institutionally corrupt? When someone is fined under the non-trier rules, or when drugs are found in a horse's system, observers may think of tips and icebergs. Barton recognises that there will always be wrongdoers, but insists that the policing of the sport is too thorough for them to thrive for long. He says: 'I think that the way racing is regulated is astonishingly good.'

LEOPARDSTOWN

Jumps (also stages flat racing)

6 March 2022

Industry day

'When's Cheltenham?' my taxi driver from Dublin airport asks. So, not a racing fan; but he is Irish, so he knows that the Cheltenham Festival is imminent. These are my assumptions, anyway. Arriving in another country, one is inclined to draw general conclusions from fragments of chat with the first person one meets.

Perhaps I should say 'I' rather than 'one', and not only to sound less pompous. The impression that Dublin is more foreign to me, a Londoner, than it was when I last visited in the nineties, may be entirely subjective. It's smarter, and buzzier, particularly in the chic area of Trinity College, Grafton Street and St Stephen's Green. But the place does not seem to be so relaxed: the people I encounter are more curt, less charming. (This is a relative verdict: by comparison with Londoners, they positively gush.) Then there is Brexit, reinforcing the severance initiated with the creation of the Irish Free State in 1922.

I am used to hearing languages of every variety when I step outside my front door, but I am struck by the multitude of tongues in the air as I stroll round the shopping district near O'Connell Street. Has Brexit diverted overseas students and workers here from London? There are a good many Eastern European voices; no Gaelic, though every sign and public announcement is in Gaelic as well as English. On the Luas tram service, each stop is named in both languages; sometimes the names are the same, so the voice says, 'Cowper; Cowper', and when we get to Ranelagh, she says, 'Ranelagh; Ranelagh', only with a throaty sound at the end of the second version.

The super-efficient Luas Green Line takes me from the centre of

Dublin to the suburb of Sandyford, about half an hour away. It's Ireland, I reflect: there will be a cohort of fellow racegoers. I get off at the Sandyford stop, and there's no one else about. I'm in the middle of a business park, cut through by numerous lanes of speeding traffic. After a succession of electronic green men – their illumination is accompanied by an electronic swooping sound, like the one triggered by the opening of the shop door in the delightful Radio 4 comedy *Fags, Mags and Bags* – have given me the go-ahead, I manage to cross these roads, find a path, and head towards the racecourse grandstand, past a large car park overlooked by a giant Microsoft building; the solitary attendant is the first pedestrian I've seen since the tram deposited me.

Following a mild kerfuffle over my ticket, which, the Leopardstown staff inform me, has already been scanned (had Aer Lingus accepted it in lieu of a boarding pass?), I enter the racecourse, which, nearly two hours before race one, has a just-waking-up atmosphere. A few yards beyond the entrance is a statue of Hurricane Fly (born 2004), who won the Irish Champion Hurdle at the course five times. It is a curious artefact: the sculptor has shown Hurricane Fly jumping a hurdle, and has attempted to convey the horse's lean fitness and muscular power; to my eyes, the attempt has failed, and what I see instead is a horse whose skin has wrinkled and collapsed over a shrunken skeleton. Further in, close to the parade ring, there's a more conventional statue, of the great filly Snow Fairy (born 2007), winner here of the Irish Champion Stakes, following victories in the English Oaks and Irish Oaks.

The founder of Leopardstown racecourse – the name indicating that this was once the location of a leper colony – was an Englishman called George Quin, who modelled it on Sandown Park. The course opened in 1888, thirteen years after Sandown, at a grand ceremony and meeting to which some 50,000 people set out to gain admittance. The railways could not cope with the volume of would-be racegoers, and the roads were gridlocked; the majority of those who did manage to get to the course found that the food and, worse, the racecards had run out. An eyewitness reported that the occasion offered good prizes and 'miserable discomfort'. A squib in a sporting paper read: 'Sacred to the memory of LEOPARDSTOWN, foully and brutally strangled at birth by gross incompetence, bungling and mismanagement, August 27, 1888.' But Leopardstown survived this memorial, as it did a scandal when owners and trainers discovered to their fury that a dedicated sprint track described by Quin as being five furlongs in length was in fact half a furlong shorter.

Leopardstown is like Sandown and like most Irish courses in being dual-purpose: it stages flat racing and jumps racing. Every British and Irish racecourse has an idiosyncrasy or two, and this is Leopardstown's: as the runners pass the grandstand, they do not turn into the back straight, but carry on galloping away from you, in the direction of the M50 and the Wicklow Mountains beyond; they are some half a mile away when they reach the turn.

On the flat, the highlights include the spring Ballysax Stakes and Derrinstown Stud stakes, both considered trials for the Irish and English Derbies; the autumn Irish Champion Stakes is often a terrific showdown between the best middle-distance horses from both sides of the Irish Sea. One of the most exciting head-to-heads took place in 2001, when the five-year-old Fantastic Light took on the unbeaten three-year-old Galileo. The pair had met in the King George VI and Queen Elizabeth Stakes at Ascot in July, when Galileo prevailed; the rivalry of their owners, the great racing powers of Godolphin (Fantastic Light) and Baldoyle/Coolmore (Galileo), added spice to the encounters. At Leopardstown, Fantastic Light tracked his pacemaker, while Galileo tracked him. As they approached the home turn, Fantastic Light was able to slip through a gap that his pacemaker had conveniently left on the inside, while Galileo had to get past on the outside. The tactic, if that is what it was, may have made the difference, because Fantastic Light entered the straight with a length advantage; Galileo pursued him all the way to the line, gaining ground by inches; the two horses, a long way clear of the others, flashed past the post side by side – almost. The judge called a photo finish; but there was not much doubt who had won, and the photo confirmed that Fantastic Light had held on, by a head.

Leopardstown's two big jumps meetings are the four-day Christmas Festival and, in early February, the two-day Dublin Racing Festival, both feasts of Grade 1 sport. All the leading Irish jumps horses – and this, in recent years, has come to mean all the leading jumps horses, full stop – compete, with the odd British-trained champion thrown in, while the novice races reveal or confirm potential champions of the future.

The winners are guaranteed to be prominent in the betting market at the Cheltenham Festival in March, and at Punchestown in April.

Inside the grandstand is a 'hall of fame': a glass-fronted display of tributes to great jockeys and horses, with racing silks, newspaper reports and other memorabilia. Among the subjects are my two favourite race-horses: Arkle (jumps) and Nijinsky (flat). There's also a section devoted to Arkle's jockey Pat Taaffe, reminding me that he also once rode Arkle's great rival, the Irish-bred but later English-trained Mill House.

Nijinsky never raced at Leopardstown: as a two-year-old in 1969, he had four victories at the Curragh, and a year later won the Irish Derby there. (His statue is outside the Curragh entrance.) But there is a Leop-ardstown race named after him, and I am certainly not going to quibble at this racecourse tribute. He was a horse with presence: 'he really filled my eye', his trainer Vincent O'Brien said, recalling his first sight of Ni-jinsky as a yearling at a Toronto stud farm. 'With Nijinsky it really was love at first sight,' said his jockey Lester Piggott, in an uncharacteristic display of effusiveness (possibly my old chum Sean Magee, Piggott's ghostwriter, had egged him on). It was a fateful meeting in Toronto, and not only because of what the horse was to go on to achieve. Nijinsky was the first advertisement for the potency of his sire, Northern Dancer, whose male line, championed by O'Brien and the Coolmore stud with which he was associated, was to become dominant in the bloodstock industry.

Nijinsky won with ease his five races as a two-year-old. He was simi-larly impressive the following year in the Newmarket 2000 Guineas, after which Romola, the widow of ballet dancer Vaslav Nijinsky, wrote a letter to Piggott: 'I was tremendously impressed with your magnificent winning of the 2000 Guineas race this afternoon on the beautiful horse Nijinsky, and I send you my congratulations. I ask of you now only one thing – please win the Derby for us!' He did. Nijinsky went on also to win the Irish Derby, and in the King George VI and Queen Elizabeth Stakes at Ascot cantered clear of a field including the previous year's Derby winner as if disdaining to make unnecessary effort. He achieved fame that not even the tremendous Frankel was to match.

Soon after, Nijinsky contracted a nasty skin condition. Nevertheless, O'Brien thought that his charge had returned to health by September, and sent him to the St Leger at Doncaster, where he became the first horse for thirty-five years to win the Triple Crown (2000 Guineas, Derby, St Leger) – and the last horse to do so. (As I mention elsewhere, Camelot was to come close in 2012.) Then came Europe's richest race, the Prix de l'Arc de Triomphe.

The Leopardstown exhibit alleges that Nijinsky lost the Arc owing to jockey error. (It does not name the jockey.) True, Piggott did not observe O'Brien's instruction to race near the front of the field; but achieving such a position is almost impossible at Longchamp if you're drawn, as Piggott and Nijinsky were, on the outside. There were only three horses behind them as the field approached the short straight. Piggott urged Nijinsky forward, but they got blocked twice, and had to go very wide. Still they flew past every rival until they reached the leader, Sassafras. But then Nijinsky faltered. A photo finish. A sick feeling in my stomach. The inevitable result: Sassafras the winner.

It's all about whether you win or lose. In the 1986 Derby, Greville Starkey on the favourite Dancing Brave found himself a long way back, overtook most of the field, failed to catch Shahrastani, was lambasted, and was replaced as Dancing Brave's jockey by Pat Eddery. In the Arc that year, Eddery had Dancing Brave almost last before the home straight, accelerated past all their rivals, and was hailed a genius. Piggott's defence following Nijinsky's defeat was that the horse was past his best: if he had been on the form he had shown in the spring and summer, he could have given his rivals an even bigger lead and still have won. The theory that Nijinsky was 'over the top' was confirmed two weeks later, when he ran in the Newmarket Champion Stakes. Racing at one pace, his extra gear not functioning, he finished second again.

I sometimes wonder if I'd love Nijinsky less if he had won the Arc. Following his career taught me about the kind of genius to which I am drawn: the kind that is accompanied by frailty. The graceful, highly gifted tennis player Hana Mandlikova would outplay the best players in the world, have victory in sight, and lose. John McEnroe was whupping Ivan Lendl in the French Open final, got two sets and a break-up, and ran out of steam. These losses, like Nijinsky's, were to partisans like me proofs of greatness, because they should have been victories. A similar principle applies to works of art: I don't want to hear Sussmayr's completion of Mozart's Requiem, or Alfano's completion of Puccini's *Turandot*. I want these works to retain their haunting state of incompleteness.

*

I seem to have drifted away from an unassuming afternoon at Leopardstown, where I enjoy the quiet and space. 'No pushing, please,' shouts a bookmaker, to an almost empty betting ring. It's not a meeting, you would have assumed, that the leading trainers would feel they needed to attend. But there are a few famous faces here. Henry de Bromhead, who next week at Cheltenham is to see his horses Honeysuckle and A Plus Tard, both ridden by Rachael Blackmore, win the Champion Hurdle (Honeysuckle) and Gold Cup (A Plus Tard), is attending to a couple of runners. Outside the weighing room, there's racing royalty: Ted Walsh, trainer of Grand National winner Papillon, and his son Ruby, who rode Papillon and many other winners. They are in conversation with a smartly attired gent in overcoat, pink tie and trilby; later, I realise that he's the veteran trainer Noel Meade (of whom more later). Top jockeys including Paul Townend and Jack Kennedy are among those in action, praying that they don't get injured with Cheltenham so close; they will both ride festival winners.

This is not the kind of occasion – an 'industry day', with racing professionals almost outnumbering members of the public – that Leopardstown chief executive Tim Husbands arrived here to oversee. Nottingham-born, Husbands has spent twenty-five years working in tourism and leisure in Belfast, most recently in charge of *Titanic* Belfast, and has an MBE in recognition of his work. (When I first meet him at Leopardstown, I seem to detect some Belfast tinges to his accent; later, when we catch up on Zoom, I can no longer hear them.) With an impressive record in attracting visitors to his venues, he arrived at Leopardstown shortly before the government forbade him, owing to Covid, from entertaining any visitors at all.

There were two compensations, apart from the help the Irish government provided. First, lockdown gave Husbands, who was a racing fan but an outsider, time to get to know the industry. 'I found the people to be brilliant,' he says. 'They're very honest, very straight – there's no hiding place in horseracing. You're either delivering or you're not, and they will not be shy in telling you what you've done wrong. But they'll also tell when they think you've done a great job.' He had not been in place for long before he started getting calls from trainers on the eve of big races: 'You need to water the track,' would be one piece of advice, from someone whose runner preferred some softness in the ground; minutes later, the trainer of a fast-ground specialist would call, with the warning: 'Don't water the ground, whatever you do.' Fellow MDs and clerks of the course would say: 'Welcome to our world.'

It took a while for the facilities at Leopardstown, owned since 1967 by Horse Racing Ireland, to reflect the premier league status of the course – until well into this century, in fact. The grandstand, which opened in 1971, was – like Sandown's, dating from roughly the same time – showing its age, until a three-phase development project transformed it, in addition to the course's other facilities. (Sandown has also had a revamp.) The second compensation from lockdown was that Husbands and his team were able to oversee the €20 million phase three of the project without disrupting the public. I'm told that the weighing room is now state-of-the-art. There are various swish bars and corporate entertainment areas. Inside the stand, there's lots of wood and glass and chrome and suspended LED lighting. The Paddock canteen offers traditional canteen fare, but from the Colts Café I buy a surprisingly excellent falafel and red cabbage wrap, flavoursome and well seasoned. The firm that produces the wrap, Fitzers, offers decent coffee from two vans near the parade ring. If you crave something more substantial than a falafel wrap, the Food Bar in the newly opened Racing Hall has a menu including 'Prime Irish' beefburger, chickpea and root vegetable tagine, 'Korean-style' crispy chicken roll, and scampi tails and chips. Outdoor and indoor children's play areas will no doubt be busy in the spring and summer.

'We have to match the expectations of the public,' Husbands says. 'They want there to be comfort, they want to feel they're having a special day out. I think a lot of racecourses are going to have to review their facilities over the next few years. It's not enough to say, "We've got a nice, small racecourse with traditional facilities." You're not going to be able to grow your racegoer audience like that.'

A race meeting on 6 March, when racing fans are obsessed by the following week's Cheltenham Festival, was never going to engender the 'sense of occasion' that Husbands aims to create at his top meetings. He will have been more heartened that at the start of February, just ten days after being given the go-ahead, Leopardstown was able to attract 25,000 people to the two days of the Dublin Racing Festival; and he will have noted the record crowds that Cheltenham entertained. A day after victory in the Cheltenham Gold Cup, Rachael Blackmore was reported to have been 'absolutely mobbed' by fans when she turned up for a single ride at Thurles. She won, of course. She's golden. When she rides at Leopardstown, she'll create the sense of occasion all by herself.

THE CURRAGH

Flat

26 March 2022

Respecting the landscape

Here, commanding a suitably awe-inspiring view – just slightly compromised by the M7 motorway – of the most venerable racing grounds in Britain and Ireland, is the most modern racecourse grandstand. It has had a few teething problems.

The Aga Khan stand cost €81.2 million, €1 million of which went on the brick-by-brick transfer to a spot beyond the parade ring of the Queen's Room, a small house built to accommodate Queen Victoria – no fan of racing – when she came over to visit the Prince of Wales, then in training at the nearby Curragh Camp. The stand consists of – and here, lacking the specialist vocabulary, I must quote the Curragh website – 'three linear planes (10,500 square metres) that are respectful to the Curragh landscape whilst cutting a dramatic and elegant silhouette'. Yes, it does look splendid. The description continues: 'Designed as a powerful floating horizontal form, the grandstand roof celebrates the horizontality of the landscape and the new racecourse structures set within it. The 39 metre diagonal cantilevered roof emphasises the contrast between the natural undulating forms of the Curragh, and the precision of the man-made.' I wouldn't have thought of that, but I am impressed.

Unfortunately, on the opening of the new development in 2019, visitors were assaulted by a terrible screeching noise, caused by the interaction of holes in the roof and the prevailing south-west wind. It took two years for the Curragh executive to announce that they had found a way to shut up this racket, with acoustic matting. A new parade ring turned out to be too small and had to be reconstructed. Racegoers complained of an 'Upstairs, downstairs' atmosphere, with upper areas of the grandstand restricted to members, owners and those with access to private boxes.

As I wait at the Curragh entrance with a growing crowd of racegoers, the clock ticking on from the official, 11.30 a.m., opening time and the delay blamed on 'problems with the turnstiles', I wonder whether the teething problems endure. Inside, as we can hear, Newbridge Gospel Choir have started their set on time, and are giving fervent performances of 'All Night Long' and other hits to an audience of zero, as racecourse staff bustle about their business. But, once we are let in, I have no further grounds to be snippy. The sun is shining, it's 17°C, the facilities are immaculate, there are large urns of flowers, and the lush green turf stretches for miles. The Curragh is already in credit, having laid on for me and a party of lads a complimentary bus service from Newbridge station; once the lads had disembarked in town, aiming to fuel themselves before heading to the racecourse, I was the sole passenger. At the end of the afternoon, the kindly driver takes me and one other racegoer on the return journey.

Why the Aga Khan stand? The spiritual leader of 15 million Ismaili Muslims has been a strong supporter of Irish racing, particularly since the Brits disqualified his filly Aliysa, first past the post in the 1989 Oaks, for having a banned substance in her system. He boycotted British racing for four years, and while he now has runners there, he keeps no horses with British trainers. He is one of the backers of the new development. The ground floor of the grandstand that bears his name is a giant atrium, with concrete pillars, a floor with pale tiling, and exposed brickwork. Escalators or lifts take you to the upper floors, which – there may have been some rejigging since 2019 – are no more exclusive than those at any racecourse. Outside the Derby Bar on the first floor is a broad, L-shaped terrace; before the majority of the crowd has arrived, I enjoy a quiet lunch here, looking out over the Curragh plain. Later, this is the view that a two-man band will also enjoy: they set up in the short arm of the L, and their audience, invisible to them, is round the corner. Up a level, there is the Lilywhites Lounge, leading out to the grandstand seats; and on the other side there are the wooden-floored Oaks Restaurant and Bar, with a terrace overlooking the parade ring. Today, when there are enough spectators to create an atmosphere but not enough to cause a crush, one can roam these facilities at leisure.

The Gaelic word 'Currech' is a generic term for racecourse, and there are records of racing here from the third century, when the sport was one of the attractions of a grand fair, the grandest of many that took place in Ireland. Laws from a few hundred years later stipulated that every Irish male be taught to drive horses, though only the nobility could ride in races. A fable called *The Voyage of Bran* promised that heaven would delight the Elect with racing 'over a glorious sweep of country'. The Irish imported Spanish horses known as hobbies, which were about the size of ponies but had a reputation as speedy racers – 'in racing wonderful swift, in gallop false and indifferent': in other words, they may not have looked graceful, but they got from A to B sharpish. The seventeenth-century writer Gervase Markham, comparing hobbies with the barbs of north Africa, wrote: 'When the best Barbaries that ever were in my remembrance were in their prime, I saw them overrun by a black hobbie at Salisbury.' Hobbies brought into England may have made a genetic contribution to the thoroughbred.

In 1634 at the Curragh, Lord Digby and the Earl of Ormond staged a match over four miles. The Earl of Cork backed Lord Digby's horse, and lost 'a new beaver hat to Mr Ferrers'. No doubt there were other gentlemen's matches at the time, and there is a record of a plate contest with a prize of one hundred guineas; but the Curragh fair was an unruly event, and attempts to regulate the sport appeared to be futile. Visiting in 1686, the Earl of Clarendon, lord lieutenant of Ireland under James II, was dismayed: 'It is sad to see the people – I mean the natives – such proper lusty fellows – poor, almost naked, but will work never but when they are ready to starve; and when they have got three or four days' wages, with them walk idly by till that be gone . . . Their habitations (for they cannot be called houses) are perfect pigsties.' He approved of the Curragh turf, however: 'much finer' than Newmarket's, was his assessment.

Despite this sorry analysis and the devastation to the country caused by the Battle of the Boyne (1690) and its aftermath, racing in Ireland did progress, and results from the Curragh appeared in the *Racing Calendar* from 1741. The most celebrated Curragh contests of the eighteenth century took place in 1749 and 1751. At the first, local heroine Irish Lass took on Black and All Black, imported from England by Sir Ralph Gore.

Irish Lass raced with a paidrín (rosary) attached to her bridle, gaining on victory national fame as 'the Paddereen Mare'. Two years later, Gore matched his horse for one thousand guineas against Bajazet, owned by the Earl of March, later to achieve notoriety as 'Old Q', the 'Rake of Piccadilly'. Before the race, the future Old Q arranged for Bajazet's jockey to jettison the weights he was supposed to carry, and to pick them up again before he weighed in afterwards. Black and All Black won anyway, his victory celebrated with the lighting of bonfires and the distribution of beer in Dublin. Despite his triumph, Gore was not inclined to ignore March's subterfuge, and he challenged him to a duel. The next morning, he arrived at the duelling ground bearing a coffin, which he presented to the earl; on it was inscribed March's coat of arms, name, date of birth, and date of death – that day. 'My dear fellow,' Gore explained to his opponent, 'you are, of course, aware that I never miss my man, and as I feel myself in excellent form this morning I have not a shadow of doubt upon my mind but this oaken box will shortly be better calculated for you than your present dress.' The earl, utterly beaten without the firing of a shot, made an abject confession and apology. Six years later, having been elected to the Jockey Club in Newmarket, he was the initiator of a rule enforcing severe punishments if jockeys failed to carry their allotted weights.

George IV, the former scapegrace 'Prinny' (of whom more in earlier chapters) and no more reputable as monarch, visited the Curragh for a race meeting in 1821. He was suffering at the time from what was described as the 'wherry-go-nimbles' – or as we might say, not putting too fine a point on it, the squits. The Duke of Leinster, George's godson, took charge of the construction of a bespoke lavatory, which proved its worth when George, caught short while a race was being run, was able to retreat to it in haste. Not allowing the ailment to darken his mood, the king donated a gold whip and an annuity of one hundred guineas as prizes for a new Curragh race.

Early attempts to introduce Irish counterparts to the Derby and Oaks did not take off. But by the mid-nineteenth century, Irish racing and breeding had advanced markedly. The Irish Derby eventually got under way in 1866. The Oaks followed, in 1895; the St Leger in 1915; the 2000 Guineas in 1921; and the 1000 Guineas in 1922. In England, the classics take place at Newmarket, Epsom and Doncaster; in Ireland, the Curragh stages them all.

Another Irish institution with a counterpart across the sea is the Turf Club, set up in 1790s as a governing body in the mould of the British Jockey Club. In 1993, the Jockey Club handed over the governance of the sport but retained its regulatory function, and a few years later there was a similar split in Irish racing; but whereas both governance and regulation are now in the hands of the British Horseracing Authority, the functions remained divided in Ireland, and are the responsibility of Horse Racing Ireland (governance) and the Irish Horseracing Regulatory Board (does what it says). They appear to disagree on the matter of whether horseracing is one word or two. They are both based at the Curragh; IHRB's HQ is a long, cream-coloured, functional-looking building beyond a racecourse fence.

The island of Ireland, one country as far as racing regulators are concerned, has twenty-six racecourses, of which two, Down Royal and Downpatrick, are in the north. That's twenty-six racecourses for a population of about seven million, while Britain has fifty-nine racecourses for sixty-five million people. Do the maths. You may infer that a higher proportion of Irish people goes racing.

Like the Jockey Club, Horse Racing Ireland is a racecourse owner: its portfolio includes Leopardstown, Navan, Fairyhouse (home of the Irish Grand National), and Tipperary. Unlike the privately owned, non-profit-making Jockey Club, HRI is, in the words of its website, 'a commercial semi-state body'. HRI and IHRB have one-third stakes in the Curragh; the Aga Khan is joined as owner of the remaining third by Coolmore Stud, Godolphin (Sheikh Mohammed, here in a rare alliance with his Irish competitors), Moyglare Stud, and J.P. McManus – financier, mighty punter, and prominent owner of jumps horses.

Irish racing is mostly in an enviable state at the moment. In jumps racing, the Irish stables are dominant. The Coolmore/Ballydoyle breeding and racing operation is formidable on the flat, although it has faced stronger rivalry in the past few years from the resurgent, Newmarket-based Godolphin. Prize money here is higher than in Britain. The lowest-class race on today's Curragh card, for example, offers a total purse almost twice as valuable as the equivalent race on the same day at Doncaster. It's cheaper to go to the races here. True, Leopardstown's premier ticket set me back €40, but my afternoon at the Curragh costs only €15, and I've paid only €26 for my Punchestown Festival ticket – a striking contrast with Cheltenham, which at its festival now charges £100 to get into the club enclosure, with a £2 booking fee on top. When I ask Suzanne Eade, HRI chief executive, what has given her the most satisfaction since starting in the job in autumn 2021, she cites in her email response various successes underlining 'the current strength and quality of racing in Ireland. We are world leaders at what we do and our industry has shown a remarkable resilience in what has been a particularly challenging few years with Covid.'

Field sizes are a problem in Britain: too many races attract only a few entries, discouraging punters and so reducing yields from their betting for the Levy. There is no such problem in Ireland. Envy on this issue, though, is tempered by memories of BBC *Panorama*'s report of the numbers of unwanted Irish thoroughbreds shipped to England for slaughter (Aintree chapter). I ask Eade whether there is overproduction in the Irish breeding industry, and about the thoroughness of tracking of racehorses once they are retired. This is her comment: 'Our annual foal crop is 25 per cent below the all-time high and we export unraced horses to over thirty countries so there is a healthy market right now. We must remain vigilant to keep the market aligned to our own strategy for fixtures.' I take this to imply that keeping track of every retired racehorse is no simple matter.

The trainer Jim Bolger has raised another issue: he has alleged that the 'number one problem in Irish racing' is cheating with drugs. Bolger, a committed Catholic of strong convictions, commands a good deal of respect, but has not found support for his assertion among his fellow trainers. Eade tells me: 'We are reassured by the recent IHRB report into antidoping activity which showed over six thousand samples analysed in 2021 [and] which revealed only twenty adverse findings, most of which derived from therapeutic mistiming and had no influence on performance.' She adds that one clear security weakness – the absence at every racecourse bar Leopardstown of security cameras at the stables – will be remedied by the end of the year.

The first race of the new flat season in Ireland is, thanks to sponsorship, a bit of a mouthful: the Alkumait Standing at Castlefield Stud with a €100,000 Bonus Irish EBF Maiden. Castlefield Stud and the

EBF (European Breeders Fund) are the race sponsors. The breeder of the winning horse gets a nomination – a breeding date – with the stud's Alkumait, whose covering fee is normally €5,000. If the product of this mating wins a top-class race, the connections receive a €100,000 bonus. The stud will be happy to pay out, because such a victory would be an advertisement worth at least a six-figure sum for Alkumait's potency.

With all ten of these two-year-old fillies seeing a racecourse for the first time, punters have as guides only the betting market, the guesses of the racecard tipster, and the horses' breeding and looks. The favourite, Finsceal Go Deo, is the daughter of a superstar racer and stallion called Kingsman and of a mare whose other offspring have performed impressively. Trying to bring to my examination of her some of what I learned from Ken Pitterson at Sandown, I am not impressed. I like the third favourite, a muscly chestnut called Forceful Speed. Finsceal Go Deo finishes out of the places in fourth. Forceful Speed is second. She is pipped at the post, but would have been a lucky winner: Shane Foley on Ocean Quest is trapped behind her, with as they say 'plenty of horse' underneath him, but spots a gap in the last fifty yards and sprints through it like an impatient queue-jumper.

In the next chapter, we'll hear from trainers Noel Meade and Jessica Harrington, but let's meet them briefly here, where they have contrasting fortunes. Meade runs Meggy Moo, who is a little slow out of the stalls, and after a couple of strides bucks her hind legs, ejecting jockey Oisin Orr. 'It was terrible for that to happen,' Meade tells me later, 'because it was a new owner [Mary Tucker] who wasn't very well, and I was looking forward to the horse having a good run and cheering her up a bit. She [Meggie Moo] had never done anything like that at home. Anyway, hopefully we'll make up for it.'

Harrington is the trainer of Ocean Quest. For this first race of the season, she did not have the filly hard trained – there are further races to come. She tells me: 'If she won, she won, and if she didn't, hopefully she would next time.' While Meade checks Meggie Moo's well-being and gets a debrief from the unlucky Orr, Harrington and companions stroll over to the Queen's Room, where winners' treats are laid on.

Harrington has mentioned another factor that racegoers must try to work out at the parade ring: whether the horses are fully fit. Few trainers, planning for a season that runs until September, will send out a horse in peak condition in March; but some trainers' runners tend to be fitter first time out than others. Aidan O'Brien may have been champion flat trainer in Ireland every year since 1999, but he does not set his sights on heading the table from the outset: in his crosshairs are the big races of the summer and autumn. When his well-bred filly Toy, odds-on favourite for race three (the Cavalor Equine Nutrition Fillies Maiden), is beaten half a length by Perfect Thunder, trained by his son Joseph, one wonders whether other horses of his will 'need the run'.* Is Mother Earth, winner of the 1000 Guineas last year and favourite for race five, the good thing that odds of 4/5 suggest? Yes, is the answer. She's the best horse in the race; don't overthink it. Perhaps she'll be fitter next time, but she gets home today by three-quarters of a length.

After the last, eighth race on the card, O'Brien gives some of his leading hopes for the 2022 classics a workout on the Curragh track; they include Luxembourg, whom we saw win at Doncaster and who is favourite for the Derby, and the filly Tenebrism, second favourite for the 1000 Guineas. I love this time of year: the tingling anticipation. For trainers, it's the same, only with a good deal of pressure thrown in. O'Brien tells the *Irish Times*: 'You're probably dreaming the whole time. You must keep yourself dreaming and at this time of year you're probably dreaming more because a lot of stuff could happen.

'But reality can set in quick. I've found [it best] to not let yourself do too much of that because you're only going to be disappointed . . . Don't set any targets. They'll come back and get you . . .

'What I've found in life is take it one day at a time. And if you're really anxious go down to one minute at a time.'†

For racing fans, though, the dreams will be interrupted. There's an old trick question in the sport: what's the longest race during the flat season? Answer (because the flat season begins before the jumps season ends): the Grand National. The most famous of jumps races, at which amateur jockey Sam Waley-Cohen, in his last race before retirement, will ride 50/1 shot Noble Yeats to victory, is still to come; and over here, a few weeks later, there's Punchestown.

---

* Toy wins next time out, by five lengths.
† Sensible caution. As mentioned, Luxembourg doesn't run in the Derby. In the 1000 Guineas, Tenebrism finishes eighth.

PUNCHESTOWN

Jumps (also stages flat racing)

27 April 2022

A fabulous buzz

I find the trainer Noel Meade outside the weighing room, thank him for having given me an interview a couple of weeks earlier, and ask him how his only runner today, the mare The Model Kingdom, will run in the last. 'Very fast,' he replies. He's joking, for the sake of the rhyme – or does he really mean it? I'm starting to wonder whether I should be backing my interviewees: Jessica Harrington, who has also kindly spoken to me, trained the winner of the first race at my trip to the Curragh, and here sends out Crosshill, who at 15/2 comes home first in race three, the Louis Fitzgerald Hotel Hurdle. Asked by the racecourse announcer whether Crosshill's victory was a surprise, Harrington says no, an answer that may explain why the gelding's price was not the generous 14/1 that the *Racing Post* had predicted. And then there was Ryan Mania at Ayr, riding three second-place finishes at combined place odds of 247/1. The point I must remember, though, is that if I were the kind of punter to back horses for reasons such as this, I'd be the kind of punter who backed a ton of losers, too.

Harrington and Meade, both in their seventies, are dual-purpose trainers, looking after jumps and flat horses. Harrington was born into a horsey family and was one of Ireland's top event riders before taking out a training permit. Meade's family were farmers; Noel rode a winner at Wexford in 1971, but concedes that he had little talent as a jockey, as well as the wrong build. If he wanted to continue working with horses, he realised, he would have to train them. Harrington has nurtured several superstars of the sport; Meade has been champion jumps trainer in Ireland seven times. Neither is going to be top trainer at Punchestown in 2022: the yards of Willie Mullins, Gordon Elliott and Henry de Bromhead have too much firepower. But here they both are, as avid for winners as ever.

> A loud hurrah for Ireland, boys,
> And louder for Kildare,
> And loudest of all for Punchestown,
> For I know you all are there.

This rhythmically challenged extract from a fifty-five-verse, 1863 celebration of Punchestown is evidence of how rapidly the April meeting here developed, from foundation thirteen years earlier into the most important jumps event in Ireland – the country that, the Cheltenham and Aintree festivals notwithstanding, can claim to be the home of the sport.

The first steeplechase on record took place in Ireland, in 1752, when Mr Edmund Blake and Mr Cornelius O'Callaghan raced over the four miles from St John's Church in Buttevant, County Cork to St Leger Church in Doneraile; the histories don't tell us who won. In 1807, the Irish *Racing Calendar* employed the word 'steeplechase' for the first time. A *Sporting Magazine* report of an accident-riddled steeplechase at Lismore in 1819 noted that this was 'a sort of racing for which the Paddies are particularly famous'. At some Irish races, a *Sporting Magazine* correspondent noted in the 1830s, jockeys and horses were at risk not only from the fearsome obstacles, but also from the crowd, who would be armed with missiles to be hurled at competitors they had not backed: 'Here a man has to run the gauntlet at the risk of martyrdom – to put himself in the way of becoming a second St Stephen, or, in plain language, being stoned to death.'

Although there had been racing in the area since the early nineteenth century, the first Punchestown meeting is usually dated to 1850, when the Kildare Hunt Club set up a raceday here. Like Leopardstown's debut, it was not an unqualified success. A *Leinster Express* journalist complained: 'There was no Stand House, the view of the running was limited, and the course very badly kept. As the day advanced the wind and rain increased in violence, and the sports, which did not commence until a quarter past two o'clock, were carried on amid a perfect hurricane.' The return journey to Dublin was 'as disagreeable as can well be imagined'. But the same paper reported that the 1853 meeting was 'one of the most brilliant affairs we have seen in the vicinity of Dublin for many years'. The Kildare Hunt added a second day of racing in 1854, and in 1860 furthered the status of Punchestown as an unmissable fixture in the calendar by hosting the Kildare Hunt Ball, at which the *Leinster Express* was thoroughly won over, enthusing over 'the brilliant and sprightly lights', 'the magnificence of the spacious ballroom', and, at the midnight supper, 'the greatest profusion of every delicacy' accompanied by wines 'of the most recherché quality'. Bertie, the Prince of Wales, did his bit too, visiting in 1868 – as always on such outings, to the disapproval of Queen Victoria: 'I much regret that the occasion should be the races as it naturally strengthens the belief, already too prevalent, that your chief object is amusement,' she admonished her son. Bertie replied, disingenuously you might say: 'Dear Mama, that you should fully understand that I do not go there for my amusement, but as a duty.' Duty drew him back here in 1885, as well as in 1904, by which time he was king.

One of the big races at the meeting, the Conyngham Cup, featured a four-and-a-half-foot wall as well as the 'big double', a bank with yawning ditches on either side. A similar though slightly less frightening bank at the contemporary Punchestown is called Ruby's Double, paying tribute to former jockey Ruby Walsh's grandfather (also Ruby); it confronts the runners in the four-mile-two-furlong-cross-country race, the La Touche Cup. Percy La Touche was a long-serving manager here. His wife Maria, who had no interest in racing, was nevertheless a fan of the festival, because it meant she could spend time undisturbed: 'One may wear one's very worst clothes and have earth all over one's hands and tools sticking out of one's pockets, with a peaceful certainty that no visitors will come,' she enthused. The La Touche Cup record, surely unbreakable, is held by actor Sean Connery's horse Risk of Thunder, who won the race seven times between 1995 and 2002. No doubt Risk of Thunder's record would have been eight victories had not the 2001 festival been cancelled, owing to an outbreak of foot and mouth disease. The Second World War also caused abandonments, as did, in 1919 and 1920, the activities of republican party Sinn Féin, which regarded hunting and its associated sport of horseracing as, in the words of a volunteer, the preserves of 'the so-called aristocrats, idlers, who have no occupation, and who have never done a day's work in their lives'.

Punchestown Racecourse sits in countryside south of Naas (which has its own course). From Dublin, you can get here by train to Sallins, just north of Naas, and then taxi; or, as I do, by a raceday coach service from Aston Quay, next to O'Connell Bridge. The coach – run, as has been every mode of transport I've experienced in Ireland, very efficiently – takes about fifty minutes.

The architecture that confronts you past the Punchestown entrance is surprising: the backs of the grandstands and the other racecourse buildings are of red brick, with gabled roofs; parade ring aside, the area resembles the forecourt of an out-of-town, four-star hotel. There is a mini-village of marquees where artists and milliners are showing off their creations; some dozen food vans include AbraKebabra, Insomnia Coffee, and Camile Thai ('healthy Thai food'). At the last-named, the racecourse announcer enthuses about the 'great smell – and the great aroma!' No doubt a sampling of Camile Thai's food would reveal that not only does it taste good, but it's flavoursome as well. To be fair, with a microphone in my hand and a brief to provide a non-stop commercial for racecourse food outlets, I'd also talk nonsense.

It's a delight to be here. The crowd of 20,000 is clued-up and friendly; by contrast with Cheltenham, there's room to move about (though it will be more congested on Friday, when 40,000 will turn up to witness Rachael Blackmore riding Honeysuckle to the mare's sixteenth straight victory); by the end of the afternoon, the ground is not strewn with discarded betting slips and food wrappers; there are no gangs of boisterous drunks sloshing lager about the place ('It may be different on Saturday,' one of my fellow coach passengers cautions).

We don't get Honeysuckle today, but we do get another special horse. Allaho, twice a dominant winner of the Ryanair Chase at Cheltenham over two miles four and a half furlongs, is 6/5 favourite for the Punchestown Gold Cup. But will he be able to pull off his usual front-running tactic over three miles, against top-class opponents, two Cheltenham Gold Cup winners among them? The answer is emphatic. The starter lowers his flag, and Allaho sets off at an uncompromising pace. Clan des Obeaux, twice a winner of the King George VI Chase at Kempton, tries to keep up, but he's going as fast as he can, whereas Allaho is coasting.

Twenty thousand people are holding their breath: it's thrilling, but is it sustainable? Allaho passes the two-and-a-half-mile mark; he's not stopping. He turns into the straight; it's a victory parade. He's pretty tired by the time he gets to the line, but he's still fourteen lengths clear.

In the winner's enclosure, it's all smiles. Everyone seems happy, including the defeated Clan des Obeaux's jockey Harry Cobden, trainer Paul Nicholls, and part-owner Sir Alex Ferguson, who are quick to congratulate the winners. 'Christ, Allaho is an absolute machine,' Cobden tells a *Racing Post* reporter. 'I was flat out everywhere and he was doing a half speed.' Nicholls says: 'We put it up to Allaho but he was just a way better horse on the day – he was awesome.' There's the spirit of Punchestown in these remarks.

The day after my visit, Meade saddles Tout Est Permis, who finishes fourth, twenty lengths behind the winner, in the La Touche Cup. Harrington's Nerverushacon is pulled up. At their training gallops, these staying chasers, nine and eleven years old respectively, exercise alongside flat racers who may start their careers as two-year-olds in five-furlong sprints. How do the trainers manage what must be varied fitness regimes? It's not complicated, is the gist of their replies. The flat and jumps horses may go to different gallops, or they may go to the same ones, Meade says; if the latter, the flat horses will do about a third of the work that the jumpers undertake. Harrington says: 'Some of the flat horses may be quite big and fat, so they do quite a lot of work' – as much, at her yard, as some of the jumpers, if that is required to get them fit. As Meade, who is largely self-taught, observes, 'It's just common sense really.' Maybe so: but it's common sense applied, in his case, to over one hundred horses in the yard (Harrington has 175): how fit is this one, what kind of regime suits her best, is she a 'morning glory' who performs well on the gallops and poorly at the races, or an 'afternoon glory' who gives no indication at home of her true ability, might blinkers or a tongue tie or cheekpieces help her to race? The top trainers – with the help of their staff, who, in Harrington's case, include her daughters Emma and Kate – understand the differing natures of the horses in their charge, and have an uncanny ability to intuit how to get the best out of them.

As Meade also says: 'Everyone does it differently.' A few weeks before Cheltenham, he and Gordon Elliott – back in the fold it seems, or perhaps never out of it, following his suspension for sitting on a dead mare on his gallops – visited the English yards of Nicky Henderson and David Pipe. 'It was quite amazing to hear their different accounts of the way they trained,' Meade says. 'Nicky's horses were bigger and rounder; Martin [David Pipe's multiple championship-winning father, now retired] didn't believe in that – he thought they'd be better lighter.'

Clearly Meade has forgiven Martin Pipe for denying him, by the shortest of margins and after an agonising wait for the judge's verdict, his first victory at the Cheltenham Festival, when in the 1998 Arkle Chase Pipe's Champleve just got the better of Meade's Hill Society. It was a sickener. 'When they called the result, I walked straight out and went back to the car park,' Meade recalled later for the *Daily Mail*. 'I talked to the attendant for half an hour about the joys of parking cars at Cheltenham. It just got me away from the whole thing.' For years, Cheltenham was his bogey track, and he was to suffer further anguish there when Harchibald, cruising up to leader Hardy Eustace in the 2005 Champion Hurdle, declined to go past him. But Meade had broken his Cheltenham duck by then with Sausalito Bay in the 2000 Supreme Novices' Hurdle, and he has since scored four further victories at the festival.

Harrington does not have as many winners on her CV, but has handled three horses of stellar quality. The first was one of my favourites, Moscow Flyer (Cheltenham chapter); I tell her that the 2004 Tingle Creek Chase, at which Moscow Flyer avenged a previous defeat by Azertyuiop, was the most exciting race I've seen live, and am delighted to find she approves of the choice: 'That was the best race,' she comments simply. Harrington's second great champion was Sizing John, whose statue overlooks the Punchestown parade ring and who in spring 2017 achieved the unprecedented feat of winning three Gold Cups – here, at Leopardstown, and at Cheltenham. A year after this seven-year-old chaser's golden season, Harrington trained the three-year-old flat racing filly Alpha Centauri to win the Irish 1000 Guineas and the Coronation Stakes at Royal Ascot.

Meade started out training flat racers; it was just the way things happened. 'I'd have trained anything that anyone would give me, to be honest,' he says. But by the late eighties and early nineties, flat

racing had become a challenging arena for a medium-sized operation: the Aga Khan's presence in Ireland, and the increasing might of
Coolmore/Ballydoyle and of Godolphin, had raised prices. 'It was getting hard to compete. I couldn't afford top flat horses, but I could afford
top jumpers, so we switched the whole thing over.' He was soon the
leading jumps trainer in Ireland. Then came the rise of Ireland's current
big three: Willie Mullins, Gordon Elliott and Henry de Bromhead.
Wealthy owners were keen to patronise them, and were willing to pay
premium sums to secure the most promising horses. 'There's nearly
been a complete reversal,' Meade says. 'Now the jumps horses have got
so expensive that it's very difficult to buy them, and the flat horses are
easier to buy. They're worldwide commodities. If you have good ones,
there are so many places they can go – America, Japan, Australia, Hong
Kong . . .'

Mullins is to have fourteen winners at Punchestown this year. Elliott
has five, and de Bromhead four. Meade and Harrington have one each.
Harrington, a no-nonsense person, has a no-nonsense attitude to this
state of affairs. 'I'm always looking to be better. I've never complained
that I couldn't buy horses. You don't complain and say, "Poor me, I
can't do it." You just try to get better at what you do. Everyone says you
can't take on Aidan O'Brien on the flat – you can, you just have to keep
pecking away, as you do with Willie Mullins.'

How does Meade feel about no longer being right at the top? 'At the
beginning, you felt you were being pushed down all right, but to be
honest I'm not sure that it didn't make life a bit easier,' he says. 'When
you're trying to win championships you're absolutely flat out, and you
can't take your foot off the pedal at all. From the time the season ends,
all you want to do is get going again and get winning. Your life is not
your own when you're running after a championship; you have to be
looking for the next winner all the time.' Perhaps I get an insight into
what he means about an easier life when I call him: there's a good deal
of chatter and laughter in the background, generated by, he explains, 'a
bit of a lunch for Nina'. It's 6 p.m. (The day before, Nina Carberry –
sister of Meade's former stable jockey Paul Carberry and a brilliant rider
herself, had won RTE TV's *Dancing with the Stars*.)

This is not to say that the fire has burned out. On the eve of Punchestown, Meade told *Kildare Live*: 'I still love it, I still get a fabulous buzz

out of training winners. To be honest, I think people that retire end up fading away. So as long as I am able to keep going I'll keep training.'

Will The Model Kingdom give him a fabulous buzz? The mare, priced at 9/2 joint third favourite for race eight, travels towards the rear of the field, heads towards the far rail as the runners turn for home, slips through a gap between two rivals, goes a length clear, and holds on to win by half a length, unbacked by me. So Meade wasn't joking about her – or was he? It turns out that she didn't have his full confidence. He tells a reporter: 'I'd say the way the race was run suited her as she was very short [of work]. She got a stress fracture behind and had to stand in her box for about two months. I don't know how she is fit but maybe she doesn't take a lot to be ready.' You can train horses for fifty years, and they'll still surprise you.

GALWAY

Jumps and flat

27 July 2022

All of one mind

The outskirts rarely flatter a city. Galway, as represented by the road from the bus station to my B&B, maintains the dispiriting architectural theme of the towns and villages I have travelled through on the way from Shannon airport: rows of concrete boxes, painted grey-pink, or grey-blue, or grey. To be fair, my concrete block of a B&B is yellow. At some point in quite recent history, something seems to have gone horribly wrong with Irish town planning.

Checked in, I return to the city centre and find a different Galway: the 'Latin Quarter', a pedestrianised area of cobbled lanes, outdoor cafés and restaurants, buskers, tourists, and young couples holding hands. It's a happening place.

One hundred thousand racing fans are not the dominating presence here, as one may, somewhat patronisingly, have expected. The west coast city, Ireland's fourth most populous, would be bustling and vibrant anyway. Accommodation would be booked up. The traffic would be, as it is all year round, atrocious.

You need to get in early. Some festival goers renew their rooms from year to year. I booked back in March, with the uncertainties caused by Covid perhaps working to my advantage. At the beginning of July, the *Racing Post* reported that only three Galway hotels were advertising vacancies for the Wednesday and Thursday of race week, and that one of them – a three-star establishment – was offering those dates at more than €1000. For my B&B room, I pay €300 for two nights– a bit more than the cost of my accommodation in Dublin, and twice what I spent in Perth and Ayr. Many racegoers are here for the full seven days, and most will emerge from the week considerably poorer, and possibly with less healthy livers.

The Galway Plate is the centrepiece of Wednesday, day three, and has been Galway's most prestigious race since the meeting began here, in the small suburb of Ballybrit, in 1869. A crowd of 40,000 turned up. Accommodation was in short supply then too, and the authorities repurposed Eyre Square in the centre of the city as a campsite. Owners and trainers transported their horses to and from the course for free, thanks to a subsidy from the Midland and Great Western Railway. The winner of the inaugural plate of 100 gold sovereigns was Absentee, having negotiated nearly two circuits of a course that included eight obstacles, two of them stone walls.

The biggest crowd ever to attend the course was 280,000 strong, here not for the races but for the visit in 1979 of Pope John Paul II, who arrived, as the grander owners and trainers at the festival do, by helicopter. The conjunction of racing and religion is natural in Ireland. Priests bless horses about to depart for the Cheltenham Festival in March; earlier in the week at Galway, the trainer Brian Duffy, having broken down on his way to the races, popped into a nearby church to pray for victory for his mare Magic Chegaga, entered in the Colm Quinn BMW Mile Handicap. She won.

I walk from my B&B, which is opposite a business park. Forty minutes later, I'm still opposite a business park, the buildings of which disfigure the view from the racecourse stands. But there is a ruined medieval tower, all that remains of Ballybrit castle, in the centre of the course; and to the right you can see Galway Bay. The circuit is about a mile and a quarter, and helpfully laid out for the viewer, who loses sight of the horses – as is the case at Punchestown – only as they turn into the straight, beyond the Killanin stand.

Entrance is about half the price of an Epsom grandstand ticket, and less than a third of what Cheltenham charges – unless, like me, you contrive to tear the ticket in two and bring the wrong half. I pay up again, though I still think they might have been generous given that they must have had a record of my booking. There's no premier or club ticket; everyone has access to everywhere, apart from the owners' and trainers' bar and viewing area.

Today, there will be about 16,000 racegoers. Tomorrow, Ladies' Day, there will be 23,000 – about the same as the attendance at Ladies' Day at Epsom, but with access to about five times as many bars, restaurants and other food outlets. The Millennium Stand (1999) and the Killanin Stand, opened by the Taoiseach, Bertie Ahern, in 2007, house bars along almost the entire lengths of their first two floors. Behind the stands, there is a champagne bar with a pianist discreetly playing show tunes, or with a view over the parade and betting rings if you prefer to sit on the terrace; a 'Guinness Village'; an area colonised by Guinness's fellow Diageo drinks company Rockshore; two food courts; long trestle tables at which people park themselves as if at a street party; and a sound stage. Here, an MC gathers enthusiastic volunteers for a line dancing class; later in the afternoon in the Rockshore Lounge, these newcomers to the activity and others are still at it, having a wonderful time and oblivious to the racing, while dance instructor Niall Doorhy treats them to country favourites.

The bookmakers' ring is, here, a square, enclosed by more than sixty pitches; there are another fifteen pitches at the far end of the course. They will turn over more than €1 million during the afternoon and evening (racing begins at 5.10 p.m.); a further €600,000 is bet with the Tote. Next door is the parade ring, around which every vantage point is occupied as the runners circle before race one, a maiden hurdle – for horses who have not won a hurdle race before – over two miles five furlongs. Learning to assess thoroughbreds starts early in these parts: a toddler in her mother's arms precociously calls out the figures she sees on the horses' number cloths and announces her conclusion: 'I like the white one.' I disagree, though not vocally – as I'm taken with Champ Kiely, the second favourite. Champ Kiely moves into the lead with a circuit to go, cruises away from his rivals after the penultimate hurdle, and passes the post twenty-one lengths clear. 'I was hoping he'd win but didn't think he'd do anything like that,' says his trainer, Willie Mullins.

Clearly I've got my eye in. Nothing grabs my attention in race two, which provides another winner for champion trainer Mullins, but Shesadream in race three looks to be in good shape. She's won two of her last three starts, she has a top trainer (Gordon Elliott) and jockey (Davy Russell): she must be worth a fiver each way at 16/1. She has only to finish in the first four and this book will have a happy ending! Alas, the doors slide shut too soon, the lovers miss their rendezvous, the letter explaining all the misunderstandings never arrives; or, to put it in the terms of this book: Shesadream finishes fourteenth.

The market might have told me: having been predicted in the race-card to start at 8/1, Shesadream was a hard sell on the course at an initial price of 12/1, and drifted to the 16/1 at which I backed her. There was, in short, no confidence in her. I end my tour as I started it, clueless.

Still, as Jane Austen wrote, let other pens dwell on guilt and misery. We shall conclude with memories of the happiness racing brings. Of the broad smile on the face of apprentice jockey Ruth Dudfield, who steers to victory another Willie Mullins horse, Dads Lad, in the 7.15. Of the delight of trainer John 'Shark' Hanlon, who runs a small stable in Bagnelstown, Carlow, and wins the Galway Plate with his seven-year-old gelding Hewick. He had bought Hewick as a two-year-old at Goresbridge sales ('hardly one of the elite thoroughbred auction houses', the *Racing Post* observed) for the nugatory sum of €1,850. He recalls the occasion: 'Paddy Mullins [Willie Mullins's father] said to me years ago that if a horse can't walk he can't run. I went to the sales to buy another horse and I met this horse coming in the back gate. I went home for a bit of grub and started thinking about the horse. Then, I came back and bought him. It's been a dream since then.'

Let us move forward to the Galway Festival card on Saturday. The dream continues when Hallowed Star gives Hanlon his second victory of the meeting. Hallowed Star's jockey is Rachael Blackmore, teaming up again with the trainer who was her first boss. Hanlon said: 'The horse was super and Rachael was super. He was keen in her hands and she had the brains to let him roll on, she was great on him as she is on them all . . . She was in my yard as a young girl and she was the most dedicated worker I ever had. She has never let the side down and she has done all of the hard work herself. She doesn't need to praise me or anyone else for the roles they have played in her rise, all she needs to do is praise herself.'

Blackmore appeared briefly at the beginning of this book. I was reporting from Wetherby but keeping an eye on the racing from Leopardstown, where I saw her adding to an impressive sequence of Grade 1 victories. Since then, she has won the Champion Hurdle twice, the Gold Cup, and the Grand National. I had to mention her in this final chapter.

During the time covered by the book, she has been out on her own as the superstar of the sport.

W.B. Yeats visited Galway racecourse in 1908, and at Lady Gregory's home, Coole Park, wrote the poem 'At Galway Races', now engraved on a plaque on the Millennium Stand. 'Here where the course is, Delight makes all of the one mind,' it begins. Not the Nobel Prize-winning poet on top form; but it does say what racing people feel. My days at the races have been a delight.

GLOSSARY

Some racing, betting and bloodstock terms

Racing

All-weather The British term and Irish for sand-based racing surfaces. In the US, they race on **dirt**. See Chelmsford City chapter.

Bay A coppery brown, the most common definition of the colour of racehorses' coats. The definition is flexible, with the bays you see at the races ranging from dark to nearly chestnut. **Brown** horses look nearly black – but **black** is also a recognised colour. **Grey** horses have mixtures of dark and white hairs, with dark ones disappearing as the horses age, leaving them almost white. **Roans** have mixtures of white and brown or chestnut hairs. Owners are required to register these colours with Weatherbys, the racing administrator, as part of their obligatory applications for horse passports.

Binoculars With racecourses showing the action on big screens, binoculars are no longer essential equipment for the racegoer. I like to have them, though. A decent pair offers a sharper image than the screen provides, particularly when the horses are in the middle distance. And it seems a shame to go to a sporting event only to watch it as one would on the telly at home.

A pair of binoculars ('bins') is advertised with a formula such as 8 x 30. The first figure represents the magnification; the second, the size in millimetres of the objective (front) lenses. A larger lens will in theory let in more light – but of course the brightness of the image also depends on the quality of the equipment. A 10x magnification may appear to be preferable to an 8x on the racecourse; in my experience, though, a slightly larger image is not necessarily a clearer one, and is harder to hold steady.

If, like me, you wear glasses, something called eye relief is an important consideration. It is a measure of how far you should be from the eyepiece lenses to get a full view. If the eye relief is less than 15, you'll probably find that with your glasses on you're too far from the lenses, even with the eyecups pushed down. If it's more than 20, you may get a blinking effect, like a shutter coming across the image. About 17 is my sweet spot.

The commentator Richard Hoiles (Exeter chapter), I noticed, avoids the eye relief issue by pushing his glasses aside when he looks through the bins. I'd send my glasses clattering to the floor if I tried that.

Wearing binoculars round your neck advertises you as a hobbyist. Trainers and most owners carry theirs by the straps, or hang them on shoulders.

Blinkers A hood with eyecups that limit a horse's range of vision. The aim is to get an easily distracted horse to concentrate. A **visor** has slits in the eyecups, allowing some lateral vision. A **hood**, worn for the parade and removed at the start, leaves the eyes clear but covers the ears. Other aids include a **noseband**, which in theory regulates a horse's head carriage but is mainly there as a reflection of a trainer's preference – the trainer Andrew Balding favours this accessory, as his father Ian did; **cheekpieces**, fitted to the side of the head, are also thought to be aids to concentration; a **tongue tie** can help a horse whose tongue is liable to inhibit breathing, or to get over the bit; **earplugs**, for horses who get upset before races, must be removed before the race begins.

Buzzy Also **fizzy**. Terms for horses that tend to get worked up.

Classics The most prestigious races for three-year-old colts and fillies. In Britain, they are the 1000 Guineas, a mile race for fillies at Newmarket; the 2000 Guineas, a mile race for colts and fillies (but no filly has run in it for a while) at Newmarket; the Oaks, a mile-and-a-half race for fillies at Epsom; the Derby, a mile-and-a-half race for colts and fillies at Epsom (fillies run in it rarely, but have won it in the past); and the St Leger, the oldest classic (founded in 1776), a mile-and-three-quarter race for colts and fillies at Doncaster. The **Triple Crown** is the 2000 Guineas, Derby and St Leger; Nijinsky was the last horse to win it, in 1970. The 'Fillies' Triple Crown' is the 1000 Guineas, Oaks and St Leger; Oh So Sharp was the most recent winner, in 1985.

Clerk of the course The official responsible for the racecourse track and for raceday management.

Draw The starting stalls berths from which horses race on the flat are determined by lot when the entries are finalised. 1 is on the inside rail – on a right-handed track (where the horses run in a clockwise direction), the number 1 berth will be on the left as you look at the stalls from the front. Some courses have pronounced 'draw biases': at Chester, for example, the tight circuit means you have a much better chance of winning if you start from near the inside rail. Connections of horses who get outside stalls in such circumstances tend to make complaints such as, 'He was drawn in the car park.' In jumps racing, with no stalls, the jockeys manoeuvre for their favoured positions.

Dress code Dressing up for a day at the races as if you were going to a wedding is no longer obligatory, and would look over the top at most race meetings nowadays. There are exceptions: the Royal Enclosure at Ascot and the Queen's Stand at Epsom on Derby day require morning dress; York asks men in the County Stand to wear ties. Racecourses invite women to dress up for 'Ladies' Days', such as the one I attended at Ripon. Some members'/club enclosures ask men not to wear shorts, jeans or T-shirts. Chester during the May meeting is a good deal dressier than Plumpton in January. Racecourse websites will advise.

Exposed/unexposed Horses are exposed if they compete in races that their form suggests they won't win. Unexposed horses could, as they say, be anything.

Form The records of horses' racecourse performances. You 'study' or may be a 'student' of the form book, which may be any medium in which these records appear.

Furlong One-eighth of a mile, or 220 yards. Britain and the US are examples of racing jurisdictions in which distances are measured by miles and furlongs. In France and Australia, the measurements are in metres. The Prix de l'Arc de Triomphe is run over 2400 metres (about a mile and a half); the Melbourne Cup is run over 3200 metres (about two miles).

Gallops The strips of ground on which horses exercise.

Genuine Genuine horses try hard. Broadcasters and journalists sometimes decide that a horse is 'likeable', perhaps meaning the same thing.

Going The state of the ground. From hard to bog-like, the terms in British racing are firm, good to firm, good, good to soft ('yielding' in Ireland), soft, and heavy. The going on all-weather tracks may be fast or slow, but more usually is described as standard or standard to slow.

'He loved the ground' is a frequent post-race comment. Whether horses 'love' galloping through mud is a moot point, but some of them certainly cope with muddy conditions better than others. They tend to lift their knees when galloping, while horses with daisy-cutter actions skim across firm ground more effectively.

Hand The unit of measurement of a horse's height. It represents 4 inches (10.16 centimetres). Arkle and Mill House (Cheltenham chapter) were, respectively, about average (16.2 hands) and giant (18 hands). You measure from the ground to the withers – the ridge between a horse's shoulder blades.

Handicap In the US, a handicapper is anyone who studies the form. In the UK, the official handicappers work for the British Horseracing Authority (BHA), keep tabs on all the racehorses in the country, and are responsible for assigning them ratings. The aim is to provide numerical representations of horses' form, and to ensure that when the numbers are converted to the weights to be carried in handicap races, all the horses in those races have fair chances. A private handicapper, such as Racing Post Ratings in the *Racing Post*, also assigns ratings, the primary purpose of which is to assist punters.

Horses are handicappers if they tend to run in handicaps, competing in a lower league than that occupied by horses that race against each other at level weights – in Group races on the flat, for example.

Let's say you own a horse who races on the flat and has a rating of 95. You enter him or her in a handicap for horses rated 0–100, and with the condition that the bottom weight – the horse with the lowest rating – will carry 8st, while the top weight will carry 10st. (I've rounded these figures for convenience: at the time of writing, minimum and maximum weights on the flat are 8st 2 lb and 10st 2lb respectively.) Your horse turns out to have the highest rating in the race, and therefore has to carry 10st – which will be the weight of the jockey, plus the weight of the saddle, plus any lead in the saddle cloth required to make up the rest. (There is a 3lb allowance for the body protectors jockeys must wear.) The next highest-rated horse is at 93, and will carry 9st 12lb – one point is the equivalent of one pound in weight. What if you have another horse, rated 65, in the race? If weighted according to ability, the horse should carry 7st 12lb. But the conditions of the race mean that the horse has to carry 8st. The horse is 2lb 'out of the handicap' or 'wrong at the weights'. (Your solution might be to book a lightweight apprentice, entitled to take several pounds off the horse's back.)

There is something counter-intuitive about handicaps. In theory, the weightings offset differences in ability, making results hard to predict. 'Anything can happen,' was once the slogan of the betting firm Bet365; a William Hill ad currently showing describes the sport as 'unpredict-able'. About which the obvious comment is: 'Exactly – that's why betting is a mugs' game.' But that's not how punters look at it, and handicap races exist in order to encourage betting, as well as to give horses below the top rank a chance to compete. Punters are happy for their task to be more difficult if it comes with potentially greater rewards.

Nevertheless, the common description of the Royal Hunt Cup (a mile handicap) as 'the big betting race' of the Royal Ascot meeting is somewhat misleading. The high rollers bet on the level weights races.

See also the Newbury chapter.

Horse Bitzer's approved definition in Charles Dickens's *Hard Times* – 'Quadruped. Graminivorous. Forty teeth . . .' – won't do here. A racehorse who is a 'horse' is an entire male of five years old and above. You do not come across many of them: by this age, the elite male racers have usually gone to pass on their genes at stud, while those left behind have been gelded (castrated). **Geldings** are, on the whole, more easy-going than racehorses for whom a sex life remains feasible. **Colts** are male horses up to the age of five. **Fillies** are female horses of up to five, at which age they become **mares**.

Horses for courses 'He loves it round here' is another favourite post-race comment about victorious horses. There is something in it. Some courses are hilly, with tight turns, suiting horses that can change gear; others have gentler turns, with longer straight sections, suiting one-paced horses who are strong gallopers. Some courses are right-handed (the horses race clockwise) and some are left-handed; certain horses have strong preferences for one direction or the other. A horse preferring to lead with the left (on) foreleg will be better suited to racing left-handed.

Jockey Club It has no jockeys in it, and it is not a club in the standard sense. Operating under what its website describes as a 'modern corporate structure', the JC manages fifteen racecourses, a good deal of land used for racehorse training, the National Stud, and the charity Racing Welfare.

Again according to its website, the Jockey Club was founded in 1750 – though some historians think the date was earlier. 'Jockey', then, could mean a horseman in general. Gradually, the Jockey Club became the governing body for all British racing, and amazingly remained so until this century, when it realised that 'criticisms can be levelled at a self-elected body', and sought to increase 'the transparency and independence of racing's regulatory responsibilities'. It handed over the policing of the sport in 2006, and its regulatory role a year later. British racing is now run by the **British Horseracing Authority**.

The Jockey Club's fifteen racecourses are Aintree, Carlisle, Chelten-ham, Epsom, Exeter, Haydock, Huntingdon, Kempton, Market Rasen, Newmarket (Rowley Mile), Newmarket (July), Nottingham, Sandown, Warwick, and Wincanton.

The Irish equivalent of the Jockey Club is the **Turf Club**, founded in 1790. The Turf Club is now the **Irish Horseracing Regulatory Board**, and the governance of the sport sits with **Horse Racing Ireland**.

Levy A tax on bookmakers' profits collected by the Horserace Betting Levy Board, a statutory body that reports to the Department for Digital, Culture, Media and Sport. The annual yield for 2021–2022 was £97 million. The fund goes towards prize money and racing welfare. Other sources of income for racing are media rights, bought by broadcasters and bookmakers; pre-race data (details to appear on racecards); sponsorship; training fees; gate receipts; and events such as weddings and conferences. Then there is the turnover of the breeding industry: stallion fees and horse sales.

In Ireland, funding for the sport comes from the Department for Agriculture, Food and the Marine, and is not directly linked to betting tax.

Off/not off I am afraid that the horse carrying your money may not always run to his or her full potential. Sometimes, this is for blameless reasons: the horse does not like the ground or the track, or may be having a bad day. Sometimes, it may be because the horse needs the race in order to get fit: you are unlikely to be tolerant of this excuse if the trainer waits until after the race to make it. And sometimes, the horse will be 'not off': the trainer and owner want to hoodwink the handicapper into assigning a low mark, enabling the horse to win at a time when gambled on by those 'in the know'.

Punters, in whom the unequal struggle with bookmakers has nurtured cynicism, will tell you that horses are not off every day of the week. Yet the truth behind even apparently blatant misdemeanours, including such cases as when in 1791 the Prince of Wales's (later George IV's) horse Escape lost a race at Newmarket and a few days later romped home at more generous odds, has often proved on examination to be impossible to untangle. All we know about racehorse training tells us that fluctuations in form are more likely than dastardly conspiracies.

On/off the bridle/bit A horse on the bridle is coasting along, with the jockey enjoying the ride. When the jockey has to start pushing, the horse is off the bridle. **'He didn't do a tap,'** as jockeys sometimes say, means that the horse never got going. He didn't find anything **'for pressure'**, is a phrase that, for some reason, I find grating: it means that the horse did not respond to the jockey's urgings.

Pattern Introduced in the early 1970s, the Pattern was designed to create a coherent programme of top-class races on the flat. The classes of race are Group 1, Group 2, Group 3, and Listed. Horses that are placed in these races earn **black type** in sales catalogues, boosting their value.

In jumps racing, the Pattern took roughly its current shape in the late 1980s. The classes here are Grade 1, Grade 2, Grade 3, and Listed. Grade 3s, unlike Group 3s on the flat, are leading handicaps such as the Grand National.

Racecard It's not a card. In horseracing, the 'card' is the runners and riders for a meeting. A racecard is the programme for the day, on sale as you enter the racecourse. The listing gives details such as the horses' colours, jockeys, form figures, owners and trainers, along with brief blurbs, tips, and betting forecasts. If you have a *Racing Post*, you get all this information and more; but a good many *Racing Post* readers buy racecards as well. It's a habit. You don't feel as if you're properly there otherwise.

Stayer On the flat, a stayer is a horse who specialises in distances further than a mile and a half. The distance of a stayers' hurdle race is three miles. But a horse can fail to stay any distance – some are so speedy that they barely last out the minimum trip. 'Will he stay?' is one of the most teasing questions for racing fans to ponder before the Derby, most of the runners in which will have at least some forebears who specialised at shorter trips.

Thoroughbred Breeders based largely in Yorkshire bred the first thoroughbreds in the late seventeenth and early eighteenth centuries, from matings between imported Eastern stallions and native mares, the latter boasting names such as Old Bald Peg and Lord Darcy's Black-legs. Today, all thoroughbreds trace their male-line descents from one of three stallions: the Byerley Turk, the Godolphin Arabian, and the Darley Arabian. The Darley Arabian's line, through the great Eclipse (1764–89), is by far the most prevalent.

The reason for highlighting the male line is that successful stallions cover (see below) a large number of mares, as do their male descendants if they are successful, therefore appearing – because thoroughbreds are inbred – many, many times in family trees. There are millions of crosses of Eclipse in the family tree of Frankel, nineteen generations down in the male line ('tail male') from his great ancestor. This is not to imply that males are more significant progenitors than females. If there are millions of copies of Eclipse in a pedigree, there must also be millions of copies of his dam, Spilletta.

Thoroughbreds – though they were not then designated as such – got their first pedigree records in 1791, when James Weatherby published *An Introduction to a General Stud Book*. Weatherbys remains a family firm as well as the authority on thoroughbred lineages in Britain and Ireland: a British or Irish horse is a thoroughbred if Weatherbys says it is.

Betting

Betting Exchange A betting operator enabled by the internet. Punters can lay as well as back. I may decide that No-Hoper will live up to his name in the three o'clock at Market Rasen. I go on to Betfair, and offer to lay him at 100, or 99/1. (The exchange's dividends, like the Tote's, are expressed as what you get back including the stake. The first figure in a bookmaker's odds is what you win; the second figure is what you stake to earn that sum. If you risk £1 on a 99/1 shot, you get back £99 plus your £1.) Perhaps you can see how this could go wrong. If lots of Betfair customers take you up on your offer, you'll be watching the race in a state of some anxiety.

The exchanges also popularised betting in-running. This can also cause some spectacular catastrophes for layers. It is not unknown for horses to look as if they have no chance, trade at 999 (1000/1) with a furlong to go, and somehow manage, with the help of erratic rivals, to win.

Such bets are not new: the great Eclipse, racing at York in 1770, was quoted in-running at 1/100.

Each way A bet consisting of two parts: win and place. A £5 each way bet does not cost £5: it costs £10. One £5 part is a win bet. The other is for the horse to be placed, and comes under the category of what is euphemistically called a 'saver', or a bet placed under the illusion that it offers insurance against a failure to deliver by your other selection.

Handicaps (see above) of more than sixteen runners offer place terms on the first four, who are said to have made the **frame**. Races with more than eight runners have three places. Races with five to eight runners have two places. There is only one place in a race with four runners or fewer. If a race has four runners, don't ask for an each way bet. The terms may be a quarter or a fifth of the win odds (so if the horse you want to back is only 2/1, don't ask the bookmaker for an each way bet): racecards and bookmakers' noticeboards have details.

It is the Grand National, a handicap with some forty runners. You put £5 each way on a horse priced at 16/1. The horse wins. HURRAH! In return, you get 16 x £5, plus your £5 stake; and, for the place part of the bet, 16 x ¼ x £5, plus your £5 stake. That is £85 plus £25 = £110: a profit of £100. What if your horse scrapes in fourth? Hurrah! You lose the £5 win part of the bet, but get back £25 – a profit of £15. (Some bookmakers pay out on more than four places in high-profile handicaps such as this.)

In general, place returns from the Tote (see below) are less generous than those from other bookmakers. But if you're backing an outsider, the Tote's win return may be larger.

It's not unusual for the favourite in a competitive handicap to be as long as 8/1 in the betting – a price at which you could back him or her each way and make a small profit. This is one of the reasons why handicaps are attractive to day-to-day punters, who leave races with small fields and short-priced favourites to those who play at a more elevated, frightening level.

The field '8/1 the field' means that 8/1 is the lowest price on any horse in a race. '8/1 bar' means that 8/1 is the lowest price on any horse whose odds haven't been quoted.

Odds on/odds against A horse priced at 2/1 is odds against. That looks like a strong favourite's price. But the market is saying that the horse is twice as likely to lose the race as to win it; to put it another way, the chances are that a horse running in three races at 2/1 each time will lose twice and win once. (Although it must be odds against that the stats will work out so neatly.) Odds on is a price such as 1/2. A near certainty then; but perhaps not, if you think of it as representing a one in three chance of losing.

Rule 4 A dreaded stipulation, though it is fair enough. Rule 4 kicks in when a horse is withdrawn from a race shortly before the start, with bookmakers unable to reframe the market. If the withdrawn horse is even money favourite and you've backed the 5/1 second favourite, you have to admit that you've suddenly got a bargain on your hands. Alas, if your horse comes home first the bookmaker will deduct about half your winnings, leaving you with what you would have earned had your horse been a favourite's price.

Tissue The morning betting forecast for each day's races. So called because of the flimsy paper on which bookmakers printed it.

Tote The pool betting service at racecourses. Set up by Winston Churchill in 1928, the Tote was a government-run body until 2011, when it was privatised under the ownership of the bookmaker Fred Done. It is now run by a consortium. In Ireland, it is run by Horse Racing Ireland.

The name is derived from totalisator, the device that calculates the pool and the value of winning bets. Elsewhere, the system is known as pari-mutuel ('mutual bet'). In France, the PMU (Pari Mutuel Urbain) was until recently the only way to bet on racing; other top racing countries, Hong Kong among them, have pari-mutuel monopolies. On many US racecourses, only pool betting is available.

You place £2 to win on No-Hoper, an outsider. At the off, there is £100 in the win pool, and only £4 of it – your bet and another punter's of the same value – on No-Hoper. No-Hoper wins! The Tote takes its share, about 20 per cent, leaving the payout to a £1 stake as £80 ÷ 4 = £20. You bet £2, so you get back £40. This will be expressed in the results as a dividend of £20. The same odds, with a bookmaker, would have been 19/1 – in this case, each £1 bet earns you back £19, plus the stake.

Racing people who regard themselves as serious punters rather than casual dabblers usually prefer to bet with bookmakers, whose margins – in other words, the profits they make from your bets – tend to be tighter than 20 per cent, and who pay out at the odds they quote.

Until recently, it was a bad idea to bet with the Tote if your horse was popular in the betting: you'd be sharing the win pool with a lot of other punters. However, the UK Tote (at most courses) and Irish Tote now guarantee that they will match bookmakers' starting prices. For win bets only, that is. Tote customers are fond of each way bets, and returns from the place portions of these bets are ungenerous.

To take an example from some time ago: Terimon, who came second in the 1989 Derby at 500/1 (so at least £100 for the place), was only £20.20 for the place on the Tote. (True, the 5/4 winning favourite Nashwan had a Tote return roughly equivalent to 13/8 – the rule I've given above is not infallible.)

Bloodstock

A **nomination** is a date for a breeder's mare with a stallion, who will **cover** her. Sending your mare to Dubawi, the most expensive stallion in Britain, will set you back £250,000.

There are dozens of sons and daughters of Dubawi in training. They are not, according to the racing industry, half siblings. Horses who are half siblings have the same dam. The term **family** refers to the female line of a horse's pedigree.

Pinhookers buy horses as foals or yearlings, aiming to sell them on as yearlings or two-year-olds. As two-year-olds, horses may come up for sale at **breeze-ups**, at which they go through their paces before prospective buyers.

Store A young horse bred for National Hunt Racing and not yet **broken** – trained to accept tack and riders.

ACKNOWLEDGEMENTS

Racing people have been very generous with their time and insights. Thank you: Richard Aldous; Paul Barton; Mike Butt; Sophie Candy; Jeannie Chantler; Simon Cooper; Suzanne Eade; Dominic Gardiner-Hill; Fraser Garrity; William Haggas; Jessica Harrington; Lydia Hislop; Gillian, Lady Howard de Walden; David Hunter; Richard Hoiles; John Hooper; Tim Husbands; James Hutchinson; Sean Magee; Ryan Mania; Noel Meade; James Millman; Robin Mounsey; Sir Anthony Oppenheimer; Mark Pariser; Ken Pitterson; Jonjo Sanderson; Graham Sharpe; Nick Smith; Philip Spink; Dan Thompson.

Thank you too: Charlie McLean; Marion Regan; Miranda Seymour.

Thank you too: Ros Edwards; Alan Samson; Ellie Freedman; Kate Moreton; Lucinda McNeile; Elizabeth Allen; Sharina Smith.

The books I have found particularly useful are: *Racecourses* by James Gill (Barrie & Jenkins, 1975); *From Epsom to Tralee* by Roy Gill (Medina, 2015); *The History of Horse Racing* by Roger Longrigg (Macmillan, 1972); *Ascot: The History* by Sean Magee (Methuen, 2002); *Vincent O'Brien: The Official Biography* by Jacqueline O'Brien and Ivor Herbert (Bantam Press, 2005); *The Heath and the Horse* by David Oldrey, Timothy Cox and Richard Nash (Philip Wilson, 2016); *Lester's Derbys* by Lester Piggott and Sean Magee (Methuen, 2004); *The Fast Set* by George Plumptre (Deutsch, 1985); *Peerless Punchestown* by Raymond Smith and Con Costello (Sporting Books, Dublin, 2000); *Irish Horse-racing: An Illustrated History* by John Welcome (Macmillan, 1982).